www.wadsworth.com

wadsworth.com is the World Wide Web site for Wadsworth Publishing Company and is your direct source to dozens of online resources.

At *wadsworth.com* you can find out about supplements, demonstration software, and student resources. You can also send e-mail to many of our authors and preview new publications and exciting new technologies.

wadsworth.com
Changing the way the world learns®

THE WADSWORTH PROFESSIONALISM IN POLICING SERIES

Samuel Walker, Series Editor

Walker: *Police Accountability: The Role of Citizen Oversight*

McDonald: *Managing Police Operations: Implementation of the New York Crime Control Model*

❖

Police Accountability

The Role of Citizen Oversight

Samuel Walker

University of Nebraska at Omaha

WADSWORTH

THOMSON LEARNING

Australia • Canada • Mexico • Singapore • Spain • United Kingdom • United States

WADSWORTH
™
THOMSON LEARNING

Executive Editor, Criminal Justice:
 Sabra Horne
Development Editor: Terri Edwards
Editorial Assistant: Cortney Bruggink
Marketing Manager: Jennifer Somerville
Marketing Assistant: Karyl Davis
Project Editor: Jennie Redwitz
Print Buyer: Robert King

Permissions Editor: Joohee Lee
Production Service: Matrix Productions
 Inc.
Copy Editor: Vicki Nelson
Cover Designer: Bill Stanton
Cover Image:
Cover Printer: Webcom Ltd.
Compositor: T:H Typecast, Inc.
Printer: Webcom Ltd.

Library of Congress Cataloging-in-Publication Data
Walker, Samuel, [date]
 Police accountability : the role of citizen oversight
 / Samuel Walker.
  p. cm
 Includes bibliographical references and index.
 ISBN 0-534-58158-7
  1. Police administration—United States—
Citizen participation. 2. Police—Complaints
against—United States. I. Title.
HV8141.W346 2000
363.2'3'0973—dc21

  00-063297

Wadsworth/Thomson Learning
10 Davis Drive
Belmont, CA 94002-3098
USA

For more information about our products,
contact us:
Thomson Learning Academic Resource Center
1-800-423-0563
http://www.wadsworth.com

International Headquarters
Thomson Learning
International Division
290 Harbor Drive, 2nd Floor
Stamford, CT 06902-7477
USA

UK/Europe/Middle East/South Africa
Thomson Learning
Berkshire House
168-173 High Holborn
London WC1V 7AA
United Kingdom

Asia
Thomson Learning
60 Albert Street, #15-01
Albert Complex
Singapore 189969

Canada
Nelson Thomson Learning
1120 Birchmount Road
Toronto, Ontario M1K 5G4
Canada

Contents

Preface

This book represents the culmination of ten years of work on the subject of citizen oversight of the police. It has been the most exciting project imaginable. During this period the subject itself has changed dramatically—and has continued to change up through the last-minute editing of this book. At times I have felt that I was functioning almost as much as a journalist, desperately trying to keep pace with fast-changing events, as a scholar attempting to dispassionately evaluate a reasonably settled subject.

During this time my understanding of the subject has changed tremendously. Many of my initial assumptions were challenged in the confrontation with the messy and often inconvenient facts of the real world. One indicator of this challenge is the fact that I had to change the basic terminology that I use. Ten years ago, I routinely used the term *civilian review*. At least midway through the project, I discovered that that term did not adequately or accurately describe the phenomenon I was studying. Eventually, *citizen oversight* became my preferred term.

The demands of reconciling my personal views on the subject of police accountability and the obligations of scholarship to pursue the facts wherever they may lead have been an enormous challenge, and a deeply rewarding one. On the personal level I regard citizen oversight, on principle, as a remedy for the historic problem of police misconduct. The research for this project has forced me to confront the fact that not all oversight agencies are effective. In large part, my research has been driven by the need to explain why certain things do not work and why some other things do work. The results of this quest can be found in the seven chapters of this book. I believe I have been true to both of the obligations that frame my life: on one hand, the obligations of citizenship to challenge and seek to correct those things that are wrong, and on the other hand, the obligations of the scholar to search for and be faithful to the truth as best we can discover it. It remains for you the reader to decide whether I have successfully met this challenge.

ACKNOWLEDGMENTS

There are many people I would like to thank for helping me with the project. Most important I would like to express my profound appreciation to the Center on Crime, Communities, and Culture of the Open Society Institute for the fellowship they awarded me in 1997. That fellowship gave me the opportunity to travel, study, write, and, most importantly, think about this complex and rapidly changing subject. I would like to thank Gara LaMarche, director of American Programs at the Open Society Institute; Nancy Mahon, former director of the Center; and Miriam Porter, in charge of fellowships at the Center. The Open Society Institute is not responsible for any of the views expressed in this book.

I would also like to thank several of my graduate students. I suspect that I would not have dug into this subject as early as I did had it not been for Vic Bumphus, an MA student at UNO in 1990 who was looking for a thesis topic. I suggested this topic, and his thesis still provides the basic framework for this book. I would also like to thank Betsey Wright Kreisel, who continued work on this project after Vic graduated. Much of this work involved simply tracking the development of citizen oversight agencies: obtaining ordinances, rules and procedures, and annual reports. In more than a few instances, local officials were not even aware of developments in their own city or county. In the last two years, Carol Archbold and Leigh Herbst have helped carry on this data collection.

I would like to thank my editor at Wadsworth, Sabra Horne, for her complete support for this book and commitment to publish it in a timely fashion while not stinting for one minute on quality. At the University of Nebraska at Omaha, I would like to thank my faculty colleagues for maintaining an academic environment that is both intellectually stimulating and unusually collegial. Bob Meier, the chair of our department, has given me all the support I have needed, for this project and for others. And of course, I need to thank Angela Patton for keeping my computer running and in times of great crisis showing me where the "On" button is.

During the course of my research, I have learned much from citizen oversight officials and law enforcement officials across the country. In particular, I would like to thank Barbara Attard in Berkeley, Merrick Bobb in Los Angeles, Lisa Botsko in Portland, Don Casimere in Sacramento, Teresa Guerrero-Daley in San Jose, Pat Hughes in Minneapolis, Katherine Mader in Los Angeles,

Pierce Murphy in Boise, and John Parker in San Diego. Eileen Luna obtained the contract for our evaluation of the oversight agencies in Albuquerque, a project from which I learned a great deal, and I would like to thank her for our continuing dialogue on citizen oversight. John Crew at the ACLU of Northern California, who has devoted his professional life to citizen oversight, has always generously shared his insights and his files with me. We have had spirited debates over some of the ideas in this book, and his challenges to my thinking have helped to make it a better book. ACLU officials in numerous other cities—Albuquerque, Baltimore, Boise, Boston, Los Angeles, New York City, Portland, Seattle, and Washington, DC, in particular but other cities as well—have also generously shared information and thoughts with me.

I'd like to thank the following reviewers of this edition for their helpful comments: Geoffrey P. Alpert, University of South Carolina; Lisa Botsko, Examiner, Police Internal Investigations Auditing Committee, Portland, Oregon; William D. Darrough, California State University, Los Angeles; Joseph J. Hanrahan, Westfield State College; Edward R. Maguire, University of Nebraska at Omaha; James E. Newman, Rio Hondo Community College; Richard J. Terrill, Georgia State University; and Robert C. Wadman, Weber State University.

Finally, I must say that I have also learned a great deal from many police officials across the country, individuals holding every rank from chief down to rank-and-file officers. It is important to state this fact because so many people across the country have the impression—derived from the news media—that police abuse pervades every department and that no police officials care. I have learned through the course of this project that this is not true. As Chapter 2 explains, the gap between the best and the worst police departments is probably greater than at any time in our history. What that means is that a number of departments have made a serious commitment to high standards of accountability—which is to say that numerous officials have undertaken the hard work of raising standards in the departments where they work. There is, in short, cause for optimism. I have learned much from these individuals, and I believe we all have much to learn from the example they have set.

Omaha, Nebraska
August, 2000

❖

PART I

What Is Citizen Oversight?

1

Introduction

POLICE MISCONDUCT IN AMERICA

Three Incidents

- In New Orleans, a woman filed a routine complaint against police officer Len Davis. Using his police radio, Davis put out a contract on the woman and had her murdered. The FBI was monitoring his radio as part of a drug corruption investigation, and he was subsequently arrested, convicted, and sentenced to death for murder.[1]

- In New York City, police officers dragged Abner Louima, a Haitian immigrant, into a precinct station bathroom and jammed a wooden stick up his rectum, inflicting injuries that required three operations to repair. The lead officer in the case was subsequently convicted on criminal charges for the assault.[2]

- In Los Angeles, officers working out of the Rampart Station handcuffed a suspect, shot him, planted drugs on him, and then arrested him for drug dealing. One of the officers involved later confessed (after being arrested himself for theft of drugs) and implicated other Rampart Station officers in brutalizing and framing suspects. As a result, about 100 convicted offenders have been released from prison (as of mid-2000), the district attorney says that as many as 3,000 criminal cases might be tainted by the corrupt activities, and dozens of LAPD officers are facing termination and criminal prosecution.[3]

These three incidents dramatize the problem of serious police misconduct in America today. While they are particularly extreme cases, abuse of citizens is a problem all across the country. A 1998 report by Human Rights Watch made the searing indictment that "police brutality is one of the most serious, enduring, and divisive human rights violations in the United States."[4] Some people believe that police conduct has actually gotten worse in recent years, despite decades of reform efforts, from police-community relations programs in the 1960s to community policing today. Some believe the police are "above the law," in the sense of being beyond the control of citizens, the courts, and even their own chiefs.[5]

Nor is it coincidental that the victims in all three of these vignettes are racial or ethnic minorities. Poor people of color bear the brunt of police abuse. Human Rights Watch concluded: "Race continues to play a central role in police brutality in the United States."[6] The problem of police abuse is primarily a problem in race relations and is one of the most volatile aspects of the national race crisis.

The alarming aspect of these three incidents is not just what individual officers did but what the events say about the departments in which the officers work. In the Louima case, the officer who committed the assault walked around the precinct station bragging about what he had done. Clearly, he did not expect to be turned in by fellow officers. The Los Angeles Police Department's own 360-page report on the Rampart scandal, meanwhile, concedes that its own internal controls had broken down. Among other things, it admits that the department's personnel evaluations are worthless and are regarded as such by members of the department.[7] The officer in the New Orleans case was caught only because the FBI was monitoring his police radio as part of a corruption investigation.

In all three of these police departments, the guilty officers apparently felt reasonably sure they would not be reported by their fellow officers and never be disciplined by their departments. The problem of police misconduct, in short, is not a few bad officers but dysfunctional police departments where accountability mechanisms have either broken down or never existed in the first place.

RESPONDING TO POLICE MISCONDUCT

What are we to do about police misconduct? What remedies work? What does not work? This book argues that the problem of police misconduct *is not a matter of a few rotten apples but of failed organizations.* In responding to serious police misconduct, it is a mistake to focus on the officers on the street. Firing or prosecuting a few officers may offer a measure of symbolic justice, but in the long run it leaves unchanged the conditions that tolerated and even fostered their misconduct. The challenge of police accountability is not how to "get" a few bad officers but how to fix organizations. Consequently, the focus of this book is on *organizational change,* about how to change the organizational culture of police departments. It argues that citizen oversight is a means to that end, a strategy for changing police organizations in order to reduce officer misconduct.

CITIZEN OVERSIGHT OF THE POLICE

Citizen oversight of the police has emerged in recent years as one remedy for the problem of police misconduct. Citizen oversight is defined as *a procedure for providing input into the complaint process by individuals who are not sworn officers.* This book examines the role of citizen oversight in promoting police account- ability. It traces the spread of oversight agencies in the United States, describes the activities of these agencies, assesses what we know about their effective- ness, and critically evaluates the arguments for and against citizen oversight.

At the outset, it is important to clarify the terminology used in this book. *Citizen oversight* is used instead of other terms that have been applied over the years: *civilian review, external review, civilian monitoring, civilian oversight,* and so on. For a variety of reasons, these other terms are either inadequate or inappropri- ate. The word *civilian* is inappropriate because it implies a civilian/military dichotomy that is inappropriate for domestic policing. The military metaphor, with its references to "wars on crime" and "thin blue lines," has had a destruc- tive effect on a government service designed to help a law-abiding domestic population.[8] Citizen *review,* meanwhile, is also not advisable because, as this book argues at great length, oversight agencies do a lot more than simply review individual complaints against the police. It is also inaccurate to speak of citizen review *boards* because a number of existing agencies do not involve a multimember board but an agency with a single director. For all these reasons, *citizen oversight* is the most comprehensive and accurate term.

The Goals of Citizen Oversight

The basic goal of citizen oversight is to open up the historically closed com- plaints process, to break down the self-protective isolation of the police, and to provide an independent, citizen perspective on complaints.[9] Internal police department procedures for handling citizen complaints have been attacked over the years as nonexistent, hostile, or inadequate. Community activists have alleged that those who try to file a complaint against a police officer often encounter additional disrespect at the police station. Substantial research and investigative reporting supports these allegations. In 1998, for example, NBC *Dateline* secretly taped the efforts of an African-American man who walked into about 30 different New York City police precinct stations and requested a copy of the complaint form. In about half of the stations, the desk sergeant refused to hand him the form, demanding to know what the complaint is

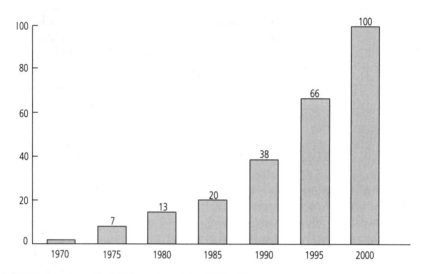

FIGURE 1-1 Growth of Citizen Oversight, 1970–2000

about. One desk sergeant became increasingly belligerent and finally ordered the man to get "out of my office."[10]

Even when complaints are accepted, the investigations are often more demeaning than the original abuse. Citizens filing complaints are asked hostile and demeaning questions. Witnesses are not contacted and interviewed. And statements by officers that defy logic are accepted at face value. Finally, even when complaints are sustained, police departments historically have failed to discipline the guilty officers. Recent investigations by both the Public Advocate for New York City and the New York Civil Liberties Union in 1999 found that only about one-quarter of all the officers against whom the Civilian Complaint Review Board sustained complaints were actually disciplined.[11]

The Recent Growth of Oversight Agencies

The movement for citizen oversight has been a major political struggle for over forty years. In recent years, it has achieved considerable success—a level of success that is largely unrecognized except by specialists in the field. In the 1960s, oversight was a highly controversial idea, dismissed as radical and dangerous by virtually everyone outside the civil rights and civil liberties communities. The two most important experiments in oversight, in New York City and Philadelphia, were abolished under pressure from local police unions. Today, however, oversight agencies are quite prevalent. Over 100 different agencies exist, covering law enforcement agencies that serve nearly one-third of the American population, and they are found in about 80 percent of the big cities of this country.[12] Figure 1-1 traces the growth of citizen oversight over the past thirty years.

Oversight, moreover, is an international phenomenon. Every law enforcement agency in the rest of the English-speaking world—the United Kingdom,

Canada, Australia, and New Zealand—is subject to some form of citizen oversight. A person filing a complaint against an officer with the Royal Canadian Mounted Police—the famous "Mounties"—has recourse to a complaint process with citizen input.[13] David Bayley, the leading expert on policing around the world, argues that "few people are aware of how general this movement has been."[14]

The growth of oversight has transformed the institutional landscape of American policing, adding a new form of accountability. In a formal organizational sense, the creation of an oversight agency means that a police department is required by law to deal with a new external agency. In many instances, formal responsibility for complaint investigations is transferred from the police department to a different agency.[15]

POLICING AND POLICE ACCOUNTABILITY

Police abuse has a long and tragic history in this country. The 1931 Wickersham Commission Report, the first systematic inquiry into the problem, concluded that what was called the "third degree" (the "infliction of pain, physical or mental, to extract confessions") was "extensively practiced" across the country.[16] Through the nineteenth century, abuse was rampant and unchecked. One hardly needs to guess how New York City police officer Alexander "Clubber" Williams earned his nickname.[17] From the nineteenth century through the 1940s, the typical victim of police abuse was a white working-class male. Today, the majority of victims of the worst abuses (as opposed to mere discourtesy) are people of color. The sad fact of American police history has been the failure, if not the absence, of meaningful procedures for ensuring police accountability.

What do we mean by *police accountability*? In theory, the police in a democratic society are accountable to the public and to the law. On one hand, they should be responsive to the people they serve and to the elected officials who are responsible for law enforcement agencies. At the same time, the police must be accountable to the law, and in particular their actions must conform to standards of due process and equal protection.

One of the central dilemmas of policing is that the two aspects of accountability often conflict with each other.[18] The public demands effective crime control, but some of the measures they ask the police to take—sweeping the streets of suspects—conflict with principles embedded in our legal system. The central question is how to achieve the proper balance between the two dimensions of accountability: serving the public while respecting the rights of citizens.

The reality, however, is that the principal mechanisms for police accountability have fallen short of their goals. Some have achieved modest successes, while others have proven to be completely inadequate to the task. The reasons for this failure are complex. There are many obstacles to police accountability. Some are inherent in the nature of policing, while others are a result of a failure of the political system to address the problem of police abuse in a meaningful way.

The Nature of Routine Police Work

The nature of routine police work creates serious potential problems for accountability. First, the police have unique and awesome powers.[19] We grant no other agency the power to take human life. Police officers may shoot to kill, and over one hundred people die in this manner every year. The police have the power to deprive us of our liberty through arrest. Several million people are arrested every year in this country. The fact that most of those arrests do not result in formal criminal prosecution, much less conviction, raises disturbing questions about who is arrested and why. Is the arrest power being used for improper purposes? Police officers may also use physical force. They may do so legally, to protect themselves, to overcome resistance to arrest, or to bring a dangerous situation under control. Unfortunately, too often officers use physical force for illegitimate purposes, to punish what they perceive as disrespect or a challenge to their authority.

Second, the day-to-day work setting of policing accentuates the accountability problem. The strategy of patrol, which has been fundamental to policing for over 150 years, disperses police officers throughout the community. On the street, they are visible to the public in a way that is not true of any other government agency. They are probably the last group of professionals who make house calls. We invite them into our homes and ask them to solve our most intimate problems: family disputes, mental health crises, and so on. Police officers perform society's dirty work, handling the problems no one else can or wants to handle. Policing is a human service activity requiring great discretion on the part of the police officer. Many of the people the police deal with are not nice: They are unruly, out of control, or have just committed some crime. Some of these people challenge police authority, and officers have to use some force to gain control of the situation.

Aggravating the problem of accountability is the fact that officers generally work alone or in pairs, free from direct observation by their supervisors.[20] In many encounters with the public, there are no independent witnesses to what happens. For these reasons, police work has been characterized as a *low-visibility* activity.[21] Thus, the work environment of policing, in short, creates ample opportunities for abuse of citizens, either as a result of an honest misjudgment or from evil motives.

Alternative Paths to Police Accountability

Our society has several different mechanisms for achieving police accountability.[22] Unfortunately, they have not been as effective as they needed to be. The following section reviews the principal accountability mechanisms, their purposes, and their limitations.

The Political System In a democratic society, the primary mechanism for holding the police accountable is the political system. Elected officials are responsible for directing the police, along with other government agencies, and for seeing that they reflect the will of the people. In this country, primary responsibility for directing the police falls on mayors and city council members, and to a lesser extent on county commissioners responsible for sheriffs' departments. They do so primarily by appointing police chiefs and controlling police department budgets.

The sad fact of our history, however, is that the political process has often failed in this area. Mayors and city council members have displayed either staggering indifference to police problems or have themselves been the ultimate source of police problems. Most of these elected officials have not cared about police misconduct. Additionally, even today those who are well intentioned lack expert knowledge about the very complex aspects of policing and police administration. Few are able to move beyond clichés about "professionalism" or "tough policing" and most fall back on purely symbolic gestures, such as putting more officers on the street. Through all of the nineteenth century and much of the twentieth, these elected officials thought about the police primarily in terms of the potential opportunities for graft or patronage.[23]

Insofar as elected officials have taken an active interest in law enforcement policies, it has been either to corrupt it or to dictate policies that have undesirable consequences. Today, these impulses express themselves in terms of posturing about "getting tough" with crime. "Zero tolerance" is simply the most popular current cliché. In a comparative study of police violence in the United States and other countries in the Americas, Paul Chevigny argues, despite enormous differences related to history and political institutions, the political pressure everywhere to control crime encourages or tolerates police abuse of human rights.[24]

The Courts Because of the pervasive failure of the political system to pursue, much less achieve, police accountability, many reformers have turned to the courts.[25] The post–World War II explosion of civil rights and civil liberties created a context for remedies for police abuse. A generation of liberals placed much of their faith in the Supreme Court to control police misconduct. The most notable landmarks in this process are such famous decisions such as *Mapp v. Ohio* and *Miranda v Arizona*. The Court's so-called "due process revolution" accomplished much, creating basic rules on searches seizures and interrogations and in the process defining general principles of accountability.[26]

The Supreme Court's many decisions related to policing eliminated many of the worst abuses, but they inevitably left much to be done. Compliance with Court decisions by police officers on the street is problematic at best. Given the nature of police work, there are abundant opportunities for evading the exclusionary rule or the requirements of the *Miranda* decision.[27] For several decades, meanwhile, the Court has cut back on constitutional protection of individuals and given the police greater leeway. Even more important, many critical areas of policing have never been addressed by the Supreme

Court. There is no Court decision barring a police officer from calling someone on the street a "scumbag" or an "asshole." There is a lead decision on
police use of deadly force, but pushing someone around in a way that is
humiliating but not physically injurious falls below the level of constitutional
scrutiny. Routine abuse and complaint procedures for responding to such incidents fall below the threshold of constitutional law.

Professional Police Administration A third strategy for police accountability is
through professional police administration. Several generations of reform-
minded police executives have attempted to control police officer behavior
and establish standards of professionalism. The police professionalization
movement accomplished a great deal, but it also faced an enormous challenge.
The first police departments in this country, created in the early nineteenth
century, were immediately immersed in politics, and the result was corruption,
inefficiency, and brutality. The dilemma was and is that politics—the very
process that is designed to ensure an accountable police—was to blame. Some
elected officials, more interested in the graft and patronage, appointed police
chiefs who would serve those goals.[28]

For nearly a century reformers fought gamely to raise the standards of
policing under the rubric of professionalization. It has been a long struggle to
raise recruitment standards, improve training, institute reasonable management
techniques. Much hope has been invested in technology, from the first paddy
wagon to today's in-car computer. Despite significant accomplishments in
many areas, however, the professionalization movement fell short with respect
to accountability. It is instructive to examine O. W. Wilson's classic text, *Police
Administration,* generally regarded as the "bible" on the subject from the 1950s
through the 1970s.[29] The book barely recognizes the subject of police discretion, the problems that arise from its misuse, or how to control those problems.
A 1997 report on police personnel evaluation systems, meanwhile, found them
to be inadequate and generally unrelated to the actual work of police officers.[30] In short, professional police administration has failed to adequately
address the critical issues of accountability.

The Rampart scandal in the Los Angeles Police Department that was
uncovered in 1999 is a particularly sobering experience. Since the 1950s, the
LAPD has generally been cited as the model of police professionalism, particularly in its high personnel standards. The standard view of the LAPD tended
to overlook allegations of excessive use of force over the years, but even the
department's critics agreed that it was free of corruption. Yet in its internal
report on the Rampart scandal, the LAPD conceded that its own internal
procedures had collapsed. The report concluded that the standard personnel
evaluations, for example, were worthless. And it listed over thirty integrity
control policies and procedures, all of which had failed to prevent the Rampart scandal from occurring.[31] In short, even in a department with a national
reputation for its high standards of professionalism and an elaborate set of
policies and procedures, serious corruption, brutality, and lying were allowed
to flourish.

A Note on Community Policing

It is impossible to talk about police accountability today without some reference to community policing. Community policing, an idea that has swept the
country since the early 1980s, represents a philosophy of policing rather than a
specific set of activities and tactics. The core principles include developing
close working relationships with neighborhood residents and responding to
particular community needs. The jury is still out on the impact of the community policing movement. It is not clear whether it has become institutionalized
as a permanent feature of American policing or is just another in a long line of
passing fads. Nor is it clear that the movement has achieved its stated goals.[32]

From our perspective, community policing raises new issues related to
accountability. To a great extent, it accentuates the problems associated with
traditional police management, primarily by decentralizing responsibility
within police departments and asking rank-and-file officers to exercise even
greater discretion than in the past. Much of the progress in police accountability in recent decades has been achieved through centralized control over police
officer discretion—that is, through court-imposed rules or internal rules and
procedures.[33] Unfortunately, the literature on community policing has given
relatively little attention to the fundamental tension between decentralized
responsibility and centralized control in policing.[34] While community policing
emphasizes partnerships with community groups, the literature on this subject
emphasizes community input into police policies (that is, *what* officers should
do) but not input regarding accountability (that is, *how* they should conduct
themselves). Potentially, citizen oversight can provide a partnership mechanism
and a process for community input with regard to accountability. To date,
however, there has been little if any discussion of this important issue.

Summary

Historically there have been several different mechanisms for achieving police
accountability. Unfortunately, most of these have not functioned as effectively
as they could or should have. And in some instances they have failed altogether. Citizen oversight of the police has arisen as both a supplement and an
alternative to these other mechanisms.

CITIZEN OVERSIGHT: PRO AND CON

As an alternative to the traditional strategies for achieving police accountability, citizen oversight combines certain aspects of each one. It represents a form
of political control by adding a new mechanism for direct citizen input into
police matters. It resembles the judicial control of police behavior by creating
a quasijudicial process of investigating and adjudicating complaints. It incorporates aspects of professional police management by strengthening the disciplinary process. And it parallels community policing by emphasizing citizen input
into policing. Whether or not it improves on these traditional strategies, or

helps to strengthen them without compounding existing problems, is of course the central question. This book argues unequivocally that it does.

Although it has grown rapidly in recent years, citizen oversight is still extremely controversial. Police unions have bitterly fought oversight proposals in every city and county. Citizen oversight raises a number of important questions about the quality of citizen complaint procedures, about police work and the nature of citizen complaints, and about our capacity to reform the police and achieve greater accountability. It is important at the outset of this book, therefore, to consider the arguments on both sides of the issue.

The Case for Citizen Oversight

Citizen oversight rests on the assumption that citizen input into the process for handling complaints against police officers will achieve a number of positive results. Specifically, advocates of oversight make the following arguments: (1) that police misconduct is a serious problem and that internal police complaint procedures fail to address this problem; (2) that citizen oversight will provide more thorough and fair investigation of complaints than those conducted by the police themselves; (3) that citizen oversight agencies will sustain more complaints; (4) that oversight agencies will result in more discipline of guilty officers; (5) that more disciplinary actions will deter police misconduct more effectively than internal police procedures; (6) that complaint review by oversight agencies will be perceived as independent and will provide greater satisfaction for complainants and also improve public attitudes about the police; and (7) that citizen oversight will help professionalize police departments and improve the quality of policing.

This is an extremely ambitious agenda, suggesting that citizen oversight will produce sweeping improvements in policing. In Chapters 3, 4, 5, and 6 we will examine in detail the assumptions underlying these arguments and the available evidence on whether the arguments are valid.

The Case against Citizen Oversight

Opponents of citizen oversight argue that it achieves none of its goals and in fact often makes matters worse. Their arguments against citizen oversight are as follows: (1) that police misconduct is not as serious a problem as people allege; (2) that police officers are capable of and do in fact conduct fair and thorough investigations; (3) that police internal affairs units sustain a higher rate of complaints than do citizen oversight agencies; (4) that police departments mete out tougher discipline than oversight agencies; (5) that internal police disciplinary procedures deter police misconduct more effectively than oversight agencies; (6) that internal police disciplinary procedures provide greater satisfaction to complainants and the general public; and (7) that external citizen oversight agencies harm policing by deterring effective crimefighting by police officers and also by undermining the managerial authority of police chief executives.

In Chapters 3, 4, 5, and 6 we will examine in detail the assumptions underlying these arguments and the available evidence regarding their validity.

A Fundamental Question: Is Citizen Input Legitimate?

At the heart of the arguments for and against citizen oversight is a fundamental question of legitimacy: Do citizens have a legitimate role in overseeing the police? Do citizens have the capacity to make judgments about the professional competence of police officers?

Opponents of citizen oversight offer arguments reflecting both practical considerations and matters of principle. First, citing the history of the police in the United States, they argue that citizen input into policing has resulted in corruption and inefficiency. Citizen input traditionally involved political interference that undermined personnel standards. The movement to professionalize the police emphasized removing improper political influence.[35] Second, opponents argue that in principle the police should be accorded full responsibility for managing their own affairs, in the same manner that other professions —doctors, lawyers, and teachers—are allowed to regulate the conduct of members of their respective professions. The underlying assumption of this argument is that police officers are professionals who by training and experience have a level of technical competence that can only be judged by fellow professionals. Only other doctors, for example, can judge whether a doctor handled a case in a professional manner or is guilty of misconduct. The third and last argument offered by opponents is that citizen oversight agencies have in fact proven to be ineffective.

Opponents cite the experience of the old Philadelphia Police Advisory Board (1958–1967) and the New York Civilian Complaint Review Board (1953–present) as evidence of this failure. We will examine the evidence regarding the effectiveness of these and other oversight agencies in the chapters that follow.

Advocates of citizen oversight respond with arguments also based on practical considerations, historical evidence, and matters of principle. First, they argue that as a practical matter police departments have failed to establish effective complaint procedures and hold their own officers accountable and therefore have forfeited any claim they can manage their own affairs without any citizen oversight. Second, they argue that as a matter of principle in a democratic society all government agencies must be subject to control by the citizenry acting through their duly elected representatives. Law enforcement agencies in the United States are already subject to citizen input through mayors, city councils, county boards of commissioners, governors, and presidents. In addition, the courts have a major impact on police policies. In this context, oversight is simply an extension of a well-established principle, according to its advocates.

Ultimately, the debate between the advocates and opponents of citizen oversight returns to the question of legitimacy: Who can and should assume responsibility for overseeing the police? This question, in turn, becomes a matter of trust: Who do you trust to oversee the police? The fact of the matter is, given the long history of controversy over police misconduct, that there is no shared consensus of opinion about trusting the police. While most

Americans consistently give the police very high ratings in public opinion polls, a large segment of the public also deeply distrusts them, particularly when it comes to investigating citizen complaints.

Failures and Successes

In the chapters that follow, we will address the question of the legitimacy of citizen oversight primarily by examining the evidence regarding its effectiveness. In brief, the available evidence indicates that some oversight agencies have very creditable records of success, while others have failed to function effectively.

New Orleans created a fully independent oversight agency, the Office of Municipal Investigations (OMI), in 1981. Yet by the mid-1990s, the New Orleans Police Department had a national reputation as one of the most corrupt and brutal departments in the entire country. There is no evidence that the OMI addressed those problems in any way.[36] In New York City, meanwhile, the New York Civil Liberties Union (NYCLU) has fought for an independent civilian review board since the early 1950s, finally achieving its goal in 1993. Yet by 1996, NYCLU Executive Director Norman Siegel was in near-despair over the results, concluding that "over its first three years of operation the CCRB has largely failed in its mission."[37] It had not proven that it could effectively and fairly investigate complaints against New York City police officers.

A somewhat related criticism of citizen oversight is that a particular agency has failed by simply not making any significant difference in the complaints process or the quality of policing. In other words, it is simply an expensive waste, and one that offers a false promise of improving policing.

Despite the shortcomings of some oversight agencies, others have established creditable records of success in improving the complaints process and effecting reforms in the police departments they are responsible for. Numerous examples are discussed in the subsequent chapters of this book, but here are a few quick examples:

- The San Jose Independent Auditor made 40 policy recommendations between 1993 and 1999, and got the San Jose Police Department to adopt 38 of them, making both complaint investigations and the handling of complaint data more professional.

- The Portland, Oregon Police Internal Affairs Auditing Committee systematically audits complaint investigations. It has identified biased or inadequate investigations, has brought these problems to the attention of the responsible police officials, and has recommended the appropriate changes.

- The Special Counsel to the Los Angeles County Sheriff's Department examines virtually every aspect of the department's operations. In one notable case, he found that the high rate of shootings by officers assigned to one troubled district were the result of a number of systemic management problems, involving the assignment and supervision of those officers.

- The Minneapolis Civilian Review Authority (CRA) created a process for receiving feedback from complainants and police officers about their experience with the complaint process. The Quality Service Audit (QSA) system provides a basis for identifying perceived problems in the investigation of complaints and for correcting them. In its first year, the CRA received extremely high ratings from both citizen complainants and police officers.

The common theme in these success stories is that the oversight agencies do more than merely investigate complaints. They take a *proactive view of their role* and actively *seek out the underlying causes of police misconduct or problems with the complaint process.* The causes of police misconduct are often deeply rooted in personnel practices—how officers are assigned to particular precincts, for example, or the level of staffing in internal affairs units. Through a policy review process, oversight agencies examine a police department's policies and procedures and recommend changes where they are needed. And perhaps most important, they monitor the implementation of those recommendations. A number of oversight agencies also have active outreach programs to meet with community groups and hear the concerns of residents.

In short, the successful oversight agencies have a *vision of better policing* and define their role in terms of bringing about *organizational change.* The relevant question, then, is not whether citizen oversight in general is a success or failure but whether particular oversight agencies are successful. If none can demonstrate success in some persuasive way, then the entire concept is suspect and it would be appropriate to consider alternative means of achieving police accountability. But if some can demonstrate success, the task then becomes one of identifying the conditions of success. What does it take to create an effective citizen oversight agency or process? Is it a question of the organizational structure of the agency? Does it involve the particular powers and resources the agency has? Is it a matter of leadership and how an agency defines its role? How critical is support from responsible elected officials? These questions are addressed in the subsequent chapters of this book.

In evaluating the role and effectiveness of citizen oversight, it is important to maintain perspective and think in terms of reasonable goals. It is a mistake to assume that citizen oversight is going to end police misconduct and solve all police problems. As Human Rights Watch cautions, "Few believe that citizen review mechanisms alone are the solution to the problem of police brutality."[38] The problem is too deeply entrenched for it to be ended by any single remedy. The argument of this book, however, is that citizen oversight is *one* important mechanism for ending police misconduct. The purpose of this book is to examine the specific ways in which it can be effective and to explore at the same time the factors that have kept some oversight agencies from being effective.

Beyond the Police: Responsive Bureaucracies

The problem of accountability is not confined to the police. It is a general problem in contemporary society, and it is particularly acute for the vast bureaucracies that administer our public schools, social welfare, and health care. It affects the traditional professions such as law and medicine, all of which have historically resisted the intrusion of outsiders into their affairs—and justified that position in the name of professionalism. Where does the hospital patient who feels mistreated go? What procedure exists for receiving and investigating that complaint? Is there a procedure at all? Is the complainant treated in a fair and respectful manner? What about the citizen who feels that his or her lawyer failed to provide proper service? Does the aggrieved medical patient feel that the doctors who investigate his or her complaint will be genuinely objective in evaluating the doctor's conduct? The questions of accountability that arise regarding complaints against the police are equally relevant to other professions.

The Plan of the Book

The plan of this book is as follows. Chapter 2 provides a history of the oversight movement: the often stormy controversies surrounding "civilian review" and the recent growth of citizen oversight. Chapter 2 traces that growth and examines the changes in public attitudes about the police and accountability of government agencies that has underpinned it.

There is much misunderstanding about what citizen oversight is and what oversight agencies do. Much of the opposition to oversight is based on fears and misinformation that have been circulating for decades. Chapters 3 and 4 describe in detail the role of oversight and the activities that oversight agencies engage in. The fact that it requires two chapters to cover this subject indicates that these activities are quite extensive. Many people believe oversight agencies investigate citizen complaints. As Chapter 3 explains, that function alone is extremely complex, with many different issues that require careful attention. Chapter 4 examines the role that oversight agencies play in monitoring the police, quite apart from investigating complaints. Many people are not aware of this role at all. Yet this book argues that the monitoring role may in fact be the most important aspect of citizen oversight.

Ultimately, people ask whether citizen oversight is effective. Usually, they want to know whether citizen oversight is more effective than traditional police internal complaint procedures. As Chapters 5 and 6 explain, the question of effectiveness is extremely complex. The first issue is, effective at what? Chapter 5 examines the effectiveness of complaint investigations by oversight agencies. The evidence and the issues considered, however, are equally relevant to police internal complaint procedures. Chapter 6 examines the evidence on the effectiveness of oversight as a monitoring role.

CONCLUSION

As a nation, we face a serious problem in police misconduct. Although many departments have taken effective steps to raise the quality of police conduct, abuse of citizens continues. In response to this problem, citizen oversight has arisen as a new strategy for achieving police accountability. Citizen oversight of police is an exciting experiment. New agencies and procedures are still being created. At this relatively early stage, we still do not understand the full potential of this experiment and its impact on policing. This book examines the experiment in citizen oversight of police in detail, identifying those procedures that work and those that do not. The end result is a road map to better policing and a more civil society.

NOTES

1. Some observers in New Orleans believe that the FBI agents did not understand what they were overhearing on Davis's radio and thus failed to prevent the murder from occurring.

2. "Officer Guilty of Helping Torture Immigrant," *New York Times,* 19 February, 1999.

3. Los Angeles Police Department, Board of Inquiry, *Rampart Area Corruption Incident* (Los Angeles: LAPD, March 2000).

4. Human Rights Watch, *Shielded from Justice: Police Brutality and Accountability in the United States* (New York: Human Rights Watch, 1998), 1.

5. Jerome H. Skolnick and James J. Fyfe, *Above the Law* (New York: Free Press, 1993).

6. Human Rights Watch, *Shielded from Justice,* 2. For a detailed discussion of this issue, see Samuel Walker, *Police Interactions with Racial and Ethnic Minorities: Assessing the Evidence and Allegations* (Washington, DC: Police Executive Research Forum, 2000).

7. Los Angeles Police Department, *Rampart Area Corruption Incident.*

8. Egon Bittner, *Aspects of Police Work* (Boston: Northeastern University Press, 1990), 132–36.

9. The best overviews of this rapidly changing subject are Peter Finn, *Citizen Review of Police: Approaches and Implementation* (Washington, DC: Government Printing Office, forthcoming 2000), and Samuel Walker, *Citizen Review Resource Manual* (Washington, DC: PERF, 1995)

10. This incident was broadcast on national television by NBC *Dateline* on August 18, 1998. Similar incidents may be

viewed on the Police Complaints Center website: www.policeabuse.org

11. New York City Public Advocate, *Investigation of the New York City Police Department's Response to Civilian Complaints of Police Misconduct—Interim Report* (New York, 15 September, 1999); "Report Says Most Officers Cited for Brutality or Misconduct Are Not Punished," *New York Times,* 30 December, 1999.

12. Samuel Walker, *Citizen Review of the Police—1998 Update* (Omaha: University of Nebraska at Omaha, 1998).

13. Andrew Goldsmith, ed., *Complaints against the Police: The Trend to External Review* (Oxford: Clarendon Press, 1991).

14. David Bayley, preface, Goldsmith, *Complaints against the Police,* vi.

15. John P. Crank and Robert Langworthy, "An Institutional Perspective on Policing," *Journal of Criminal Law and Criminology* 83:2 (1992): 338–63.

16. National Commission on Law Observance and Enforcement, *Report on Lawlessness in Law Enforcement* (Washington, DC: Government Printing Office, 1931), 4.

17. Samuel Walker, *Popular Justice: A History of American Criminal Justice,* 2nd ed. (New York: Oxford University Press, 1998).

18. The classic examination of this issue is Jerome Skolnick, *Justice without Trial,* 3rd ed. (New York: Macmillan, 1994).

19. The classic discussion is Egon Bittner, "The Capacity to Use Force," *Aspects of Police Work* (Boston: Northeastern University Press, 1990), 120–32.

20. The best discussion of this aspect of police work is still Albert Reiss, *The Police*

and the Public (New Haven: Yale University Press, 1971).

21. Joseph Goldstein, "Police Decision Not to Invoke the Criminal Process: Low Visibility Decisions in the Criminal Process," *Yale Law Journal* 69: 4 (1960): 543–88.

22. An illuminating comparative perspective on the various alternative strategies for achieving accountability is found in Paul Chevigny, *Edge of the Knife: Police Violence in the Americas* (New York: The New Press, 1995).

23. Samuel Walker, *A Critical History of Police Reform* (Lexington: Lexington Books, 1977).

24. Chevigny, *Edge of the Knife.*

25. Samuel Walker, "Historical Roots of the Legal Control of Police Behavior," in David Weisburd and Craig Uchida, eds., *Police Innovation and Control of the Police* (New York: Springer Verlag, 1993), 32–55.

26. Walker, *Popular Justice.*

27. See, for example, Richard A. Leo and George C. Thomas III, eds., *The Miranda Debate: Law, Justice, and Policing* (Boston: Northeastern University Press, 1998).

28. Walker, *Critical History of Police Reform.*

29. O. W. Wilson and Roy C. McLaren, *Police Administration,* 4th ed. (New York: McGraw-Hill, 1977).

30. Timothy N. Oettmeier and Mary Ann Wycoff, *Personnel Performance Evaluations in the Community Policing Context* (Washington, DC: Police Executive Research Forum, 1997).

31. Los Angeles Police Department, *Rampart Area Corruption Incident.*

32. The literature on community policing is vast and rapidly growing A good overview is David Bayley, *Police for the Future* (New York: Oxford University Press, 1994). The best case study is Wesley Skogan and Susan M. Hartnett, *Community Policing, Chicago Style* (New York: Oxford University Press, 1997).

33. Samuel Walker, *Taming the System: The Control of Discretion in Criminal Justice, 1950–1990* (New York: Oxford University Press, 1993).

34. But see George L. Kelling, *Broken Windows and Police Discretion* (Washington, DC: Government Printing Office, 1999).

35. Walker, *Critical History of Police Reform.*

36. "Officer Linked to Killing, Shocking a Jaded City," *New York Times,* 19 December, 1994.

37. New York Civil Liberties Union, *Third Anniversary Overview of the Civilian Complaint Review Board* (New York: NYCLU, 1996), 1.

38. Human Rights Watch, *Shielded from Justice,* 55.

2

❖

The Rise, Fall, and Revival
of Citizen Oversight

INTRODUCTION

Citizen oversight of the police in the United States today is widespread and growing (see Chapter 1, Figure 1-1). This development, however, is the result of a long and bitter struggle, one that is closely intertwined with the nation's race problem. The history of the movement for citizen oversight of the police falls into three broad periods. Between the 1920s and the mid-1950s, oversight first emerged as a radical idea, and after World War II it was eventually embodied in a few experimental agencies. In the second period, from the late 1950s through the 1960s, civilian review—as it was called—became one of the major demands of civil rights leaders. Extremely bitter conflicts over this issue erupted in Philadelphia and New York City. The demise of review boards in those two cities by the end of the decade appeared to signal the death of citizen oversight. The third period began with the quiet revival of oversight in 1969 with the creation of the Kansas City Office of Citizen Complaints and continues to the present day.

The contours of the history of the oversight movement reflect deeper changes in American society: the rise and development of the modern civil rights movement, the changing role of the police in society, and new public concern about accountability of government agencies, including but not limited to the police.

BEGINNINGS: 1920s–1950s

In the 1920s, police brutality was a serious and pervasive problem, as it had been since the creation of the first modern police departments nearly a hundred years earlier.[1] Officers freely beat citizens on the street, knowing that they would rarely if ever be punished for doing so. Brutal and coercive measures were used to extract confessions from criminal suspects. The 1931 Wickersham Commission report on *Lawlessness in Law Enforcement* found that the third degree, which it defined as the deliberate infliction of pain, was widespread across the country. It reported numerous instances of police beating confessions out of criminal suspects. In one case, officers hung a suspect out of a window by his heels until he confessed. The chief of the Buffalo, New York, Police Department expressed open contempt for the Constitution.[2]

Although incidents of police brutality were regularly reported in the press, neither the courts nor responsible elected officials took action to end it. The courts took a "hands-off" posture toward the police, as they did toward prisons, regarding them as beyond the scope of constitutional protection of individual rights. One legal scholar has characterized the pre-1930s era as the "stone age" of the constitutional law of criminal procedure.[3] Local elected officials, meanwhile, mainly saw the police as a source of graft and patronage and expressed little if any concern about brutality.

Within the police profession, a small group of reformers, led by August Vollmer from Berkeley, California, desperately fought to raise standards of professionalism. In all their reports, articles, and books, however, there is scarcely a word about physical abuse of citizens and no mention of citizen complaints about police conduct. There is no record of any police department's having a formal citizen complaint process until the 1940s.[4] In fact, the 1977 edition of O. W. Wilson's textbook on *Police Administration,* for a generation regarded as the authoritative work on the subject, devotes less than a page to the subject of internal police investigation of alleged officer misconduct.[5]

In this context of neglect, only a few radicals dared suggest that citizens should have some input into the handling of complaints against police officers. The idea first appeared in Los Angeles in 1928, when the Los Angeles Bar Association created a Committee on Constitutional Rights. Volunteer attorneys received and investigated complaints, and they referred them to the Los Angles Police Department for official investigation.[6] The Los Angeles Police Department was probably no more brutal and corrupt than any other big city department at that time, although its "Red Squad" was particularly aggressive in spying on political groups.[7] The local ACLU affiliate devoted much of its slender resources to fighting abuse by the LAPD. In the larger political context, however, the ACLU and its few allies in Los Angeles were lonely voices in the wilderness.[8] The bar association committee had no official status, of course, but it succeeded in planting the idea of citizen involvement in the complaint process.

The idea of oversight slowly began to spread. The 1931 Wickersham Commission endorsed it, recommending the creation of "some disinterested agency" in each city to assist people with their complaints against the police.[9] Created by President Herbert Hoover, the Wickersham Commission was the first comprehensive study of the entire criminal justice system, Its report on *Lawlessness in Law Enforcement* was a devastating exposé of police brutality and gave police reformers an important boost. The three authors of the report— Zechariah Chafee, Walter Pollack, and Carl Stern—were all closely associated with the ACLU. Chafee, who was also the preeminent authority on freedom of speech, included a similar recommendation in his preface to *Our Lawless Police,* a popular expose of police brutality in 1931. He recommended: "There should be in each community an untrammeled body . . . to which complaints of brutality and other official lawlessness can be brought, and by which such complaints will be energetically and fearlessly investigated."[10]

The next proposal for citizen oversight arose in the aftermath of a one-day race riot in New York City in 1935. The riot had been sparked by rumors that a young African-American man had died in police custody. Mayor Fiorello LaGuardia, one of the leading progressive reformers of the 1920s and 1930s, responded by appointing a commission to study the riot—one of a long series of riot commissions.[11] The commission included Arthur Garfield Hays and Morris Ernst, both lawyers and co-general counsels for the ACLU. Both were deeply committed to racial justice and refused to join the American Bar Association because it did not admit African Americans.[12]

Hays and Ernst persuaded the commission to recommend that the New York City Police Commissioner appoint "a committee of from five to seven Harlem citizens of both races to whom people may make complaint if mistreated by the police." This committee would "sift" the complaints and take those with "merit" to the commissioner. The committee would also serve as an "advisory committee" to the commissioner on relations with the Harlem community.[13] This proposal was stronger medicine than LaGuardia was prepared to swallow, however. Despite his deserved reputation as a progressive on many issues, he was not ready to challenge the prerogatives of the police department, and he simply ignored the commission's recommendation.

In the context of the times, LaGuardia's response was not surprising. Few mainstream politicians expressed any interest in police brutality. The police issues that did arouse their concerns were corruption and the nonenforcement of laws regulating gambling and drinking. Police reform efforts concentrated on eliminating political influence over the police and on raising personnel standards. Little thought was given to administrative controls over on-the-street police behavior. The leading experts on police professionalism, notably August Vollmer and Bruce Smith, did not even mention the issue of citizen complaints.[14] Indeed, the reformers' campaign to eliminate "political" interference translated into a strong bias against any citizen input into policing, an attitude that professional-minded police chiefs retained for decades.

War and Race: Changes in the Wind

World War II radically altered the politics of race relations in America and in the process transformed the issue of police abuse. The war years gave birth to the modern civil rights movement as a broad-based interracial effort. The rhetoric of the war effort, with its denunciation of Nazi racism, encouraged African Americans to press for equality at home. A threatened march on Washington in 1943, the first national public civil rights protest, forced President Franklin D. Roosevelt to take the first tentative steps to end race discrimination in employment. The rising expectations of the African-American community, together with the dislocations caused by the domestic war effort, aggravated racial tensions in local communities across the country.

These tensions finally exploded in race riots in New York City, Detroit, and Los Angeles in the summer of 1943. Near-riot situations developed in Washington, D.C. and a number of other cities.[15] The Detroit riot lasted nearly a week and left thirty-four people dead and $2 million worth of property destroyed. Even more important, it disrupted production in the crucial automobile factories for nearly a week. Coming in the midst of World War II, the riots in Detroit and other cities were an alarm bell to the American political establishment, which feared that the Germans and the Japanese would exploit racial tensions in the United States. In response to the riots, civic leaders across the country organized "unity" campaigns, emphasizing racial and religious tolerance.[16]

One aspect of the wartime unity effort was the first police-community relations movement in the sense of an organized effort to improve relations between the police and racial minority communities. Several police departments conducted the first race relations training programs for their officers. California, under the leadership of Governor Earl Warren, published a series of community relations manuals for the police. Breaking new ground, these manuals instructed police officers to treat all citizens equally and not to discriminate on the basis of race. The police-community relations movement introduced the first serious attention to the issue of citizen complaints against the police.[17]

The riots of 1935 and the World War II years established the social and political dynamic that would drive the citizen oversight movement over the next half century. Oversight, and the demand for control of police brutality, became part of the emerging national civil rights movement. It is significant that although police brutality was a serious problem in the first hundred years of American policing, no serious movement for better citizen complaint procedures appeared until the issue was defined in terms of race. The subsequent history of the oversight movement is inseparable from the history of the post–World War II civil rights movement.

Washington, D.C.: A Halting First Step

One of the first tangible results of the wartime police-community relations effort was the creation of the Complaint Review Board (CRB) for the Metropolitan Police in the District of Columbia in 1948. A historic but halting first step in the oversight movement, the board consisted of three citizens who reviewed complaints referred to them by the police chief and made recommendations about the proper disposition. In practice, the board had little visibility and handled very few cases. With no staff of its own, it was entirely dependent upon the investigative files compiled by the police department, which did not even create its own specialized complaint unit until 1966. A 1966 report concluded that the CRB had "functioned quietly and infrequently," handling a total of only fifty-four cases between 1948 and 1964. Only eight cases were ever referred to the chief for action. Nor did the board "see fit to question the small number of cases referred to it by the Chief of Police."[18]

The low visibility of the CRB also accounts for the lack of strenuous opposition from either the police chief or the rank and file. They had no reason to feel threatened by an agency that played such an insignificant role. As the civil rights movement escalated in the 1960s, however, pressure increased for a more active CRB. In June 1965, its procedures were revised, making it easier for citizens to file complaints and giving the board more power to initiate investigations on its own. The number of complaints increased to thirty-nine in 1965–66, but this was still an extremely low number by the standards of later years.[19]

Other cities also took tentative steps regarding oversight in the late 1950s. Review boards were created in Minneapolis, Rochester, and York, Pennsylvania, but none ever became fully operative. The legal status of the Minneapolis board was immediately challenged, for example, and it never began operating. These half-hearted steps suggest that while there was increasing concern about police brutality and police-community relations among some community leaders, there was not yet strong political support for better citizen complaint procedures. In fact, concern about citizen complaints was so limited that most police departments did not even create formal complaint procedures until the early or mid-1960s.[20]

BREAKTHROUGH: THE PHILADELPHIA POLICE ADVISORY BOARD

The first significant oversight agency was the Philadelphia Police Advisory Board (PAB), created in 1958. The idea of the PAB originated with the Greater Philadelphia Branch of the ACLU, which charged that in sixteen years no Philadelphia police officer had been disciplined "for a wrong done to a civilian as a result of a complaint that was originated by a civilian."[21] The election of Richardson Dilworth as mayor in 1952 created new possibilities for reforming the police. A member of the city's social elite, he had been active with the local ACLU and appointed like-minded people to his administration. The director of the Philadelphia ACLU affiliate explained to national ACLU leaders that "Philadelphia has an administration sympathetic to civil liberties. The Police Commissioner himself is an enlightened man, apparently sensitive to the importance of protecting the citizen from police excess." Police Commissioner Thomas Gibbons made a serious effort to reform the police department and worked with the Philadelphia ACLU on several issues.

By late 1956, however, the ACLU concluded that trying to improve the police department's internal Police Board of Inquiry (PBI) was a "futile" effort and proposed creating a civilian review board. Only the local NAACP endorsed the ACLU proposal, as the local bar association and other civic groups regarded it as dangerously radical. City Council member Henry W. Sawyer, III, a prominent attorney and president of the ACLU affiliate, introduced a bill to create a review board in early 1957, but it died in a hostile committee. The ACLU then turned to Mayor Dilworth, who created the PAB by executive order on October 1, 1958.[22] This was a historic step, but in the long run the elitist origins of the PAB ultimately proved to be a fatal weakness. Subsequent events proved that what one mayor could create by executive order another mayor could just as easily abolish.[23]

The PAB consisted of a board of citizens who would receive citizen complaints, refer them to the police department for investigation, and after reviewing the department's reports make a recommendation to the Police Commissioner for action. The initial board members included several luminaries: Nobel Peace Prize winner Clarence Pickett and the renowned criminologist Thorsten Sellin. The PAB was extremely weak, however. It had no budget during its first two years and relied entirely on the volunteered time of its board members. It obtained a part-time executive secretary in 1960 and a full-time staff member only in 1963.

The Fraternal Order of Police (FOP), representing the rank and file, was initially slow to respond to the PAB but in 1960 sued to enjoin its operations. The suit was settled by a compromise that altered some of the PAB's procedures to protect the rights of police officers. As the civil rights movement escalated in the 1960s and African-American criticisms of police brutality increased, however, the FOP launched a more aggressive attack. It filed a second suit in March 1967 and prevailed on the grounds that the executive order creating the PAB violated the city's Home Rule Charter. The state supreme court overturned this decision in 1969, but Mayor James Tate, a conventional Democratic Party figure beholden to the police union and the white ethnic communities it represented, simply refused to reactivate the PAB.[24] With that, the first significant citizen oversight agency passed into history.

Because it was such an important innovation and managed to survive for nearly a decade, the PAB received an enormous amount of attention, both during its lifetime and after its demise. The first serious study of police complaint procedures, a 1964 *Harvard Law Review* article, concluded that it successfully introduced an innovative "citizen judgment to police policies and activities" and had helped develop new police department policies on such potentially contentious issues as the use of handcuffs.[25] Opponents of citizen oversight argued that it was a failure, citing evidence that the PAB sustained fewer allegations against police officers than did the departments internal affairs unit (this evidence and the controversy surrounding it is examined in detail in Chapter 5). Even its staunchest supporters conceded that the PAB was far from perfect and did not significantly reduce police brutality or improve police-community relations. In later years, both the President's Crime Commission and the American Bar Association cited the alleged failure of the PAB in recommending against citizen oversight.[26]

THE POLICE-COMMUNITY RELATIONS CRISIS OF THE 1960S

The police-community relations crisis of the 1960s thrust the issue of citizen oversight of the police into national prominence. In city after city, as the tempo of the civil rights movement escalated, African Americans confronted the police over alleged brutality and unjustified shootings. Civil rights groups challenged racial discrimination across the spectrum of American life—education, housing, employment—but the issue of police brutality had special significance. Because of the high visibility of the uniformed police officer, the white cop in the ghetto became the symbol of racial oppression.

It is doubtful that police brutality actually increased in these years. Rather, in a dynamic that would continue through the 1990s, the civil rights movement steadily raised expectations about the quality of police behavior. Incidents that had been allowed to pass without protest in the past now became the source of angry confrontations. The more radical critics of the police pinned the offensive stereotype of "pigs" on them, caricaturing them all as uneducated, reactionary bigots.

In truth, as the President's Crime Commission reported in 1967, big city police officers were poorly educated, inadequately trained, and barely supervised. Even the best police departments did not take seriously issues of race, brutality, and citizen complaints. In the Los Angeles Police Department, reputedly the most professional in the nation, an officer might face serious discipline for damaging a patrol car but hardly an inquiry for shooting and killing someone. LAPD Chief William Parker dismissed all critics of the police—the NAACP, the ACLU, and others—as dangerous radicals bent on undermining the LAPD's "thin blue line" between civilization and anarchy.[27]

The escalating conflict between the police and ghetto residents finally exploded in a series of riots that swept the country between 1964 and 1968. Nearly all of these riots were sparked by an incident involving a white police officer. The first major riot, in New York City in the summer of 1964, followed the fatal shooting of an African-American teenager by a white off-duty officer. A routine traffic stop triggered the devastating 1965 riot in the Watts community of Los Angeles. A police raid on an after-hours bar in the African-American community set off the even more devastating Detroit riot of 1967. The Kerner Commission, appointed by President Lyndon Johnson to study the national race crisis, counted 164 disorders in the first nine months of 1967 alone.[28]

To curb police abuse, civil rights groups demanded the hiring of more African-American officers and the creation of civilian review boards to handle complaints. The latter demand focused attention on existing police complaint procedures. The Kerner Commission concluded: "The manner in which complaints of police misconduct are processed has become a deep concern to minority communities."[29] Its investigations found that there was an "almost total lack of effective channels for redress of complaints against police conduct" and that this was one of the three major causes of African-American hostility toward the police.[30] In Milwaukee and Plainfield, New Jersey, for examples, police chiefs "reject all complaints out of hand." A New Haven review board was considered "worthless." Top police officials in Detroit had seemingly good intentions but there were "no real sanctions" for officers guilty of misconduct. A 1967 U.S. Civil Rights Commission report found that persons attempting to file complaints were often threatened with criminal charges. Police officers generally had "little fear of punishment" and enjoyed "a degree of immunity from their departments."[31]

In response to these problems, the Kerner Commission recommended "external review" of citizen complaints—specifically, a "specialized agency, with adequate funds and staff, should be created separate from other municipal agencies." It argued that a police internal review procedure "regardless of its efficiency and fairness, can rarely generate the necessary community confidence" to be effective. "Making a complaint should be easy," the commission continued, with complaint forms readily available throughout the community. It also recommended that these external agencies review general police policies, "since many complaints concern departmental policies rather than individual conduct."[32]

The Debate over Civilian Review

The police-community relations crisis sparked a national debate over civilian review boards. ACLU affiliates in Philadelphia, New York, and other cities took the lead in the fight for civilian review, working closely with the NAACP and other local civil rights groups. In 1964, the national ACLU adopted an official policy endorsing "the adoption by municipalities of independent civilian police review boards," arguing that "this technique is not only a desirable method for dealing with civilian complaints of illegal police practices in a way that will preserve community confidence in the police."[33]

Not unexpectedly, the police chiefs adamantly opposed citizen review as an infringement on their professional autonomy and a threat to effective crime control. In response to the Philadelphia PAB, the International Association of Chiefs of Police (IACP) adopted an official statement in 1960 declaring its "unequivocal and vigorous opposition to and rejection of the creation and existence of such so-called police practice review boards." In a strategy that would prove to be very effective, the IACP played upon public fear of crime, warning that civilian review "would result in the impairment of law enforcement," including the "harassment, weakening, and usurpation of the legally constituted and vested administration of law enforcement personnel, all to the great detriment of efficient police performance." The chiefs expressed confidence in their own internal complaint mechanisms, arguing that "an aggrieved citizen . . . has recourse to the existing, established and tested civil and criminal processes of justice."[34] This assertion overlooked the fact that in 1960 most departments did not have any formal complaint review procedure at all.[35]

The IACP restated its opposition again in 1964, provoked by the *Harvard Law Review* study of police internal affairs units. The article was in fact not very critical of the police. It took at face value police department descriptions of their complaint procedures and as a result probably exaggerated their openness to complainants. Four years later, the Kerner Commission found that many of these procedures were in fact very hostile to complainants. The IACP dismissed civilian review boards as "devoid of both responsibility and authority" and "a superficial attempt to deal with more complex problems" of police administration. Without realizing the implications of its own argument, the IACP pointed out that the Chicago police department received six times as many complaints per officer as Philadelphia, in part, it argued, because of "the confidence the Chicago citizen places in the police department's ability to clean its own house." The point was well taken, but it was also a devastating commentary on most police departments, which did not have open and accessible complaint procedures.[36]

President Lyndon Johnson responded to rising public concern about crime and justice by creating the President's Crime Commission in 1965. The commission's 1967 report, *The Challenge of Crime in a Free Society,* rejected civilian review, arguing that it was "unreasonable to single out the police" for "special scrutiny,"[37] and cited the Washington, D.C. and Philadelphia review boards as evidence of their ineffectuality. The American Bar Association's (ABA) *Standards for the Urban Police Function* also rejected civilian review boards, arguing that the concept had "inherent defects." The ABA objected to the fact that review boards "focused solely on the police, ignored other agencies; second, procedures for determining proof . . . require many procedural safeguards." It claimed that the Philadelphia PAB "never was able to achieve its purpose." The ABA subsequently dropped some of the most critical language but still did not endorse citizen oversight.[38]

The authors of the Crime Commission report and ABA *Standards* represented the most knowledgeable and progressive-minded experts on policing. While they recognized the urgent need for greater police accountability and were deeply concerned about race discrimination by the police, their reform strategy, inherited from the early professionalization movement, was highly skeptical about external input into policing. They preferred to pursue better policing through higher police personnel standards, better training, and modern management techniques. Citizen review looked to them as a dangerous step backward to the bad old days of political influence.

Backlash: The Police Union Movement

The most significant and lasting impact of the oversight movement was to foster the creation of what would prove to be its major opposition: police unions. The demand for external oversight galvanized rank-and-file officers and spurred the creation of local police unions. Recognized police unions existed in a few major cities in the early 1960s; ten years later, they were virtually universal in cities outside the southeast. Oversight was hardly the only cause of police unionism. Police officers were angry about many things by the mid-1960s: low pay, punitive management practices, Supreme Court decisions such as *Mapp* and *Miranda,* the persistent charges of police brutality, and a general sense that they were not respected by the general public and actively hated by black leaders and white student radicals. Citizen oversight became a convenient focal point for all of these grievances. As one scholar observes, "Opposition to civilian review boards has been one of the major rallying points in organizing policemen."[39]

In the bitterly polarized atmosphere of the police-community relations crisis, the rank and file opposed even the most elementary forms of accountability. Officers in many cities refused to identify themselves by name or badge number to citizens who requested such information. The mayors in several cities had to order officers to wear name tags. In some cases, however, officers covered them up during confrontations. Boston police officers, for example, removed their name tags during a 1969 demonstration, offering the excuse that they could be hurt by the tags' pins. Boston Mayor Kevin White suggested sewing the tags on.[40]

The police unions offered a grab-bag of objections to citizen oversight. The most common was to deny the charge that brutality was widespread and to accuse oversight advocates of being professional agitators and/or communists. As one put it, the demand for civilian review was "merely the hue and cry of a number of vociferous and articulate anti-police groups and their representatives."[41] Police union spokespersons also declared, as the chiefs did, that police departments were quite capable of handling individual complaints themselves. Police officers particularly resented being made the scapegoats for the nation's racial crisis and objected to being "second-guessed by those who have no experience in police work." Finally, they argued that oversight was a strategy for intimidating officers on the part of criminals who have been arrested. Attacking civilian review as a threat to "law and order" proved to be the most effective strategy.[42]

The rise of the police unions had enormous consequences for police management, stripping chiefs of the autocratic power they had historically enjoyed. And as the New York Civil Liberties Union concluded in 1990, "Staunch opposition from police unions is the single greatest reason why civilian-controlled systems are not commonplace around the country."[43]

The unions, however, mainly spoke for white police officers. African-American officers often supported oversight. When black officers in New York City supported the independent CCRB in the 1960s, union president John Cassese attacked them, saying, "It's unfortunate they put their color before their oath of office."[44] In the 1990s, the National Black Police Officers Association published a brochure on police misconduct, urging officers to report abuse by other officers. A national survey of police officers, meanwhile, found that about 70 percent of the black officers believe "civilian review boards are an effective means of preventing police misconduct," compared with only about one-third of white officers.[45] This represents a historic break in the traditional solidarity of the police subculture, and is indicative of the deep racial divide within the rank and file.

Crisis in New York City

Nowhere was the controversy over citizen oversight more bitter or protracted than in New York City. The New York City Civilian Complaint Review Board (CCRB) grew out of a U.S. Justice Department investigation of corruption in the NYPD in the early 1950s. The investigation also uncovered allegations of police brutality and the failure of the NYPD to discipline officers guilty of misconduct. Congressman Adam Clayton Powell, representing Harlem and emerging as a national civil rights leader, quickly took up the issue. The New York Civil Liberties Union (NYCLU), meanwhile, pressed for a better citizen complaint procedure.[46] The issue burst into the headlines in 1953 with the revelation that the Justice Department under President Harry Truman, reluctant to embarrass New York City Democrats, had made a secret agreement with city officials not to investigate alleged civil rights complaints if the NYPD would institute internal reforms. The revelations forced Mayor Vincent Impellitterri to create the CCRB in 1953.[47]

The CCRB consisted of three NYPD deputy commissioners who would review complaints and make recommendations for disposition to the police commissioner. Structurally, it was part of the police department and not a form of citizen oversight. As was the case with the Washington, D.C., CRB, it had little visibility and handled few cases. In 1953 and 1954, it reviewed an average of about eighty complaints a year, sustaining 20 percent of them.[48] According to one report, the small number of complaints resulted from the fact that precinct-level police officials exercised "great discretion" in receiving complaints. Many people were discouraged from filing complaints, and even if they persisted, their complaints were often not formally recorded.[49]

The next decade witnessed a steadily escalating struggle to reform and strengthen the CCRB. The complaint procedure was gradually centralized and subject to bureaucratic controls. Partly as a result, the average annual number of complaints doubled to about 160 per year by 1957. If anything, however, dissatisfaction with the CCRB increased as the civil rights movement escalated. NYCLU Director Aryeh Neier commented in 1966 that "the public perceived the CCRB as a 'whitewash agency' which could not be trusted to deal fairly with grievances brought before it."[50] Neier added that "there is no more convincing evidence of the need for civilian review than the strength of police opposition" to it. NYCLU attorney Paul Chevigny, who operated a neighborhood law office in Harlem that handled police complaints, found "grotesque abuses" with the official complaints process. Complainants were discouraged from filing complaints and officials often sought to explain an officer's actions without fully investigating. The entire process, including the CCRB, was "too secretive" to inspire public confidence.[51]

A race riot in the summer of 1964, sparked by the fatal shooting of an African-American teenager by a white off-duty police officer, further inflamed race relations in the city and focused even more attention on the police. In

1965, mayoral candidate John V. Lindsay, running as a liberal sympathetic to civil rights, promised to create a citizen-dominated CCRB. After Lindsay was elected, new Police Commissioner Howard Leary issued General Order #14 in May 1966, adding four nonpolice members to the CCRB, thereby giving it a 4-3 civilian majority. Leary declared, "It is essential that the entire community has confidence in the impartiality of the administrative machinery which supervises the exercise of police power." In a statement representing a reversal of the traditional police attitude toward complaints, he explained, "It is the policy of this department to encourage the public to bring forward legitimate grievances regarding police misconduct."[52] This was a bold position to take at a time when most police chiefs followed the lead of the LAPD's William Parker in dismissing allegations of brutality as the work of professional malcontents and dangerous radicals.

The new CCRB board members were drawn from the city's liberal elite and included NYCLU activist Algernon D. Black as chair and Franklin Thomas, an African-American attorney and future president of the Ford Foundation. An expanded staff included forty sworn NYPD officers as investigators. Although Lindsay's CCRB was both hailed and attacked as an "independent" review board, it remained essentially a unit of the NYPD but with some added citizen input. The enormous controversy over the CCRB raised public awareness of it and helped produce a dramatic increase in the number of complaints. After averaging 200 complaints a year (231 in 1964), it began receiving 100 complaints per month in 1965.

The Policeman's Benevolent Association (PBA), the local police union, wasted no time in attacking Lindsay's CCRB and quickly gathered enough signatures to place a referendum on the November 1966 ballot to abolish it. The measure would amend the city charter to require that each member of any review board be "a regularly appointed, full-time member or full-time administrative employee of the Police Department."[53] The campaign over the CCRB referendum quickly became a bitter and racially divisive contest. The PBA played the "law and order" card, warning that the CCRB would undermine effective policing and lead to a rise in crime. The attacks were not explicitly racist, but in the political context of the time, "crime" had become a code word for an opposition to civil rights. The Independent Citizens Committee Against Review Boards was dominated by the PBA but also included prominent conservative groups such as the American Legion, the Conservative Party, and the John Birch Society. In support of the CCRB, the NYCLU organized a coalition of groups as the Federated Associations for Independent Review (FAIR).[54]

On November 8, 1966, the voters abolished Lindsay's CCRB by an overwhelming 2-1 margin. Only in Manhattan did a majority of the voters support the board, with primary support coming from African-American and Jewish voters. Analysis of voting patterns found that the most frequently cited reason for voting against the CCRB was that it "makes law enforcement more difficult; it hampers the police." In a clear statement of priorities, 80 percent of those voting against the board agreed with the statement, "Unfairness and brutality may have to be tolerated if the welfare of the community is at stake." Even more shocking, 60 percent of those voting *for* the board also agreed with the statement.[55] Crime control, in short, was a more salient issue for most New Yorkers than was control of police abuse. Voters' positions on the CCRB correlated very strongly with their attitudes toward the civil rights movement, with hostility to civil rights generally translating into support for the police.[56]

After the referendum the CCRB was reconstituted, with the former civilian members being replaced by civilian employees of the NYPD.[57] Following its demise, even the staunchest supporters of Lindsay's CCRB conceded that it had been weak. One analyst concluded: "No independent 'civilian' point of view developed. Civilian members became 'police buffs,' highly supportive of the police officers' point of view."[58] Algernon Black concluded that the CCRB had made some contribution to resolving the police community relations problem in the city but that the agency was hardly a "panacea."[59]

The 1966 referendum left a lasting scar on city politics. The PBA remained an implacable opponent of any form of citizen oversight, while the NYCLU and its allies continued to press for a truly independent CCRB. Interviewing NYCPD officers almost ten years later, Nicholas Alex found that the "emotional impact" of the battle still remained, with the idea of a civilian review board a lightning rod for all of the officers' grievances. He found that for them "it is not a question of whether a review board includes civilians. It seems that a review board, whatever its shape or form, is seen as interfering with police affairs."[60]

The End of the 1960s

With the demise of both the Philadelphia PAB and Lindsay's CCRB in New York City, the citizen oversight movement seemed dead by the end of the 1960s. The lesson of the struggles in those two cities seemed to be that when push came to shove, police unions could flex their political muscle and defeat proposals for citizen oversight.

THE REVIVAL OF CITIZEN OVERSIGHT
IN THE 1970s

Quietly and with little publicity, citizen oversight revived in the 1970s. The idea picked up momentum through the decade and by the early 1980s was a full-fledged national and international movement. Although there were few riots after 1968, police brutality remained a simmering controversy in virtually every city. Civil rights organizations continued to press for control of police misconduct and did not abandon the demand for civilian review. The rebirth of the oversight movement was largely the result of changing public attitudes about accountability, not just for the police but for all government agencies. Perhaps more than anything else, the Watergate scandal heightened the awareness of Americans to the threat of "lawless" government agencies. As a consequence, the oversight movement acquired new and important support among white Americans who had previously been indifferent to the issue of police brutality.

In 1969, Kansas City created the first citizen oversight agency to survive to the present day. After a racial disturbance in April 1968 sparked by the assassination of Dr. Martin Luther King, the mayor appointed a local Commission on Civil Disorders. It recommended a new complaint procedure for the police department, and the following year the city council created the Kansas City Office of Citizen Complaints (OCC).[61]

The OCC was significant in two important respects. First, unlike the Philadelphia PAB and Lindsay's CCRB, it was created by ordinance, which put it on a firmer legal footing than those established by executive order. Second, in an important sign of changing attitudes, Police Chief Clarence Kelley endorsed the OCC. Kelley already had a national reputation as a reformer and would become director of the FBI in 1973. At a community meeting in 1970, he explained that the OCC was "the most effective tool in stopping alleged police harassment."[62] Kelley's position was a significant break from the tradition of police hostility to external oversight, and in the years ahead an increasing number of chiefs would follow his lead.

The OCC received citizen complaints and forwarded them to the police department for investigation. The police would return completed investigative files to the OCC, which would review them and make recommendations for disposition to the police chief.[63] Lacking independent investigative authority, and with no strong leadership, the OCC was at best marginally successful. In a critical assessment in the mid-1990s, Douglas Perez gave it "low marks for openness and availability."[64] Despite its weaknesses, the OCC survived, something neither the Philadelphia PAB or Lindsay's CCRB had achieved, and in this respect alone it represented the future of citizen oversight.

Berkeley, 1973

The first oversight agency with independent authority to investigate complaints was the Berkeley Police Review Commission (PRC), created by referendum in April 1973. Given the city's tradition of radical political activism, it was hardly a surprise that Berkeley would be the first to take this step. Since the early 1960s, there had been numerous clashes between the police and demonstrators over issues related to the Vietnam War, civil rights, and campus political issues at the University of California. In 1971, radical activists placed on the ballot a referendum to establish community control of the police. This proposal would have divided the city police department into a series of neighborhood-level departments, each governed by elected boards of commissioners. Community control, a popular idea among radical activists in the 1960s and early 1970s, was seen as a way of reducing the power of unresponsive public bureaucracies and returning control of government to the people. An experiment in community control of the public schools in New York City in the late 1960s resulted in one of the bitterest political controversies of the decade.[65] In April 1971, Berkeley voters rejected community control by a 2-1 margin, with even the African-American neighborhoods opposing it.[66] Two years later, voters approved the far less radical referendum creating the PRC.

The PRC consisted of a board of nine citizens, each appointed by a member of the city council, and a staff of investigators. It was empowered to investigate complaints against police officers, hold public hearings on specific complaints, and send recommendations for disciplinary actions to the city manager and the police department. The internal affairs unit of the Berkeley Police Department remained in place, giving the city two citizen complaint mechanisms.[67]

The PRC soon proved to be less independent of the police department than its supporters had hoped, however. It adopted a policy of advising officers subject to complaints that they had a right to remain silent, and as a result many officers simply refused to cooperate. (This limitation was ended some years later.) In a critical analysis of the PRC, Douglas Perez argued that it was expensive, duplicated the police department's internal affairs unit, and sustained a smaller percentage of cases than internal affairs.[68]

As time passed, the PRC slid into ineffectuality and by the late-1990s had fallen into a state of disarray. The staff fell from six to three and a half positions, including only one full-time and one half-time investigator by 1997. The number of complaints received, meanwhile, also fell by half. On the positive side, the PRC maintained a small but creditable policy review program. It published an extensive report opposing the use of pepper spray by the Berkeley Police Department, which recommended that it not be used; staffed a working group to develop guidelines related to medical marijuana (which had been legalized by the California voters in 1996 but remained illegal under federal law); and sponsored a forum on police interaction with people with disabilities.[69]

The PRC's problems lay not so much with the concept of oversight as with the culture of radical politics in Berkeley. After the successful 1973 referendum, the radical community evidently did not follow through with sustained attention to the many practical problems related to the administration of a citizen complaint agency. Symptomatic of much of the radical politics of the 1960s, activists emphasized purely symbolic issues and neglected the complex and often difficult issues of administrative detail. The activists' neglect allowed a succession of city councils and city managers to erode the agency's budget and not give it sufficient political or financial support. By the 1990s, the once-pioneering PRC had been outstripped by other, newer oversight agencies. Barbara Attard, an experienced former staff member of the San Francisco Office of Citizen Complaints, was appointed Director of the PRC in 1997, and she launched an effort to revive the agency.

The Detroit Board of Police Commissioners

The voters of Detroit created the third important new oversight agency by referendum in 1973. Creation of the Board of Police Commissioners (BPC) was part of a broader political upheaval in the city and the rise of African-American political power. Coleman Young was elected the city's first African-American mayor in the same election. Young was a long-time civil rights activist and made eliminating police brutality one of his major campaign planks.[70] Police brutality had been a bitter issue in the city for a quarter of a century, and the 1967 riot was one of the two worst in the 1960s in terms of both property destruction and lives lost.[71]

The history of citizen complaint procedures in Detroit was typical of developments in other cities. Prior to 1961, the police department "had no systematic process through which a citizen could lodge a complaint against a police officer." A desk sergeant would take the information from a complainant and turn it over to the lieutenant or inspector. As one officer later explained, "There would be a very cursory investigation and it would always come out where the officer was justified in whatever he did. . . . It was always a whitewash situation."[72] In response to increasing protests from the African-American community, the police department created a Community Relations Bureau (CRB), which eventually evolved into the official complaints unit.[73] These reforms failed to produce significant improvements in either police performance or the handling of complaints, however, and local African-American leaders decided on a fundamental change in the governance structure of the police department.

In the early 1970s, the city undertook a revision of its city charter, and a revised charter creating a Board of Police Commissioners to govern the police department was approved in 1973 (taking effect on July 1, 1974). The board, whose members were appointed by the mayor, had full authority over the Detroit Police Department. In this respect, it was a return to a form of political control of the police common in the nineteenth century.[74]

To handle citizen complaints, the BPC established an Office of the Chief Investigator (OCI) with a staff of nonsworn investigators. Individual complaints were investigated by "mixed" teams of sworn officers and civilian investigators. The OCI was independent of the police rank and file, and as a unit of the BPC it had full access to all police department records. This included the power to interview police officers. At the same time, however, as a part of the BPC it was formally a part of the governing structure of the police department. Edward Littlejohn characterized the status of the BPC/OCI in terms of an "'inside' position . . . composed of 'outsiders.'"[75]

OVERSIGHT AS A NATIONAL
MOVEMENT: THE 1980s AND 1990s

The number of new oversight agencies continued to grow through the late 1970s and early 1980s, and by the middle of the eighties a full-fledged national movement had emerged. The U.S. Civil Rights Commission conducted hearings on brutality in Philadelphia, Memphis, and Houston, and its 1981 report, *Who is Guarding the Guardians?*, made the unambiguous recommendation that "it is imperative for [the complaints] process to be subject to some outside review."[76]

Two changes in American politics fostered support for citizen oversight of the police. At the municipal level, African Americans steadily gained political power, capturing mayor's offices and seats on city councils. At the same time, there was a significant shift in public attitudes among all Americans about government and the control of official misconduct. In an indirect but vitally important way, the Watergate scandal and the subsequent revelations of misconduct by federal agencies—spying by the FBI, assassination plots by the CIA, politically motivated IRS audits—created a new public consciousness about the need for controlling government agencies. This new mood expressed itself in many forms: federal and state privacy laws, state open records laws, and a system of inspector generals for federal agencies.[77] Revelations about the mistreatment of patients in medical experiments led to a federal law and complex administrative regulations designed to protect human subjects in research.[78] Across the country, state and local agencies were subject to input from new citizen advisory boards. All of these developments reflected a new political culture of government accountability and protection of citizen rights. The police oversight movement was one part of this general trend and directly benefited from the new public mood.

The growth of oversight agencies in the 1980s and early 1990s was marked by several characteristics. First, there was considerable experimentation with the form of oversight, often as a result of political compromise forced by the continuing opposition from police unions. Neither the ACLU nor the NAACP, the two principal national organizations working on the issue, had an "off-the-shelf" model of oversight, and local leaders often created their own versions. Political compromise produced both weak forms of oversight that were not really independent of the police department and genuine innovations such as the auditor model of oversight. Second, in several cities, notably Portland and Minneapolis, initial oversight agencies proved to be less than satisfactory but were subsequently strengthened by new ordinances. Thus, the experience of stagnation and decline that occurred in Kansas City and Berkeley was not always repeated in other cities.

The San Francisco Office of Citizen Complaints

The voters of San Francisco created an independent Office of Citizen Complaints (OCC) by referendum in November 1982.[79] The campaign over Proposition A included a novel political twist indicative of the changing dynamics of the oversight issue. The ballot also included an issue related to police officers' salaries. The police union struck a deal with the politically powerful gay community and agreed not to oppose the OCC in return for gay community support for police salaries. The police union, in effect, decided that money was more important than citizen oversight, or at least that oversight was not a life and death issue.

The OCC was a fully independent agency, with its own staff of investigators. It had to struggle for many years to establish itself as an effective agency, however. The police union, after not opposing it in the referendum, fought the OCC in the courts and delayed its effective operation for several years. Even more serious was the lack of strong support from a succession of mayors. Some community activists even suspected that several mayors deliberately appointed OCC directors with a covert mandate to limit the agency's role. By the mid-1990s, both John Crew of the local ACLU and Van Jones of the Lawyers Committee for Civil Rights dismissed the OCC as ineffectual.[80] The election of Willie Brown as mayor of San Francisco in November 1995, however, marked a turning point for the OCC. Brown was strongly committed to oversight and appointed Mary Dunlap, a prominent civil rights attorney, as OCC director. In the same election the voters also approved a referendum mandating additional staff for the OCC. Proposition G, requiring the OCC to have one investigator for every 150 San Francisco police officers, not only passed by a 64-36 percent margin but marked the first time that any city had established minimum standards for staffing oversight agencies.[81]

By the late 1990s, the OCC appeared to have established a good working relationship with the San Francisco Police Department. In the 1980s, police chiefs rejected about half of all OCC determinations of sustained complaints. By 1997, however, the chief of police accepted all of the OCC determinations.[82] This development suggested that, over time, police suspicion and hostility toward oversight could be overcome, at least in some cities.

The Portland Auditor

The Portland, Oregon, Police Internal Investigations Auditing Committee (PIIAC) introduced the auditor model of oversight, an important innovation in the field. PIIAC originated out of a series of police scandals in 1980 and 1981. In one incident, narcotics officers were caught planting drugs on suspects and then lying to their superiors about it. In another, a police officer threw a dead possum in front of a restaurant in the African-American community. Outraged, civil rights leaders demanded oversight of the police, and the city council responded by creating PIIAC. Following the lead of the New York City PBA, the local police union fought back by sponsoring a referendum in November 1982 to abolish PIIAC. Although the union and its allies, operating as the Committee for a Safe Portland, outspent PIIAC supporters by $70,000 to $12,000, the voters rejected Measure 51 by a narrow margin. In an important sign of changing public attitudes, the crime issue that had been so successful in New York City failed to sway a majority of Portland voters.[83]

The nine-member PIIAC board began operating in December 1982. PIIAC's primary role did not involve investigating individual complaints but rather monitoring the police department's internal affairs unit (hence the name "auditing committee"). PIIAC also served as an avenue of appeal for persons unhappy with the outcome of their complaint, and it had the power to send cases back for further investigation.

With no precedent to guide them, PIIAC's members struggled to define their role. The chair of PIIAC observed that "we have no standards for comparison [of our performance], we are a first-of-its-kind and a one-of-its-kind committee." There was some confusion over PIIAC's role, as many citizens thought it was intended to investigate their complaints. The chair of PIIAC, however, noted: "Clearly, the approach of the Portland committee is to identify ways in which the police *organization* has contributed to a bad situation."[84] This statement represented an important shift in the focus of oversight agencies, away from individual officers and toward more systemic organizational problems.

In its first year, PIIAC handled seventeen appeals, made nine recommendations for change in complaint process, and filed three reports. Most important, it found that citizens were more "exercised" about their treatment in the complaint investigation than they were about the original police misconduct. It also found a general failure of internal affairs to explain police procedures to complainants, and more seriously a failure even to interview officers who were the subject of complaints. In short, there was a clear indication of "[lack of] interest in the citizen's complaints" on the part of internal affairs.[85]

Despite its innovative role, PIIAC was widely regarded as ineffectual. Many of the criticisms were justified, as PIIAC struggled with no staff and confusion over its role. Criticisms increased after a significant increase in fatal shootings of citizens by police between 1989 and 1992. In 1993, Portland Copwatch, a community-based watchdog group, called for a review board with independent powers of investigation. PIIAC's powerlessness, it argued, "impairs public trust."[86] A series of newspaper articles quoted critics accusing PIIAC of being a charade.[87] An investigation by the Office of the City Auditor was equally critical, concluding that "PIIAC has not accomplished its objectives," and that both PIIAC itself and the city council had "failed to conduct adequate oversight of the police internal investigations system." Many duties required by ordinance had simply not been carried out.[88]

The election of Vera Katz as mayor in 1993 led to major reforms and pointed PIIAC in a new direction. A veteran political leader, and most recently speaker of the Portland house of representatives, Katz made strengthening PIIAC one of her campaign issues. Her recommendations included easier citizen access to the complaints process, including neighborhood sites where people could file complaints, formal training of internal affairs staff in customer service and complaint handling, a community outreach strategy, timelines for completing investigations, and a series of quarterly reports. Most important, she recommended a full-time staff person for PIIAC. Katz's recommendations indicated not only a commitment to oversight of the police but a grasp of the administrative details necessary for making oversight work effectively that was unique among elected officials.[89]

Mayor Katz's recommendations were adopted by the city council in January 1994, and Lisa Botsko was hired as a full-time PIIAC staff member. Formally on the staff of the mayor's office, she also reported to the PIIAC Citizen's Advisory Committee and to City Council. PIIAC soon distinguished itself as an innovative instrument of police reform. Botsko's quarterly reports provided a window into the police department, regularly identifying problems that needed attention, and monitoring implementation of recommendations for change.[90] The revised PIIAC did not satisfy everyone. Portland Copwatch, although applauding many of the changes, continued to press for an independent investigation of complaints.[91]

Minneapolis: Two Chapters

As in Portland, the development of oversight in Minneapolis underwent two distinct phases. Despite the city's reputation for good government, the police department had a bad history of excessive force. Even the news media used the term "thumpers" to describe Minneapolis police officers.[92] In 1983, Mayor Donald Fraser, a former member of Congress with a national reputation as a liberal, created an internal affairs review team to audit the police department's handling of complaints. The review team found a number of problems, including several cases where Police Chief Anthony Bouza did not discipline officers where excessive force complaints had been sustained. This finding was particularly surprising since Bouza was a maverick among police chiefs, with a national reputation as a reformer.[93] An analysis of public opinion data, meanwhile, found that the existence of the review team had a positive effect on the perception of the handling of complaints by the police department. The review team itself, however, felt that it had no real power to implement changes and, seeing no changes in the police department, simply ceased functioning.[94]

   Police abuse continued to be a serious issue in Minneapolis. There were a number of highly publicized incidents, and one officer who cost the city about $2 million in brutality suits remained on the force despite two attempts to fire him. Finally, in 1990, the city council responded by creating the Civilian Review Authority (CRA) with independent investigative power. After initially struggling, the CRA established a positive working relationship with the police department and even won the grudging respect of the police union. By the late 1990s, the union recommended that officers choose the CRA's mediation program to resolve complaints, and a number of officers opted to forego public hearings over their complaints and submit their cases directly to the chief for discipline, implicitly indicating that they accepted the CRA investigation as fair. The CRA established a Quality Service Audit system allowing both complainants and police officers to evaluate how they were treated, and both groups gave the CRA extremely favorable ratings.[95]

Other Auditor Systems

Several other cities and counties joined Portland in creating auditor systems of oversight in the early 1990s. San Jose established the Independent Police Auditor (IPA) in 1993. As in other cities, this step was the end result of a long controversy over police brutality, with the San Francisco ACLU office leading the fight for oversight. The issue came to a head in 1992, when a Citizen Review Ad Hoc Committee recommended the creation of an oversight agency with independent power to investigate complaints.[96] Not surprisingly, the police department objected, and the ensuing debate led to a compromise in the form of the Independent Police Auditor. The ACLU's John Crew strenuously objected, citing press accounts about the ineffectuality of the Portland and Seattle auditor systems.[97]

The most notable auditor system was the Special Counsel to the Los Angeles Sheriff's Department, created in 1993. As Special Counsel, Merrick Bobb operated under a series of three-year contracts with the County Board of Supervisors and hired staff on an as-needed basis. Bobb's primary mandate was to reduce the costs of civil litigation arising from misconduct by deputy sheriffs. Between 1988 and 1992, the county paid out $18 million in police-related misconduct litigation.[98] Bobb took an expansive definition of his mandate and investigated virtually every aspect of the sheriff's department, including recruitment and training, officer assignment patterns, and sex discrimination in the department as well as use of physical and deadly force. His lengthy semiannual reports found that in many cases use of force problems were the result not of a few bad officers but of flawed management practices. Thus, he shifted the focus of reform away from the proverbial "bad apples" and toward management issues.[99]

A historic breakthrough for oversight in Los Angeles occurred in April 1995, when, by referendum, the voters authorized creation of the Office of the Inspector General to oversee the Los Angeles Police Department. For decades the organizational culture of the LAPD had been highly resistant to citizen oversight. The Los Angeles Police Commission, which nominally controlled the LAPD, had been a largely supine agency, deferring to a succession of strong police chiefs. The sensational Rodney King incident in 1991 finally set change in motion. The Christopher Commission produced a devastating report on the lack of accountability in the LAPD and, among other things, recommended the creation of an inspector general. After much stalling by the city, the voters mandated creation of an IG's office in 1995, authorizing it "to audit, investigate, and oversee the Police Department's handling of complaints of misconduct . . . and perform such other duties as may be assigned by the Board."

After additional delay, Katherine Mader, an attorney with the district attorney's office, began functioning as IG in mid-1996. Following Merrick Bobb's lead in adopting a broad vision of her role, she investigated such issues as the handling of domestic violence by police officers and the department's response to officers with repeat complaints. In perhaps her most important initiative, Mader examined the problem of "false and misleading testimony" by police officers, or what others preferred to call police lying.[100] Not surprisingly, the LAPD resisted her efforts, and Mader characterized its compliance with her office as "sporadic, delayed, and occasionally confused."[101]

Mader's efforts eventually proved to be a little too vigorous even for her employers, the Police Commission. In late 1998, the chair of the commission attempted to restrict her authority, and Mader resigned. Her angry departure provoked a public debate on the role of inspector general, with the result that the mayor, leading members of city council, and the Los Angeles Times all supported changes to ensure an independent inspector general.[102]

Not all auditor systems were effective, however. The Albuquerque Independent Counsel (IC) failed to fully utilize its authorized powers or play much of a public role.[103] The Seattle auditor, meanwhile, was limited by ordinance to a very narrow role and had no authority to review the policies and practices of the police department. Nor did all oversight advocates endorse the auditor approach. The ACLU's John Crew and leaders of Portland Copwatch, in particular, continued to insist on oversight agencies that had independent investigatory power.[104]

In 1999 and 2000 yet another variation in citizen oversight appeared. Seattle created an Office of Police Accountability (OPA) through which the police department's internal affairs unit would be directed by a civilian employee appointed by the police chief. Nashville created a similarly mixed system that includes elements of both external and internal accountability. By the end of the century the oversight movement had matured to the point where there were competing models of oversight that could be evaluated on the basis of their track records.

OVERSIGHT AT THE END
OF THE CENTURY

By the end of the 1990s citizen oversight of the police was firmly established as an important feature of American policing. There were about 100 separate oversight agencies, with new ones being established on a regular basis. This represented a substantial growth from only 13 in 1980 and 38 in 1990 (see Chapter 1, Figure 1-1). About 80 percent of the police departments in the fifty largest cities had some form of oversight. There were also oversight agencies for county sheriffs departments, state police agencies, a number of Native American tribal police departments, and at least one university campus police department. The Iowa Citizens' Aide/Ombudsman was authorized to handle complaints against any government official in the state, which included the many small town and rural sheriff's departments.[105]

The Growth of Oversight

Perhaps the most notable aspect of the oversight movement was its experimental and often ad hoc character that produced a tremendous variety among oversight mechanisms. The classic civilian review board, as found in San Francisco and Minneapolis, was very different from the auditor model found in Portland and Los Angeles County. Moreover, none of the review boards were exactly identical, as was also the case with the various auditor systems. The debate over oversight was no longer whether it was a good idea, but which form to adopt.

There were also clear differences in the effectiveness of the various forms of oversight that were not related to formal structure. Some review boards with independent investigatory power had creditable records, such as Minneapolis and the reinvigorated San Francisco OCC. Others, such as the New York CCRB, had little to show for themselves. There were strong auditor systems, as in Portland and San Jose, and weak ones, as in Seattle. The differences were more often the result of political leadership, which in turn reflected the civic culture of a community, and the quality of the leadership in the agency itself.

Federal law enforcement agencies were conspicuously absent from the oversight movement. This state of affairs contrasted sharply with that in other English-speaking countries, where all law enforcement agencies were subject to some form of citizen oversight by the 1990s. The Commission on the Restructuring of the Internal Revenue Service (IRS) received a proposal for oversight of its complaint process but did not adopt it. A similar proposal related to federal law enforcement agencies was presented to the Commission on the Advancement of Federal Law Enforcement (CAFLE) in 1998.[106]

The growth of oversight was an international phenomenon, and developments in other countries paralleled those in the United States. In England, for example, the issue of police accountability arose in the 1960s and led to a number of changes in complaint procedures that culminated in the creation of the Police Complaints Authority (PCA), a national complaint review board. In Canada, Australia, and New Zealand a similar scenario played out, with the result that by the mid-1980s every law enforcement agency in those countries was subject to some form of external oversight.[107]

By 1985, the oversight movement had matured to the point where its leaders established a professional association, the International Association for Civilian Oversight of Law Enforcement (IACOLE). Membership consisted of both paid staff and unpaid lay board members of oversight agencies in the United States and other countries. Without a staffed office, however, IACOLE's activities remained rather limited. By the 1990s, significant divisions appeared within IACOLE, and a group of Americans established the National Association for Civilian Oversight of Law Enforcment (NACOLE) to focus on purely American concerns. A few years later, the Canadian Association for Citizen Oversight of Law Enforcement (CACOLE) was established. And by the late 1990s there were enough oversight agencies in the San Francisco Bay Area of California to support a regional professional association, the Bay Area Police Oversight Network (BAPON).[108]

Public Opinion and the Politics of Oversight

All but a handful of the oversight agencies were created by ordinance or referendum. This represented a major shift from the 1960s, when both the Philadelphia PAB and the citizen-dominated CCRB in New York City were established by mayoral executive order in the face of opposition or indifference from city councils. In those two cities, police unions had sufficient political clout to have them abolished and they were able to block proposals in other cities.

A number of factors contributed to the shift in public opinion on police accountability between the 1960s and the 1990s. Even though public fear of crime remained high and had a significant impact on other criminal justice policies, police unions were steadily less able to use it to defeat oversight proposals. The highly publicized beating of Rodney King by Los Angeles police officers in March 1991 gave the oversight movement a boost, but it largely strengthened a trend that already had considerable momentum. In San Francisco (1982), San Diego County (1991), Portland (1982), and a few other localities, oversight was established (or at least not abolished) by popular vote. A 1992 Harris Poll found overwhelming support for citizen involvement in the review of police complaints. Only 4 percent of whites supported the idea that the complaint process should be handled only by police. Fifteen percent supported an "all civilian" process. An overwhelming 80 percent favored a mixed system of citizens and police.

A division of opinion along racial lines also exists among police officers. A national survey of about 1,000 officers in 1998 found that almost 70 percent of African-American officers agreed that "citizen review boards are an effective means of preventing police misconduct," compared with 33.3 percent of white officers (although most observers are surprised by the level of support among the white officers).[109]

The shift in public opinion was partly the result of growing African-American political power at the municipal level. In Detroit and New Orleans, for example, oversight agencies were created with the strong support of African-American mayors with strong civil rights backgrounds. In many other cities, support came from African-American and Hispanic city council members. A study of civil rights activity in several California cities in the 1970s and early 1980s found that citizen oversight correlated with the strength of African-American (but not Hispanic) participation in city government: "The only cities to establish police review boards as of 1980 were cities where blacks had gained control of independently elected mayoral offices and led the dominant coalition in city council."[110]

Growing racial and ethnic minority political power was not the sole factor in the growth of the oversight movement, however. Oversight agencies were also established in cities such as Minneapolis and Seattle, where African Americans and Hispanics are a relatively small percentage of the voting population. And, ironically, oversight was particularly weak in Washington, D.C. and Atlanta, where African-American political power was strongest.[111] In their history of civilian review in Washington, D.C., in fact, Cheryl Beattie and Ronald Weitzer observe that race has played a less prominent role in the creation of review boards in recent years, or what they refer to as "second wave" review boards.[112]

The most important development was the steadily growing support for police accountability beyond its traditional base in the civil rights movement. Accountability was increasingly seen as important by a broader spectrum of Americans. Rising concern about the accountability of government agencies was an important theme of American politics following the Watergate scandal of the early 1970s. Revelations about abuses of power by the Nixon administration, the FBI, the CIA, and other agencies spawned a number of new laws designed to hold officials accountable.[113] The oversight movement was a direct beneficiary of this new mood.

The community policing movement also contributed indirectly to the growth of oversight. Born in the early 1980s, the idea of community policing became virtually the gospel among police chiefs and politicians by the 1990s. Although community policing advocates said almost nothing specifically about citizen complaints, their emphasis on developing "partnerships" between police departments and community residents undermined the traditional police argument that citizens are unqualified to make judgments about police policy.[114] Community policing helped to change the attitudes of many police chiefs, fewer and fewer of whom actively fought oversight proposals. The chief of the Minneapolis Police Department stated that he liked having the Civilian Review Authority (CRA), in part because it relieved his internal affairs unit of the burden of handling all the routine inquiries that did not rise to the level of a formal complaint.[115] To be sure, some of the lack of opposition from chiefs may have reflected a cynical view that the proposed agency wouldn't make any difference either way and that a weak review board lends a gloss of legitimacy to the complaints process.[116]

Police unions continued to fight oversight, but it was increasingly a losing, rear-guard action. In Seattle, for example, the union, realizing that some form of oversight would be created, participated in the negotiations to create the auditor system. In other cities, the union challenged specific aspects of the oversight agency, such as its subpoena power. But in San Diego County, the courts rejected the union's claims and upheld the subpoena power of the Citizens' Law Enforcement Review Board. In Philadelphia, however, the recalcitrant and uncooperative posture of the Fraternal Order of Police reduced the new Police Advisory Commission to virtual ineffectiveness.[117]

Setbacks

Despite its significant growth, the oversight movement suffered a number of notable setbacks. The District of Columbia Civilian Review Board was abolished in 1995. Although the immediate reason was the financial crisis of the district, virtually everyone realized that the board was a dismal failure—taking as long as three years to investigate complaints. A 1995 report by the ACLU affiliate found a total of 885 complaints that had not yet been disposed of. Incredibly, 135 of these (or 15 percent) were four years old. And in one case, the U.S. District Court held the district liable for damages because the CCRB had a "policy or custom" of inadequate review of complaints. The ACLU report found that the CCRB had very low visibility in the community, a point supported in part by the relatively low rate of complaints (between 400 to 500 a year). The problem in Washington was not a lack of material resources. In 1993, the CCRB had a budget of $1.1 million and a staff of twenty-five. The problem, according to the ACLU, was "the inefficient allocation of existing resources." A new review board was authorized by the District City Council in 1998.[118]

In Atlanta and Boston, meanwhile, oversight agencies had been established some years earlier but were essentially nonfunctional by the late 1990s. In Boston it was clear that neither mayors nor a majority of city council members supported oversight. Atlanta was a more curious situation, since city politics were dominated by the African-American community, which had been the driving force behind the oversight movement across the country.

Equally troubling was the evident weakness of a number of oversight agencies. The New Orleans Office of Municipal Investigations (OMI) was a dismal failure. Created in 1980 with power to conduct independent investigations of citizen complaints, it had nothing to show for its efforts. By the mid-1990s, in fact, the New Orleans Police Department had a notorious national reputation as perhaps the most corrupt and violent department in the country. The New York City CCRB, although finally separated from the police department in 1993, had a poor record and was severely criticized by the New York Civil Liberties Union, which for forty years had led the fight for an independent CCRB. In 1996, the NYCLU concluded that "over its first three years of operation the CCRB has largely failed in its mission." It found "a relentless abdication of leadership—by the mayor, the city council, and by the agency's thirteen appointed board members."[119] The Offices of Municipal Investigation in Pittsburgh and Cincinnati also had weak records and were replaced by new oversight agencies in 1997 and 1998.

CONCLUSION

Citizen oversight of the police was an established fact of life in American law enforcement by the end of the century. It existed in nearly all big cities and was steadily spreading to smaller communities. The spread of oversight marked a momentous change since the tumultuous 1960s. Most important, citizen involvement in the complaint process was increasingly recognized as an important means for achieving police accountability. The police were no longer able to persuasively argue that they were immune from outside scrutiny.

Impact of the Oversight Movement

The impact of oversight on policing was difficult to assess, however. Events such as the Rodney King beating in Los Angeles, two murders of citizens by New Orleans police officers, and the brutal assault on Abner Louima by New York City police officers in 1997 led many people to conclude that nothing much had changed and that police abuse was even getting worse. These highly publicized events, however, occurred in cities that had either been most resistant to oversight (Los Angeles and New York City), or where an existing oversight agency had clearly failed. In other cities there had been long-term improvements in the quality of day-to-day policing. The number of fatal shootings were down in most cities since the 1970s, and grotesque incidents of physical brutality were rare rather than common events. Many observers, including this author, believe that with the exception of certain departments police behavior has in fact improved in most cities and counties over the past ten to twenty years. Many agree with Herman Goldstein's observation that the gap between the best and the worst police departments is greater than at any time in history.[120]

What role had the oversight movement played in this change? It is impossible to provide a definitive answer. The central purpose of this book is to examine in detail the role and impact of citizen oversight. As Chapters 3 and 4 explain, the role of citizen oversight is far more varied and complex than most people recognize. And as Chapters 5 and 6 explain, evaluating the effectiveness of oversight is extremely difficult.

NOTES

1. Samuel Walker, *A Critical History of Police Reform* (Lexington: Lexington Books, 1977).

2. National Commission on Law Observance and Enforcement, *Lawlessness in Law Enforcement* (Washington, DC: Government Printing Office, 1931).

3. Yale Kamisar, *Police Interrogation and Confessions: Essays in Law and Policy* (Ann Arbor: University of Michigan Press, 1980).

4. Walker, *Critical History of Police Professionalism.*

5. O. W. Wilson and Roy C. McLaren, *Police Administration,* 4th ed. (New York: McGraw-Hill, 1977).

6. Cheryl-Ann Beattie Repetti, "The Politics of Civilian Review: Police Accountability in Washington, DC, and New York City, 1948–1974," unpublished Ph.D. dissertation, George Washington University, 1997, 94–95; Cheryl Beattie and Ronald Weitzer, "Race, Democracy and Law: Civilian Review of Police in Washington, DC," in Andrew Goldsmith, ed., *Civilian Oversight of Policing* (London: Hart, 2000); Ernest Hopkins, *Our Lawless Police* (New York: Viking, 1931), 13, 156–57, 360.

7. Frank Donner, *Protectors of Privilege* (Berkeley: University of California Press, 1990).

8. Samuel Walker, *In Defense of American Liberties: A History of the ACLU* (New York: Oxford University Press, 1990).

9. National Commission on Law Observance and Enforcement, *Lawlessness in Law Enforcement,* 192. Repetti, "Politics of Civilian Review," 94. Samuel Walker, *Popular Justice: A History of American Criminal Justice,* 2nd ed. (New York: Oxford University Press, 1998), 155.

10. Hopkins, *Our Lawless Police,* xii.

11. A useful collection of excerpts from riot commission reports and commentary is Anthony M. Platt, ed., *The Politics of Riot Commissions,* (New York: Collier, 1971).

12. Walker, *In Defense of American Liberties.*

13. *The Complete Report of Mayor LaGuardia's Commission on the Harlem Riot of March 19, 1935* (New York: Arno Press, 1969).

14. For example, Bruce Smith, *St. Louis Police Survey* (New York: Governmental Research Institute, 1942).

15. Dominic J. Capeci, Jr., *The Harlem Riot of 1943* (Philadelphia: Temple University Press, 1977); Alfred McClung Lee and Norman D. Humphrey, *Race Riot* (New York: Dryden, 1943).

16. Samuel Walker, *Popular Justice: A History of American Criminal Justice,* 2nd ed. (New York: Oxford University Press, 1998), 170–72.

17. Samuel Walker, "The Origins of the American Police-Community Relations Movement: the 1940s," *Criminal Justice*

History—An International Annual, 1 (1980): 225–46; Walker, *Popular Justice,* 170–72.

18. President's Commission on Crime in the District of Columbia, *Report on the Metropolitan Police Department* (Washington, DC: Government Printing Office, 1966), 77, 80; Repetti, "Politics of Civilian Review," 111–19, 176–95; Beattie and Weitzer, "Race, Democracy and Law." The board was also severely criticized in "Administration of Complaints by Civilians against the Police," *Harvard Law Review* 77 (1964): 510.

19. Beattie and Weitzer, "Race, Democracy and Law"; Repetti, "Politics of Civilian Review."

20. President's Commission on Law Enforcement and Administration of Justice, *Task Force Report: The Police* (Washington, DC: Government Printing Office, 1967), 200; "Administration of Complaints by Citizens against the Police," 510–11.

21. Edward Littlejohn, "The Civilian Police Commission: A Deterrent of Police Misconduct," *University of Detroit Journal of Urban Law* 59 (Fall 1981): 15 (citing Hudson).

22. Spencer Coxe, letter to Morris Ernst, November 24, 1958, in ACLU of Greater Philadelphia Papers, Temple University, Box 26; Richard J. Terrill, "Police Accountability in Philadelphia: Retrospects and Prospects," *American Journal of Police* 7 (1988): 79–97.

23. Terrill, "Police Accountability in Philadelphia."

24. Ibid., 84; S. A. Paolantonio, *Frank Rizzo: The Last Big Man in Big City America* (Philadelphia: Camino Books, 1993).

25. "Administration of Complaints by Civilians Against the Police," *Harvard Law Review* 77 (1964): 513–14.

26. James R. Hudson, "Organizational Aspects of Internal and External Review of the Police," *Journal of Criminal Law, Criminology, and Police Science* 63 (September 1972): 427–32.

27. On police personnel standards, see President's Commission, *Task Force Report: The Police;* on Los Angeles, see Paul Jacobs, *Prelude to Riot* (New York: Vintage Books, 1968), 13–60.

28. National Advisory Commission on Civil Disorders [Kerner Commission], *Report* (New York: Bantam Books, 1968), 112–13.

29. U.S. Commission on Civil Rights, Wisconsin Advisory Committee, *Police Isolation and Community Needs* (Washington, DC: Government Printing Office, 1972), 77.

30. Kerner Commission, *Report,* 310.

31. Ibid.

32. Ibid., 311.

33. American Civil Liberties Union, *Policy Guide* (New York: ACLU, nd), Policy #204 (14 September, 1964).

34. IACP Resolution, "Police Review Boards," 6 October, 1960; published in *Police Chief,* (February, 1964): 34.

35. The President's Crime Commission reported in 1967 that only about half of all police departments had a special unit for handling complaints. President's Commission, *Task Force Report,* 195.

36. IACP, "Police Review Boards," *The Police Chief* (February 1964): 12.

37. President's Commission, *Task Force Report,* 198.

38. American Bar Association, *Standards Relating to the Urban Police Function,* Approved Draft, 1973" (New York: American Bar Association, 1973), Standard 53, 160–61. The second edition of the *Standards* deleted some of the critical language, including the phrase "inherent defects." American Bar Association, *Standards for the Urban Police Function,* 2nd ed., Standard 5.3 (6)(c)(1).

39. Stephen C. Halpern, *Police-Association and Department Leaders* (Lexington: Lexington Books, 1974), 87; Walker, *Popular Justice,* 199–200.

40. Hervey Juris and Peter Feuille, *Police Unionism* (Lexington; Lexington Books, 1973), 139–40.

41. Americans for Effective Law Enforcement, *Police Civilian Review Boards,* Brief #82–3 (San Francisco: AELE, 1982), 10.

42. Ibid.

43. New York Civil Liberties Union, *Police Abuse: The Need For Civilian Investi-*

gation and Oversight (New York: NYCLU, 1990), 11.

44. Cassese quoted in New York Civil Liberties Union, *Police Abuse: The Need for Civilian Investigation and Oversight,* 14–15. [Original quote in *New York Times,* 30 June, 1966].

45. National Black Police Association, *Police Brutality: A Strategy to Stop the Violence* (Washington, DC: NBPA, n.d.). David Weisburd and Rosann Greenspan, with Edwin E. Hamilton, Hubert Williams, and Kellie A. Bryant, *Police Attitudes Toward Abuse of Authority: Findings From a National Study* (Washington, DC: Government Printing Office, 2000).

46. Aryeh Neier, "Civilian Review Boards—Another View," *Criminal Law Bulletin,* 2: 8 (1966): 11–12.

47. Ronald Kahn, "Urban Reform and Police Accountability in New York City, 1950–1974," in R. Lineberry and L. Masotti, eds., *Urban Problems and Public Policy* (Lexington: Lexington Books, 1975), 107–27; Repetti, "The Politics of Civilian Review".

48. Kahn, "Urban Reform and Police Accountability," 111–12.

49. Ibid., 112.

50. Neier, "Civilian Review Boards," 15.

51. Paul Chevigny, *Police Power* (New York: Vintage Books, 1969), 260–61.

52. Algernon Black, *The People and the Police* (New York: McGraw-Hill, 1968), 77–78.

53. Copy in David W. Abbott, Louis H. Gold, and Edward T. Rogowsky, *Police, Politics, and Race: The New York City Referendum on Civilian Review* (New York: American Jewish Committee, 1969), appendix A.

54. Neier, "Civilian Review Boards," 10.

55. Abbott, Gold, and Rogowsky, *Police, Politics, and Race,* 26.

56. Ibid., 36–37; Black, *People and the Police,* 216.

57. Abbott et al., *Police, Politics, and Race.*

58. Kahn, "Urban Reform and Police Accountability," 118.

59. Black, *People and the Police,* 223.

60. Nicholas Alex, *New York Cops Talk Back* (New York: John Wiley, 1976), 77.

61. Kansas City, Office of the City Auditor, *Preliminary Review: Kansas City, Missouri Police Department* (Kansas City, June, 1996), 188.

62. Clippings in Sid Willens, *Ombudsman Handbook* (3 August, 1979). Mimeographed document provided by author.

63. Douglas Perez, *Common Sense about Police Review* (Philadelphia: Temple University Press, 1994), 164–91.

64. Ibid., 176.

65. Maurice R. Berube and Marilyn Gittell, eds., *Confrontation at Ocean Hill-Brownsville* (New York: Praeger, 1969).

66. Jerome H. Skolnick, "Neighborhood Police," *The Nation* (March 22, 1971): 372–73. Red Family, *To Stop a Police State: The Case for Community Control of Police* (Berkeley: Red Family, 1971).

67. A critical analysis of the PRC is in Perez, *Common Sense about Police Review,* 124–63.

68. Ibid., 138–39.

69. Berkeley Police Review Commission, *Statistical Report* (1997, January 1998–June 1998), 2; interview, Barbara Attard, Director, PRC, 1999.

70. Coleman Young and Lonnie Wheeler, *Hard Stuff: The Autobiography of Coleman Young* (New York: Viking, 1994).

71. Kerner Commission, *Report;* Leonard Gordon, comp., *A City in Racial Crisis: The Case of Detroit Pre- and Post- the 1967 Riot* (Dubuque: W. C. Brown, 1971).

72. Littlejohn, "Civilian Police Commission," 25.

73. Ibid., 26.

74. Walker, *A Critical History of Police Reform.*

75. Littlejohn, "The Civilian Police Commission," 14.

76. U.S. Commission on Civil Rights, *Who is Guarding the Guardians?* (Washington, DC: Government Printing Office, 1981), 163.

77. Paul C. Light, *Monitoring Government: Inspectors General and the Search for Accountability* (Washington, DC: Brookings Institution, 1993).

78. David J. Rothman, *Strangers at the Bedside* (New York: Basic Books, 1991).

79. Memorandum, "Background Information on Charter Amendment to Create an Office of Citizen Complaints" (San Francisco: n.p., 22 July, 1982).

80. John Crew, interview, 1996; Van Jones, interview, 1996.

81. "In San Francisco Proposition G Passes," *Policing by Consent* (December 1995): 6.

82. San Francisco Office of Citizen Complaints, *1997 Annual Report* (San Francisco: Author, 1998).

83. Annette I. Jolin and Don C. Gibbons, "Policing the Police: The Portland Experience," *Journal of Police Science and Administration,* 12 (September 1984): 315–22.

84. Ibid., 320.

85. Ibid., 321–22.

86. Portland Copwatch, *Proposal for an Effective Civilian Police Review Board,* 3rd ed. (Portland: Copwatch, Spring 1996), iii. The third edition reprints the original 1993 report along with an update.

87. ACLU of Northern California, *A Campaign of Deception: San Jose's Case Against Civilian Review* (San Francisco: ACLU-NC, 1992).

88. Portland, Office of the City Auditor, *Portland's System for Handling Citizen Complaints about Police Misconduct Can Be Improved* (January 1993): 34, 35, 38.

89. Mayor Vera Katz, Memo, Police/Citizen Accountability Initiative, Discussion Draft, 17 November, 1993.

90. These activities are described in detail in Chapters 3, 4, 5, and 6.

91. Portland Copwatch, *Proposal for an Effective Civilian Police Review Board,* 3rd ed.

92. See, for example, David Brauer, "Screening the Thumpers," *City Pages* (21 June, 1995) This author found the term routinely used by persons inside and outside the police department.

93. Anthony M. Bouza, *The Police Mystique: An Insider's Look at Cops, Crime, and the Criminal Justice System* (New York: Plenum, 1990).

94. Wayne A. Kerstetter and Kenneth A. Rasinski, "Opening a Window into Police Internal Affairs: Impact of Procedural Justice Reform on Third Party Attitudes," *Social Justice Research* 7: 2 (1994): 107–27; Minneapolis, Internal Affairs Unit Review Panel, "First Report" (Minneapolis, 1985).

95. Bruce Johnson, "CRA Mediation: Is it the Way to Go?" *Show Up* (August 1998); interviews, Pat Hughes, Director CRA, 1998; interview, Darryl Lynn, CRA Board President, 1998.

96. Citizen Review Ad Hoc Committee, *Citizen Review of Police Conduct: Task Force Report* (San Jose: Santa Clara Bar Association, 1992).

97. Crew, *Campaign of Deception,* 4–8.

98. James G. Kolts, *The Los Angeles County Sheriff's Department* (Los Angeles: Los Angeles County, 1992), 25.

99. Special Counsel, *Semiannual Reports.* The nature and impact of Bobb's work is examined in Chapters 3, 4, 5, and 6.

100. Office of the Inspector General, *Six-Month Report* (Los Angeles: Board of Police Commissioners, January 1997)

101. Ibid.

102. "Police Watchdog Resigns: Los Angeles Set for Debate" *The New York Times,* 15 November, 1998.

103. Samuel Walker and Eileen Luna, *A Report on the Oversight Mechanisms of the Albuquerque Police Department* (Albuquerque: City Council, 1997).

104. ACLU of Northern California, *A Campaign of Deception—San Jose's Case Against Civilian Review.*

105. Samuel Walker, *Citizen Review of the Police—1998 Update* (Omaha: University of Nebraska at Omaha, 1998); Samuel Walker, *Citizen Review Resource Manual* (Washington, DC: Police Executive Research Forum, 1995).

106. Samuel Walker, presentation, Commission on the Advancement of Federal Law Enforcement, *Commission Hearings, August 24, 1998* (Washington, DC, 1998).

107. Andrew Goldsmith, ed., *Complaints against the Police: The Trend to External Oversight* (Oxford: Clarendon Press, 1991).

108. San Jose, Independent Police Auditor, *Year-End Report, 1997* (San Jose, 1998), 3.

109. "Public Solidly Favors Mixed Police/Civilian Review Boards," *Law Enforcement News* (31 October, 1992), 1. David Weisburd and Rosann Greenspan, with Edwin E. Hamilton, Hubert Williams, and Kellie A. Bryant, *Police Attitudes Toward Abuse of Authority: Findings From a National Study* (Washington, DC: Government Printing Office, 2000).

110. Rufus P. Browning, Dale Rogers Marshall, and David H. Tabb, *Protest Is Not Enough* (Berkeley: University of California Press, 1984), 152–56.

111. The District of Columbia CCRB was abolished in 1995 for financial reasons, although virtually everyone regarded it as ineffectual. The Atlanta oversight agency, meanwhile, was nonfunctional.

112. Beattie and Weitzer, "Race, Democracy and Law."

113. Paul Light, *Monitoring Government: Inspectors General and the Search for Accountability* (Washington, DC: The Brookings Institution, 1993).

114. The literature on community policing is vast. The best introduction is David Bayley, *Police for the Future* (New York: Oxford University Press, 1994). See also Wesley Skogan and Susan M. Hartnett, *Community Policing, Chicago Style* (New York: Oxford University Press, 1997).

115. Interview, police chief (anonymity requested).

116. Paul Chevigny, *Edge of the Knife* (New York: The New Press, 1995), 95.

117. Philadelphia Police Advisory Commission, *Annual Report, 1998* (Philadelphia, 1998).

118. Piper and Marbury, *Analysis of the District of Columbia's Civilian Complaint Review Board and Recommendations for its Replacement* (Washington, DC: ACLU-National Capitol Area, 1995), 28, 30–31. *Cox v, District of Columbia,* 40 F.3d 475 (DC Cir. 1994).

119. New York Civil Liberties Union, *A Third Anniversary Overview of the Civilian Complaint Review Board* (New York: NYCLU, 1996), 2.

120. Interview, Goldstein.

PART II

The Role
of Citizen Oversight

3

The Independent Review
of Complaints

INTRODUCTION

The basic role of citizen oversight of the police, as originally conceived by its advocates, is to provide an independent review of complaints against police officers. In this context, "independent" means having complaints reviewed by persons who are not sworn police officers. For many people, however, the idea of independent review of complaints is little more than a slogan. This chapter examines the many complexities and problems that are involved in implementing this idea. It is also important to keep in mind that independent review of complaints is only one role for citizen oversight of the police. The monitoring role, and the various activities associated with that role, is examined in detail in Chapter 4.

Having complaints investigated by people who are not sworn police officers is intended to break down the closed and self-protective bureaucratic ethos of American police departments and ensure that investigations are fair and unbiased. The most extreme form of the self-protective ethos is the so-called "code of silence" by which officers refuse to testify against other officers and in some cases even lie to protect them. Considerable scholarly and contemporary evidence supports the idea of the code of silence. William Westley's classic work on the police subculture found that police officers were willing to lie to protect illegal behavior by their colleagues.[1] More recently, the Christopher Commission investigation of the Los Angeles Police Department (LAPD) in 1991 concluded that the code of silence is "perhaps the greatest single

barrier to effective investigations."[2] The Mollen Commission investigation
into corruption and brutality in the New York City Police Department in the
mid–1980s reached a similar conclusion.[3]

Complexities

The idea of independent review of complaints is sound in principle but far
more difficult to achieve in practice than is generally recognized. The term
independent review itself is ambiguous in two basic respects. First, as Richard J.
Terrill warns, independence is a "nebulous term" that has many different
meanings in this context.[4] A complaint review agency may be formally independent, in the sense of being a separate agency from the police department,
but may not act independently of the police, and/or may not be perceived as
being independent. Second, the "review" of complaints can take many different forms. In existing citizen oversight agencies, citizen input takes a
number of different forms and occurs at different stages in the complaint
process.

Too often in the debate over citizen oversight these complexities are
ignored and "independent review" (or "civilian review") becomes nothing
more than a slogan. For advocates of citizen oversight it is a panacea for police
problems, while for opponents it is a bogeyman that threatens to destroy effective policing.

The purpose of this chapter is to examine what genuinely independent
review of citizen complaints against the police entails. The first section examines the assumptions underlying the demand for independent citizen review,
along with the assumptions underlying the opposition to it. The second section explores the various meanings of the term *independent* as it applies to
complaint review procedures. The third section covers the administrative
details necessary for effective complaint review. As explained in Chapter 1, the
theme of this book is organizational change: how police departments can be
changed to the point where they routinely operate with high standards of
accountability and the role that citizen oversight can play in effecting that
change. Consequently, this chapter addresses the extent to which the independent review of citizen complaints plays or might play some role in changing police organizations.

INDEPENDENT REVIEW: PRO AND CON

At the outset, it is useful to examine the standard arguments for and against the
independent review of complaints. As the discussion that follows will make
clear, the arguments on both sides rest on certain assumptions about the complaint process that have not been verified. The arguments on both sides are
summarized in Figure 3-1.

ARGUMENTS FOR:	ARGUMENTS AGAINST:
1. Police misconduct widespread	1. Police misconduct not a serious problem
2. More thorough and more fair investigations	2. Less thorough and less fair investigations
3. Higher sustain rate	3. Lower sustain rate
4. More disciplinary actions	4. Fewer disciplinary actions
5. Deter police misconduct	5. Deter effective police work
6. Improve public attitudes	6. Less public satisfaction
7. Promote police professionalism	7. Undermine police professionalism

FIGURE 3-1 Arguments For and Against Independent Review

The Arguments for Independent Review

First, advocates of independent review argue that *police misconduct is widespread,* in large part because police departments have consistently failed to investigate allegations of misconduct and to discipline guilty officers. This argument assumes that thorough investigations are inhibited by bureaucratic self-protectiveness within police organizations and the code of silence among individual officers.

Second, advocates of independent review argue that investigations conducted by persons who are not police officers will be *more thorough and fair* than investigations conducted by police officers because the latter are improperly influenced by the norms of the police subculture.

Third, advocates of independent review argue that more thorough and fair investigations will lead to a *higher rate of sustained complaints.* Police departments sustain an average of about 10 percent of all citizen complaints, and oversight advocates cite this low figure as evidence of the need for independent review of complaints.[5]

Fourth, advocates of independent review assume that a higher rate of sustained complaints will result in *more disciplinary actions* of officers who are factually guilty of misconduct. More officers will suffer meaningful discipline, in the form of suspension and termination, as opposed to relatively meaningless verbal reprimands or warnings.

Fifth, advocates of independent review argue that more disciplinary actions will *deter future police misconduct* more effectively than weak or nonexistent patterns of discipline. Deterrence includes both special deterrence involving officers who are disciplined and general deterrence of other officers who will learn from the example of others.[6] Deterrence, in turn, will lead to a long-term improvement in the quality of on-the-street policing.

Sixth, advocates of independent review argue that it will *improve public attitudes toward the police.* This includes two groups of citizens. Individuals who file complaints will be more satisfied with their experience because they will believe that their complaints have been thoroughly and fairly investigated. The general public, meanwhile, will give the police more positive ratings because they will no longer suspect that misconduct is covered up. The improved quality of policing resulting from greater deterrence of misconduct will further improve public attitudes. Finally, because a disproportionate number of complainants are African Americans, these improvements in attitudes will result in better police-community relations and a reduction in racial conflict.

Seventh, advocates of independent review assume that all of the above factors will combine to *improve the level of professionalism* in a police department. On-the-street misconduct will be reduced, new standards of performance will develop, and the norms of the police subculture will evolve in a positive direction.

The Arguments against Independent Review

The arguments against independent review are essentially reverse-mirror images of the arguments in favor of it. These arguments are also based on a number of closely linked assumptions about the operation and impact of complaint review procedures.

First, opponents of independent review argue that it is not needed because *police misconduct is not a serious problem*. The Americans for Effective Law Enforcement (AELE), a legal defense organization for police officers, declares that "police misconduct is simply not the problem that the proponents of review boards would have us believe."[7] The AELE dismisses demands for oversight as "merely the hue and cry of a number of vociferous and articulate anti-police groups and their representatives."[8]

Second, opponents of independent review argue that investigations by people who are not sworn police officers will be *less thorough and less fair* than those conducted by police officers. Outsiders, they argue, do not understand police work, are not competent to assess the dynamics of police-citizen interactions, and consequently cannot make good judgments about alleged misconduct. Opponents of independent review also argue that some nonpolice investigators may be biased against the police.

Third, opponents of independent review argue that police *internal review procedures sustain a higher rate of complaints* than do citizen oversight agencies. The evidence that supports this argument, along with the data that comprise sustain rates, is examined in detail in Chapter 5.[9]

Fourth, opponents argue that independent review will result in *fewer disciplinary actions* of officers because citizens tend to be more lenient toward officers than are the police. They generally cite data from the old Philadelphia Police Advisory Board in the 1950s and 1960s. This evidence is examined in detail in Chapter 5.

Fifth, opponents argue that instead of deterring misconduct, independent review of complaints will *deter officers from effective police work*. The net result will be an increase in crime. As the AELE puts it, police officers "do not want to be second-guessed by those who have no experience in police work."[10] Closely related to this point is the argument that independent review singles out the police for special treatment, subjecting them to a form of scrutiny not applied to other public employees.[11]

Sixth, opponents of independent review argue that it *will provide less satisfaction to complainants*. This argument logically follows from the two previous arguments: that complainants will be dissatisfied by the low sustain rate provided by independent review procedures and will conclude that they are not genuinely independent.

Seventh, opponents of independent review argue that it *undermines police professionalism* by intruding on the professional autonomy of the police and disrupting effective management. This argument assumes that the police are entitled to the same kind of professional autonomy that the classic professions of law, medicine, and education enjoy.[12]

Assessing the Arguments for and against Independent Review

The arguments for and against independent review rest on assumptions that are largely untested and unproven. On several issues there is simply no research whatsoever. If the arguments in favor of independent review are valid, it is safe to assume that positive changes in the organizational culture of a police department will result from the creation of an independent review process. If, on the other hand, the arguments against independent review are valid, then it can be assumed that negative organizational changes will result and the interests of police accountability will be set back.

The *first* issue is whether police misconduct is sufficiently serious to indicate that the police are unable to investigate themselves and that independent investigative review is needed. The traditional police argument that misconduct is not a serious problem cannot be sustained in the face of numerous independent investigations that have found serious police problems. Both the Mollen Commission in New York City and the Christopher Commission in Los Angeles, for example, found not only patterns of serious misconduct by police officers but also a consistent failure of those departments to investigate allegations and discipline guilty officers.

An investigation by the Office of the Public Advocate found that the New York City Police Department consistently failed to discipline officers against whom complaints were sustained by the Civilian Complaint Review Board. It disciplined only 48.8 percent of officers with sustained complaints in 1995, and only 21.1 percent in 1996 (but did increase the rate to 61 percent in 1999). Moreover, three-fourths of those officers who were disciplined received "the lightest possible penalties," essentially "little more than a letter in their personnel files."[13] Police internal review procedures are often *perceived* to be inadequate, to the point of being whitewashes. As Susan Watt argues, even if an internal complaints process is fair, "it does not intrinsically appear fair."[14] Creating and maintaining the appearance of fairness is one of the central justifications for citizen oversight.

The *second* issue involves the question of whether investigators who are not sworn officers conduct fairer and more thorough investigations than police officers. On this issue there is no conclusive evidence one way or another, and the debate has failed to address the factors that contribute to high-quality investigations. Common sense, however, suggests that the quality of investigations depends on such factors as the qualifications of individual investigators and the quality of the training and supervision they receive. Or, to put it another way, the question is whether complaint investigators themselves are held accountable. It cannot be assumed that all outside investigators do a thorough job or that all police departments consistently fail to investigate alleged misconduct.

This issue leads to more fundamental questions about the criteria that should be used in assessing the quality of complaint investigations. What constitutes a thorough and fair investigation? What criteria should be used to make determinations of thoroughness and fairness? There has been surprisingly little discussion of these questions in the debate over complaint review. The issue is complicated by the fact that controversies over police conduct are so often matters of perception: one side sees excessive force while the other sees justifiable force. Additionally, perceptions of particular incidents are heavily influenced by underlying feelings of trust in the police that are, in turn, the legacy of historical experience. Put simply, many people do not trust the police and are immediately suspicious of investigations that fail to find misconduct.

Developing appropriate criteria for assessing the quality of complaint investigations is not a hopeless task, however. Several oversight agencies have developed and currently use criteria for determining the thoroughness and fairness of complaint investigations. These criteria efforts are examined in detail in Chapter 6.

The *third* issue is the question of whether independent investigators or internal police investigators sustain a higher rate of complaints. The entire issue of the sustain rate as a performance measure is a matter of great controversy. Many experts, including this author, argue that it is not a valid performance measure and that others are more appropriate. Chapter 5 includes a detailed discussion of the problems associated with the data that comprise the sustain rate.[15]

On the *fourth* issue, whether citizen oversight or internal police affairs units impose more discipline, opponents of oversight frequently cite James Hudson's 1972 study of the Philadelphia Police Advisory Board (PAB), which found higher sustain rates and more disciplinary actions in cases handled by the internal PBI than for those handled by the external PAB. Hudson's findings are often misinterpreted, however, and opponents of oversight willfully ignore his explicit conclusion that internal and external complaint procedures cannot be compared, in large part because they handle very different kinds of cases.[16] Hudson's study and the larger issue of the sustain rate as a performance indicator are discussed in detail in Chapter 5 (pp 137–138).

The *fifth* argument, that independent review of complaints will deter police misconduct, is unproven. For that matter, there is no research on whether internal review of complaints deters misconduct (although an evaluation of early warning systems suggests that those procedures do have a positive impact on subject officers).[17] The counterargument that independent review deters officers from effective law enforcement is equally unproven. There has been no research on the impact of complaints themselves or different complaint review procedures on officer performance. There is no evidence on the question of whether officers who are disciplined because of citizen complaints become less active and make fewer arrests or write fewer traffic tickets. The problems associated with attempting to measure on-the-street police behavior and the deterrent effect of any change in police discipline procedures are examined in detail in Chapter 5.

On the *sixth* issue, whether independent review of complaints provides greater satisfaction for complainants, there is some evidence but it is very ambiguous. Some complaint procedures do result in high levels of satisfaction, while others do not. The relevant question is: What aspects of complaint review procedures lead to higher levels of satisfaction than others?

Whether or not independent review of complaints contributes to a general improvement of public attitudes toward the police is more difficult to determine. Surveying public opinion about a police department is relatively easy, but isolating the impact of a complaint procedure on the attitudes of people who have not had direct contact with it is extremely difficult. Their attitudes are likely to be affected by aspects of policing unrelated to the complaint procedure. Chapter 5 examines the existing evidence on both of these questions.

The *seventh* issue, whether independent review of complaints improves police professionalism or undermines effective management is the most complex of all the issues. Not only is there presently no evidence either way on the issue, but it would be extremely difficult to determine in the best of circumstances. Many factors affect the quality of management in a police department. Some of these factors are external to the police department: political influence, the community environment, budgets, and so on. Others are internal to the police department: the quality of leadership, the formal and informal standards of discipline, the norms of the local police subculture, and so on.

The police themselves have undermined their traditional argument that independent review of complaints improperly intrudes on the professional autonomy of police managers in several ways. First, the community policing movement emphasizes the development of creative partnerships between the police and community groups.[18] The philosophy of community policing has enjoyed almost universal support in the law enforcement community over the past fifteen years, which means that police chiefs have conceded the importance of significant citizen input into important departmental issues.

Second, police officers routinely appeal adverse disciplinary actions through established civil service procedures. These appeals are heard by politically appointed board members who do not have law enforcement experience. In some jurisdictions, appeals are heard by independent arbitrators.[19] It is hypocritical of police officers to then argue that people of similar backgrounds cannot evaluate alleged complaints against the police. A study of arbitration decisions of officer suspensions (1 to 30 days) in Chicago found that arbitrators fully reversed the police department as often as it fully upheld the disciplinary action (about 40% of all cases in both categories). In short, police officers do not object to the involvement of outsiders when it serves to mitigate punishment on a regular basis.[20]

Third, our legal system routinely asks ordinary citizens to rule on complex legal matters through the jury system, and police officers have never argued against the jury system. Evaluating a citizen complaint does not require any great legal expertise. It simply asks a person to hear two sides of a case and to decide, for example, which side has more credibility and whether a police officer used excessive force given the circumstances.

Finally, it is hypocritical of police officers to object to review by outsiders, because historically they have opposed internal review as well. Part of the folklore of policing is the enormous hostility that rank-and-file officers feel toward internal affairs units. Assignment to internal affairs has been regarded as the least desirable of all assignments and one that officers resist at all costs.[21] They have traditionally regarded investigators as "snitches," headhunters, or worse. In many departments they believe that internal affairs is biased and protects favored officers. A 1998 New York City Council report, for example, found that many people believed that officers who "befriend powerful Departmental officials or union leaders can receive more lenient sentences than others or get a case thrown out altogether."[22]

In short, police officer opposition to citizen oversight is really part of a general opposition to any inquiry into their conduct regardless of the source of that inquiry.

CRITERIA FOR EVALUATION

To place the goals of independent review of complaints in a broader perspective, it is useful to consider the criteria that should be used to evaluate complaint procedures. Douglas Perez identifies three criteria: integrity, legitimacy, and learning.[23] *Integrity* refers primarily to the thoroughness and fairness of the complaint investigation process. *Legitimacy* refers to how the complaint investigation process is perceived by its clients, stakeholders, and audiences. These include complainants, officers who are subject to complaints, the community at large, the police department, and elected officials ultimately responsible for the process. *Learning* refers to the extent to which the process provides meaningful feedback to responsible officials in such a way that allows them to make improvements in both the complaint process and the police department.

These criteria are directly related to the theme of citizen oversight and organizational change. The entire controversy over citizen oversight exists because many people do not believe that police complaint procedures have integrity. Thus, these procedures lack legitimacy in the eyes of important segments of the community. There is also the widespread belief that police

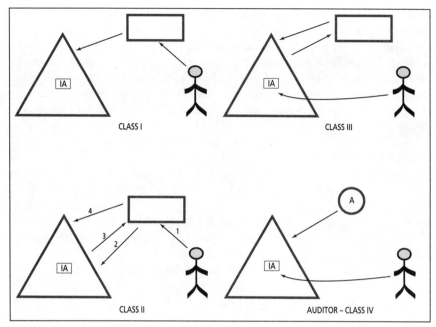

FIGURE 3-2 Four Models of Citizen Oversight

departments do not use individual complaints as a means of learning about and correcting problems.

ASPECTS OF INDEPENDENCE

With respect to complaints against the police, the concept of *independence* has three separate dimensions: structural independence, process independence, and perceived independence.[24]

Structural Independence

External or citizen review of complaints against the police is intended to be independent in the sense that it involves an agency that is structurally separate from the police department for which it is responsible. As the following section explains, existing citizen oversight agencies vary tremendously in terms of their formal structure. They differ in terms of where in the complaint review process citizen input occurs and in terms of the exact nature of the citizen input. From the standpoint of *structural independence,* there are four basic models of citizen oversight.[25] Figure 3-2 provides a schematic diagram of the different models of oversight systems.

In what are termed *Class I* systems, responsibility for investigating individual complaints is given to a separate agency external to the police department. The critical factor is that *persons who are not sworn officers conduct the initial fact-finding investigation of complaints.* Their investigative reports are reviewed by other nonsworn officials, who then forward a recommendation to the police chief for final disposition. The Minneapolis Civilian Review Authority (CRA) and the San Francisco Office of Citizen Complaints (OCC) are examples of Class I systems.

In *Class II* systems, citizen complaints are investigated by the police department and citizens have some input in the review of the investigative reports. In Kansas City, for example, complaints are initially received by the Office of Citizen Complaints (OCC) and then are forwarded to the police department for investigation. Completed investigative reports are sent back to the OCC for review and a recommendation that is then forwarded to the police chief. Class II systems, in short, have some citizen input but the citizens are dependent upon the investigations done by the police.

Class III systems are essentially appellate review procedures. Police departments remain responsible for receiving, investigating, and disposing of complaints. If the complainant is not satisfied with the result, he or she may appeal to the oversight agency. If the agency disagrees with the disposition or feels the investigation was inadequate, it may refer the case back to the police department for further investigation. It cannot, however, overturn a disposition and substitute its own judgment about the case. Obviously, Class III systems are the least independent and involve the lowest level of citizen involvement. The Omaha Citizen Review Board is an example of a Class III system.

Class IV systems, which are also known as auditor systems, do not investigate individual complaints, but are authorized to review, monitor, or audit the police department's complaints process. The Portland Police Internal Investigations Auditing Committee (PIIAC) and the San Jose Independent Police Auditor (IPA) are examples of the auditor model. Both have the authority to recommend that individual complaints be sent back for investigation, but they also play a larger role in reviewing the policies and procedures of the police department and in making recommendations for change. The Special Counsel to the Los Angeles Sheriff's Department has a broader auditing mandate and engages in a comprehensive review of management practices.

The four classes of oversight systems have developed through an ad hoc process of compromise and experimentation. Additional variations have recently appeared. New forms of oversight were created in Seattle, Washington (1999) and Nashville, Tennessee (2000) that do not fit into any of the four classes just described. In Seattle the new Office of Professional Accountability is responsible for the police department's internal affairs unit, including the handling of complaints, and is directed by a civilian employee appointed by the chief.[26] Nashville adopted a similar arrangement. The Seattle and Nashville systems are hybrids. On one hand, they are "internal" because responsibility for handling complaints remains with the police department. On the other, there is an element of citizen oversight to the extent that the citizen complaint process is directed by someone who is not a sworn officer.

Variations of Structural Independence

The four models described here are generic. In practice, each one includes enormous variations in roles and responsibilities, staffing and resources, complaint procedures, and other administrative matters.[27] The New York City Civilian Complaint Review Board (CCRB) and the New Orleans Office of Municipal Investigations (OMI) are both Class I systems but are structured very differently.[28] The CCRB includes a board of politically appointed citizens that appoints the professional staff, while the OMI involves a civil service-protected office with a single director. The San Jose, Portland, and Los Angeles County Special Counsel are all auditor systems but are structured very differently. The San Jose Independent Police Auditor is an independent agency with a single director; the director of the Portland PIIAC is on the staff of the mayor's office but reports to the mayor, city council, and a board of citizens; the Special Counsel to the Los Angeles County Sheriff's Department is an attorney employed under a fixed-term contract.

The four models described here vary considerably in terms of the degree of their independence. Class I systems are structurally the most independent model because they conduct their own fact-finding investigations. Class II and III systems are structurally far less independent because they do not conduct their own independent fact-finding investigations. As a consequence, they are often perceived as being less independent. A grand jury report, for example, concluded that the San Diego (City) Civilian Review Board, a Class II system, "cannot conduct independent interviews and is hampered by its total dependence on Police Department internal investigations." Moreover, because the agency's staff and budget were then a part of the police department, it gave "the impression that CRB is simply another division of the police department."[29]

Terrill argues that some oversight agencies have little more than symbolic independence. They have the appearance of independent review of complaints but in fact are dependent upon internal police investigations. Some observers regard these essentially powerless agencies as window dressing; some may even represent a form of "consumer fraud" in the sense that they promise independent review of complaints without in fact achieving it.[30] Class II and III systems basically provide more symbolic than substantive independence. While they do in fact "review" complaints, in practice they only review material developed by the police. And as later chapters of this book argue at length, the critical issue is the investigative fact-finding process and whether or not that process is thorough and fair. Class IV auditor systems are independent of the police, but in a very different way than Class I systems.

The true independence of an auditor system depends not just on the language of the authorizing statute or ordinance, but on seemingly minor administrative matters, particularly with respect to access to police department documents. This point was well illustrated by a controversy in late 1998 that culminated in the resignation of inspector general of the Los Angeles Police Department. Inspector General (IG) Katherine Mader resigned when the Police Commission attempted to limit the IG's access to completed investigations, denying her access to investigations still in progress, and to subject the IG's reports to review (and possible editing or censorship) by the executive director of the Police Commission.[31]

Process Independence

The fact that an oversight agency is structurally independent does not by itself guarantee that it functions in a way that is genuinely independent of the police department it is responsible for. This aspect of independence is referred to as *process independence.*

One of the frequent criticisms of some oversight agencies is that the members of a review board are more lenient with police officers than police internal review procedures.[32] As some critics put it, "the watchdog becomes a lapdog." Although there is no evidence to support the conclusion that all citizen oversight agencies are more lenient (see the extended discussion of this extremely important issue in Chapter 5), there is indeed a problem that lay members of oversight boards will become co-opted by the police. Many people are easily awed or intimidated by the police and impressed by testimony about the danger and difficulty associated with being a police officer. Review board members may begin to lean over backward to see things from the police point of view and in this sense lose their independence. Or it may be the case that the individuals appointed to serve on a review board are inclined to favor the police in the first place.

The Los Angeles Police Commission is an excellent example of an oversight agency that is structurally independent but has not functioned independently of the police department it is responsible for. By city charter, the commission has full responsibility for the Los Angeles Police Department (LAPD). And yet, as numerous observers have concluded, it has always deferred to the LAPD police chief on important issues. The Christopher Commission concluded in 1991 that the Police Commission had neither sufficient powers nor resources to adequately play an effective oversight role. It specifically recommended that the Police Commission assume "a direct, major role in handling citizen complaints."[33] The situation did not appear to improve over the next eight years. In 1999 a new scandal was uncovered in the LAPD, and an internal LAPD Board of Inquiry report found that accountability procedures within the LAPD had completely broken down. The Police Commission had not only failed to ensure that the recommendations of the Christopher Commission were implemented but allowed other procedures to lapse.[34]

The Milwaukee Fire and Police Commission (FPC) is another example of structural independence without process independence. The FPC was created by state law in 1885 and has full authority to run the Milwaukee Police Department (MPD). It receives citizen complaints and conducts trials over alleged misconduct. It has the power to "suspend, demote, or discharge Department members for conduct in violation of Department rules and regulations."[35] Yet the Milwaukee FPC receives very few complaints and is widely distrusted by the African-American community. It received only 42 complaints in 1987; the number rose to about 100 in 1991 and fell to about 50 in 1992. San Francisco has almost the same number of officers (1,800 in 1992) but the OCC averages about 1,000 complaints per year.[36] Attorney James Hall told the U.S. Civil Rights Commission in the mid-1990s that potential complainants in Milwaukee "are intimidated to even go to the fire and police commission. . . . There is this whole history that there is no relief available." Another witness told the Civil Rights Commission that "minorities were intimidated from complaining" and that "complaints at the districts were ignored."[37]

Along the same lines, the then-director of the New Orleans Office of Municipal Investigations could not in 1998 cite a single example of a police department policy or procedure that he had helped to change.[38] During the course of this person's tenure as OMI director, corruption and excessive force by New Orleans police officers became a national scandal. In short, the full structural independence of the OMI, including civil service protection for the director, did not guarantee that the agency would operate independently and effectively.

How can we determine whether a structurally independent oversight agency is in fact operating independently? There is no easy answer to this question. Later sections of this chapter and the next describe the various roles and responsibilities that oversight agencies can and do engage in, while Chapter 5 and 6 discuss alternative strategies for evaluating effectiveness.

Perceived Independence

A third dimension of independence is whether a given agency is *perceived* to be independent. An oversight agency may be structurally independent and may have a high degree of process independence but not be perceived as being independent, particularly by those segments of the community that are suspicious of the police and have demanded the creation of an oversight agency.

Perceived independence is as complex as the other two dimensions of independence. Perceptions of an oversight agency are influenced by a variety of factors that may have little to do with the actual performance of the agency. One controversial incident can damage the reputation of an oversight agency just as it can with police departments. Appointed members of oversight boards may be criticized by opponents of the officials who appointed them.

One particularly thorny question is the issue of who represents particular groups in the community. Who, for example, represents the African-American or the Hispanic community? There are often allegations that a particular African-American member of an oversight board does not truly "represent" the African-American community because of close ties to white political leaders or the police department. Such controversies are particularly difficult. It may be the case that a board member's critics are simply political rivals or have some personal grudge.

The issue of who "truly" represents particular communities is not confined to the subject of citizen oversight of the police. It lies at the heart of ideas proposed by law professor Lani Guinier, whose nomination for the position of Deputy Attorney General by President Clinton in 1993 touched off a national controversy. Guinier was attacked by her critics as an advocate of racial quotas in voting districts. A close reading of Guinier's articles and books reveals that her proposals were prompted by her profound disappointment that the election of many African-American officials since the 1965 Voting Rights Act had not produced officials who addressed deepseated issues of poverty and other social problems. Her proposals for changing election procedures, in short, are designed to produce elected officials who she feels are more representative of the African-American community.[39] Suffice it to say, however, that skin color alone does not automatically guarantee a particular point of view on policing —or any other social or political issue, for that matter.

Another feature affecting the perceived independence of a review board is the presence of police officers on the board. Officers serve on the boards of about a quarter of all oversight agencies.[40] The 1998 ordinance creating a new review board for the Washington, D.C. police department mandated that one member of the board would be a police officer.

The police and their allies argue that the presence of an officer brings a necessary element of police expertise to the board's deliberations. Most oversight advocates, however, argue that it compromises the perceived independence and probably even the process independence of the agency. The Baltimore Complaint Evaluation Board (CEB) is a special case, since seven of the twelve members are public officials, and most of them police or prosecutors. The U.S. Civil Rights Commission concluded: "The domination of the CEB by enforcement agencies . . . combine to cast doubt on the credibility of the existing system. . . . The CEB seems to many to be merely an extension of the police department."[41]

The fate of the Flint ombudsman in the mid-1990s suggests how perceived independence often becomes entangled in racial and political controversies. For several years, the ombudsman was a white attorney with strong connections to the local Democratic party and the politically powerful United Automobile Workers. This individual functioned in a diligent but low-key manner. When he returned to private practice, he was replaced by an African American who took a high-profile public role, speaking to community groups about police misconduct. African-American community leaders spoke highly of him and thought his predecessor was too much a part of the local political establishment. Whites, however, were generally critical of the new ombudsman, particularly with regard to the public role he played, and cited a failure to administer the office effectively. In fact, he prepared no annual reports and was eventually fired for alleged misconduct in office (he appeared at his office after being fired and was then barred from the premises by a restraining order). Which of the two Flint ombudsmen was the more effective? The evidence suggests that the former was, but the latter's public role won more favor with the African-American community.[42]

The task of evaluating the actual and perceived independence of an oversight agency is not impossible. The appropriate yardsticks are the various activities outlined later in this chapter and the next. Thus, for example, it is possible to determine whether an oversight agency has sufficient resources to accomplish its tasks, whether there is any documented evidence of an active outreach program or policy review process. Chapters 5 and 6 examine ways of evaluating the effectiveness of such programs.

INDEPENDENT OVERSIGHT
AND THE DILEMMA OF DEMOCRACY

In some instances, long-time advocates of citizen oversight have become disillusioned with the very agency they fought to create, perceiving it as a part of the "system." Many of these people are deeply alienated from the political system, often for understandable reasons after years of fighting police abuse and encountering resistance from the police and city hall. At the 1998 NACOLE meeting, for example, a member of the review board in one west coast city, pointing out that their board is dependent on attorneys from the city and receives its budget from the city, asked plaintively whether there were any way their board could be made less dependent on the "system."[43] At a meeting in Des Moines, Iowa, where this author spoke in 1997, several African-American citizens in attendance complained that a proposed oversight agency was still "part of the loop" and therefore could not possibly be effective.[44]

These criticisms bring us to one of the fundamental dilemmas of accountability in a democratic society. The dilemma can be stated succinctly: How can we create a form of oversight that is independent of the police and yet responsive to the public through the normal channels of democratic government? As an agency of local government, the police are a part of the local political system; and any form of oversight must also be a part of that very same political system. In the nineteenth century, the police were *too* responsive to the political system. The professionalization movement in the twentieth century sought to reduce improper political influence but in many ways went too far in isolating the police from the public.[45]

It is understandable that people who have been fighting police abuse and an unresponsive political system would begin to think in terms of an oversight system that would be fully independent of that political system. Unfortunately, such an approach is completely unacceptable in a democratic society, where all government agencies must be answerable to the public they serve. Oversight advocates who want an oversight agency that is completely independent of local politics have simply not thought through the basic question of how the members of such an agency would be selected. Many seem to imagine that *they* will get to pick the board members, thereby circumventing the mayor and city council whom they distrust. But, of course, if one group can claim to control an oversight agency, why can't other groups make similar claims? Why can't the police union get to control the agency? The point is that no group or faction has any such right. In a democratic society, control of public agencies is accomplished through the normal institutions of representative government. This, if course, brings us back to the original problem: the failure of these institutions to hold the police accountable.

The dilemma of balancing independence and responsiveness is not unique to the subject of citizen oversight of the police. Indeed, it is a fundamental aspect of democratic self-government. How do we ensure good government when the majority and their elected representatives either don't care or, worse, desire bad things?[46] Our constitutional system of government deals with some aspects of this problem through the Bill of Rights, which imposes some basic limits on majority rule. We give judges a certain degree of independence for the same reason. Unfortunately, many police misconduct issues lie far below the scope of lofty constitutional issues, and involve a number of mundane but nonetheless critical political and administrative issues: Who is to be police chief? Should this officer be disciplined for certain behavior? Who should command the internal affairs unit? It is these often mundane administrative details that shape the culture of a police department and, with that, the level of misconduct out on the street.

The dilemma facing so many advocates of citizen oversight is that the political establishment is often unresponsive. Thus, for example, many observers believe that even though the voters approved the San Francisco OCC in 1982, a succession of mayors undermined the agency by appointing directors with a clear mandate not to pursue oversight too vigorously. And by the same token, many observers believe that the OCC became more active and effective after the election of Willie Brown as mayor in 1995. The New York City Council created a fully independent CCRB in 1993, but because of hostility and indifference from the mayor's office and the police department itself, its effectiveness has been severely hampered.[47]

The recent history of the federal Independent Counsel Act dramatizes the difficulties and the dangers of creating an investigative authority that is independent of constituted political authority. The law was enacted in an effort to create some mechanism for investigating alleged lawbreaking by members of a presidential administration (including the president himself or herself) that would be independent of the Justice Department, which is controlled by that administration. Independent Counsel Kenneth Starr's investigation of President Bill Clinton, however, raised serious questions about whether his office was dangerously out of control. Questions have been raised about whether Starr's investigation represented a political vendetta, moved far beyond its original mandate, and used unacceptable methods. Because of these questions, Starr's major legacy is likely to be the demise of the Independent Counsel law itself. The point is that an out-of-control investigation is an inherent danger with any agency that is designed to be free of the normal checks and balances of constituted political authority.[48]

Alternative Means of Achieving Independence

The lesson of the independent counsel experience is that investigative authorities, whether prosecutors or complaint investigative bodies, must ultimately be answerable to responsible political authority. The dilemma is that this answerability will necessarily involve some degree of political control. The challenge is how to achieve the desired aspect of independence with the necessary element of political accountability.

There are several possibilities for achieving that balance with respect to oversight agencies for the police. One approach is to create state-level oversight agencies. Ample precedent for such agencies already exists. The Iowa ombudsman has authority to investigate complaints of any public agency in the state. England has a national oversight agency, the Police Complaints Authority (PCA).[49] In Canada and Australia, provincial level oversight agencies exist.[50]

State-level agencies in the United States have the virtue of not being directly controlled by the local political authorities responsible for the police departments under investigation. State-level agencies are also a reasonably efficient approach to accountability for the thousands of small law enforcement agencies in the United States. This approach has three dangers, however. First, the agencies could be so removed from the local context that they would be unresponsive to specific police problems. Second, the plain facts of American geography could hamper their efficient operations. Imagine, for example, a state-level agency in Ohio that attempted to serve Cleveland, Columbus, and Cincinnati, not to mention the many smaller cities. Third, this approach changes but does not solve the problem of politics. A state-level agency would be responsive to a different set of political forces. To be sure, it would be less subject to local political pressures but, as already noted, it might be less responsive to local problems for precisely the same reason.

Some oversight advocates have suggested that to circumvent the existing political establishment, members of a civilian review board should be elected directly by the people. At first glance, this proposal has the appeal of direct democracy and a strategy for allowing "the people" to assert control over the police. Upon closer examination, however, this idea is not likely to be a solution and in fact could result in less independent oversight of the police than currently exists. There is no reason why the elected members of a review board would be any more independent of the police than current city council members. And, in fact, police unions are well positioned by virtue of their organizational resources to dominate the elections. The result could very well be a highly "pro-police" review board. Direct democracy, in short, is not always the best solution for difficult problems. The best approach remains the appointment of oversight officials, with candidates screened in a fashion similar to the screening of judicial nominees. The results will, of course be far from perfect, but it will ensure that oversight officials are neither aggressively "pro-police" nor "anti-police."

ASPECTS OF THE COMPLAINT
REVIEW PROCESS

The formal structure of an oversight agency is really only the starting point for analyzing its role in the investigation of complaints. There are a number of legal and administrative aspects of complaint review that affect an agency's capacity to handle complaints effectively.

Scope of Authority

Although the demand for citizen oversight has primarily involved the police, some oversight agencies also investigate complaints against the employees of other agencies. The Cincinnati Office of Municipal Investigations (OMI) and the New Orleans Office of Municipal Investigations (OMI) have this authority.[51] The Iowa ombudsman can investigate complaints against any public official in the state. In 1994, about 6 percent of its cases involved law enforcement agencies, including small police and sheriffs' departments, the state patrol, and the state Division of Criminal Investigation.[52] Much of the work of the San Diego County Citizens Law Enforcement Review Board (CLERB) involves complaints arising from the detention facilities operated by the sheriffs' departments.[53] By the mid-1990s, about 17 percent of all oversight agencies handled complaints against the police and other city or county departments.[54]

Giving an oversight agency responsibility for departments other than law enforcement is appropriate for several reasons. First, police officers are hardly the only government officials about whom complaints are made. As Walter Gellhorn pointed out more than thirty years ago, poor people probably "find themselves in controversy with welfare and educational authorities than with the police."[55] The principle of accountability applies to all public employees, and it is appropriate to have effective accountability mechanisms in place to deal with complaints.

Second, broadening the scope of authority of an oversight agency responds to the traditional criticism by the police that citizen oversight unfairly singles them out for special scrutiny.[56] The American Bar Association did not not endorse citizen oversight, in part because it "focus[es] solely on the misdeeds of policemen while ignoring the potential for abuse of discretion and impact on minority groups of other administrative agencies."[57] Recent developments in broadening the scope of authority for oversight agencies render the ABA criticism out of date.

Third, creating state or county-level oversight agencies with responsibility for all agencies in that jurisdiction is a reasonable method of providing oversight for the many small law enforcement agencies in the United States. About 80 percent of all law enforcement agencies have ten or fewer sworn officers;[58]

most are small-town and rural police and sheriffs' departments. Creating an oversight agency for each one would be administratively inefficient because these small departments do not generate enough complaints in any given year to justify it. Complaints against officers in these small departments do arise, of course, and some oversight mechanism is appropriate. A state-level agency along the lines of the Iowa ombudsman is an appropriate solution.

Possible Prosecution for False Statements

Some complaint procedures require complainants to sign a statement indicating their understanding that they can be prosecuted for making false allegations against a police officer. California has a state law, the Boland Amendment, to this effect. Most experts on citizen complaints believe that such a requirement unnecessarily intimidates potential complainants and deters them from filing complaints. Although there is no empirical research on the subject, most experts believe that very few complainants knowingly file false allegations against officers. Most complaints involve legitimate differences of perception about the events in question: e.g., that the officer used excessive force, that the citizen threatened the officer, etc. Complaints of this nature do not involve criminal intent to knowingly file false statements. On the contrary, advocates of citizen oversight and an increasing number of police departments themselves argue that the complaint process should be as open as possible and that each and every potential complaint should be given at least some formal consideration.

Requiring Officer Testimony

One of the most bitterly contested issues in the struggle over oversight is whether an oversight agency should have subpoena power to compel the testimony of police officers. Subpoena power is essentially a means to an end: obtaining the truthful testimony of police officers about allegations against other officers.

Obtaining the testimony of police officers is absolutely essential for Class I oversight systems. They are responsible for the initial fact-finding investigation of complaints, and this process cannot be effective or meaningful if investigators are unable to obtain all relevant information about an alleged incident. In many cases, the testimony of one or more other officers is crucial. A Class I system that cannot require officers to testify is doomed to ineffectuality. The Michigan Court of Appeals, upholding the subpoena power of the Flint ombudsman, held that without this power, "the ombudsman could become a kind of toothless tiger, as ineffective as a nonvoting member of a debating society."[59] A 1997 San Diego grand jury report concluded that the operations of the San Diego County CLERB had been "thwarted since its inception by incessant litigation brought by the Deputy Sheriffs Association," including a suit over subpoena power.[60]

Subpoena power is a more complex matter for Class II and III systems since they do not conduct their own fact-finding investigations and only review police investigative files. These systems are weak by design, limited to reviewing original complaint investigations conducted by the police. Giving them power to subpoena officers, complainants, and witnesses would in effect transform them in to Class I systems with independent investigatory power.

Class IV or auditor systems do not conduct the initial investigations of complaints, and therefore the power to subpoena officers is not as crucial as it is with Class I systems. Nonetheless, access to all relevant information in and about the police department is essential for auditor systems. Without such authority, they are unable effectively to monitor the operations of the internal affairs unit and the rest of the police department. Merrick Bobb, the Special Counsel to the Los Angeles Sheriff's Department, examines virtually every aspect of the department's operations. Most auditor systems are given this power by statute.

Police unions have fought subpoena power in legislatures and in the courts. Generally, they have lost this battle. The courts upheld the subpoena power of the Flint ombudsman, and in 1994 the California Supreme Court rejected a challenge to the subpoena power of the San Diego County CLERB.[61]

A different approach to obtaining officer testimony is to make cooperation with complaint investigations a condition of employment. In Minneapolis, for example, all city employees, including police officers, "shall, except as expressly prohibited by law, respond promptly to any and all reasonable requests for information, for participation in evidentiary hearings, and for access to data and records." Failure to cooperate "shall be deemed an act of misconduct."[62] In Oakland, California, police officers were originally allowed to not appear at 40 percent of the hearings conducted by the Citizens' Police Review Board (CPRB). After much criticism of the CPRB by the ACLU and PUEBLO, a local human rights organization, a new ordinance was enacted in 1996 giving it subpoena power in all cases.[63]

Although essential for the investigation of complaints, mandatory testimony by officers—either as a condition of employment or through subpoena—does not settle the issue of police officer cooperation with investigations. Historically, one of the main obstacles to police accountability has been the so-called "code of silence," the refusal of police officers to testify truthfully about their own behavior and to testify against other officers, and their willingness even to lie to cover up misconduct by fellow officers.[64] Some oversight agencies have undertaken efforts to combat false and misleading testimony by police officers. These efforts are examined in Chapter 4.

Public Hearings

In a number of oversight agencies, the investigation of a complaint culminates in a public hearing. The hearing is essentially a trial where the evidence against the officer is presented and the officer has an opportunity to rebut the charges. In some oversight agencies—the Minneapolis CRA, for example—hearings before the CRA Board are not public.[65] In Denver, the police union sued to prevent the Public Safety Review Board from mentioning police officers by name at public hearings. The board adopted its own policy of voluntarily not mentioning names.[66]

Many advocates of oversight regard public hearings as essential for bringing to light the facts of officer misconduct. Public hearings are not necessarily the panacea their advocates believe them to be, however. First and perhaps most important, public hearings do not provide the largest window into either the police department or the complaint process. In a way that is analogous to trials in the criminal process, public hearings inevitably involve only small and unrepresentative samples of all complaints. In the criminal process, where only about 10 percent of all cases go to trial, most of the important decisions are made in the pretrial stages, beginning with arrest. By the same token, the complaint process involves a series of critical decisions involving the intake, recording, classification, and investigation of complaints. Public hearings on the small percentage of complaints that reach the hearing stage shed little if any light on the practices that affect most cases.

Second, the adversarial nature of formal hearings results in the loss of much information. To be sure, an officer can be compelled to testify about the incident under investigation, but the rules of evidence severely restrict the scope of the inquiry to that incident. As is argued in other parts of this book, however, complaints are often symptomatic of deeper problems within a police department. Focusing on particular incidents tends to deflect attention away from these deeper problems and make the individual officer the scapegoat. An active auditor system, by contrast, can inquire into the full range of police practices that underlie on-the-street misconduct incidents.

Third, hearings are extremely time consuming and place enormous burdens on the lay members of review boards, most of whom face demands on their time from their own careers and private lives. The requirement that all cases go to a hearing was one of the reasons why the old Washington, D.C., CCRB became hopelessly backlogged in the early 1990s, to the point where many cases languished for three years or more.[67]

There are other ways of opening a window into a police department and getting systematic and useful information about police practices and the complaint process. Some of the auditor models of oversight undertake wide-ranging investigations of police practices. Merrick Bobb's reports on the Los Angeles Sheriff's Department (see Chapter 4, pp. 96–97) are comprehensive in scope, examining the various administrative practices and problems that underlie many complaints. We learn far more about the sheriff's department from Bobb's semiannual reports than we ever would from an adversarial public hearing over a citizen's complaint.

Some oversight agencies, meanwhile, routinely provide brief but detailed descriptions of individual complaints. The 1997 annual report of the Oakland CPRB, for example, contains narrative descriptions of cases heard by the board, including the names of the complainants and the officers involved, the alleged misconduct, and the decision of the board.[68] The San Diego CLERB provides similar descriptions of incidents in its minutes. These brief accounts also explain the rationale for the CLERB disposition. In one case, for example, it explained that "there is not enough evidence to prove whether or not this incident actually happened." In several others, it noted that the allegation was not proved "due to the fact that the majority of the deputies refused to cooperate in the investigation." In another, "there was no physical evidence or testimony to corroborate the complainant's allegation."[69] Information of this sort not only provides a window into the police department but allows the public to judge the performance of the oversight agency.

Finally, developments in Minneapolis suggest that hearings are not always necessary once a police department establishes a serious commitment to accountability and the oversight agency has established its credibility with police officers. By the late 1990s, an increasing number of Minneapolis police officers began choosing to forego their right to a public hearing. In 1996 and 1997, half of the complaints sustained by the CRA were completed with the officer stipulating to the charge(s) and the case going directly to the police chief for discipline without a hearing.[70] In effect, these officers admit their guilt and implicitly acknowledge that CRA investigations are fair and that nothing is to be gained (and perhaps much is to be lost) by contesting the case in a hearing.

Standard of Proof

After a complaint investigation is completed, what standard of proof should be used to determine whether or not to sustain the allegation(s) against the officer? The complaint process is administrative rather than criminal, and therefore the *proof beyond a reasonable doubt* standard is inappropriate. Two other standards are generally used. The lower of these is *preponderance of the evidence.* Somewhat higher is the *clear and convincing* standard. The 1996 ordinance revising the Oakland CPRB, for example, requires that "the burden shall be placed upon the complainant to prove, by a preponderance of the evidence, the allegation(s) of the complaint."[71] The rules of the Berkeley Police Review Commission, on the other hand, state that "no complaint shall be sustained unless it is proven by clear and convincing evidence presented at the hearing."[72] The preponderance of the evidence standard, which most oversight advocates prefer, is the appropriate standard.

The "Tie Goes to the Officer" Issue

A related issue that disturbs many oversight advocates is the situation known as "the tie goes to the officer." Where there is insufficient evidence that the officer committed the alleged misconduct (that is, the preponderance of the evidence does not support the complainant), a complaint is not sustained. In a five-year follow-up to the Christopher Commission report, Merrick Bobb noted that this issue arose in "many" of the cases he reviewed.[73] "In a typical case," he explained, "there are two main witnesses to the alleged misconduct, the complainant and the officer."[74] The result is that the case becomes a "swearing match," and in the absence of any other evidence against the officer the complaint is not sustained.[75]

Bobb concedes that this is "a difficult issue." Always allowing the officer to avoid discipline allows much misconduct to go unpunished. Some oversight advocates have suggested that some alternative mode of disposition is needed, although no specific alternative has been offered.

Any alternative to not sustaining a complaint when the evidence results in a "tie" would set a dangerous precedent, however. A citizen complaint has potentially serious consequences for an officer. In addition to discipline in the immediate case, there are potential future implications, particularly in departments that use early warning systems or disciplinary histories in making promotion decisions. The prospect of permitting discipline in cases where there is not even a preponderance of the evidence is extremely dangerous in a society where one of the cornerstones of the legal system is that a person is innocent until proven guilty. Potentially, it could result in discipline in cases where there are only unverified allegations.

The proper approach is not to weaken the standard of proof but to *improve the quality of investigations* to ensure that all relevant facts are gathered and that the resulting disposition is reasonably related to the facts.

Disciplinary Power

When a complaint is sustained, oversight agencies generally forward their decision to the police chief as a recommendation. With the few exceptions explained later, this is only a recommendation and not a disciplinary action itself.

There is considerable variation on the exact status of these recommendations. In Minneapolis, CRA dispositions are binding on the police chief. The chief has some leeway on what disciplinary action to take but may not reverse a CRA determination that a complaint is sustained. In San Francisco, on the other hand, the chief may reject an OCC recommendation. An interesting pattern developed regarding police chief responses, however. In the early years of the OCC during the 1980s, chiefs reversed about half of all OCC recommendations, changing sustained complaints into unsustained or exonerated dispositions. By the late 1990s, however, San Francisco chiefs were accepting most if not all OCC recommendations. An ACLU report found that as late as 1994 the chief of police was taking disciplinary action in only 49 percent of OCC sustained cases, compared with 90 percent of cases sustained by internal affairs.[76] The 1997 OCC *Annual Report,* however, indicated that the chief had sustained 100 percent of all OCC sustained complaints.[77]

The greater acceptance of OCC recommendations is the result of several factors. In part, the attitude of the police chief reflected the priorities of Mayor Willie Brown, first elected in 1995 and a strong supporter of the OCC. At the same time, the relationship between OCC and the police department had matured over the years, with the police gradually coming to accept the oversight role of the OCC.

Whether oversight agencies should have the power actually to discipline officers is an extremely complex matter.[78] Three issues need to be considered. First, in most jurisdictions it is not legally possible since the power to discipline is specifically given to the chief of police by state law or local ordinance. A change in city charter or state law would be necessary to transfer that power to another agency.[79]

Second, in those cities with police commissions, the appointed boards have the ultimate power to impose discipline.[80] The Milwaukee Fire and Police Commission (FPC) has full power to hire, demote, suspend, or terminate Milwaukee police officers. The San Francisco Police Commission also has ultimate disciplinary authority over police officers. The Detroit Board of Police Commissioners was created in 1973 as part of a general movement to enhance accountability and reduce police brutality.[81]

Some comments need to be made about these police commissions, however. First, several of them have not used their powers effectively. The Milwaukee FPC has a dismal record of handling citizen complaints. The Los Angeles Police Commission was a supine entity for decades, deferring to the authority of LAPD police chiefs. The Christopher Commission labeled the L.A. Police Commission's authority "illusory."[82] The San Francisco and Detroit police commissions, on the other hand, have more creditable records of asserting control over their respective police departments.[83]

These examples illustrate the point that structural independence does not guarantee process independence. Meaningful accountability depends upon a number of different factors, including effective political leadership and a vision of police accountability on the part of the commission or agency. An oversight agency that is structurally independent can be rendered ineffective by a lack of political will and administrative leadership.

Taking disciplinary power away from the police chief and giving it to an external agency, moreover, may be detrimental to accountability in the long run. Many oversight experts, including the author of this book, argue that such a move undermines the power of the police chief, and with that the chief's sense of responsibility. This arrangement tends to create situations where a chief could say, in response to a particular incident, "I have no power to discipline that officer." The long-term result is irresponsibility on the part of chiefs.

At the same time, it should be noted that citizens have a significant role in police disciplinary actions and have had it for many years. All law enforcement agencies in this country operate under some form of civil service. These procedures allow an officer to appeal disciplinary actions. Generally, appeals are heard by a civil service or personnel board, consisting of citizens appointed by elected officials.[84] Many of these boards have consistent records of mitigating or overturning disciplinary actions by police chiefs (e.g., a three-day suspension reduced to a one-day suspension). In fact, police chiefs bitterly complain about cases where they have fired an officer for serious misconduct only to have him or her reinstated by a civil service agency. An officer in the Minneapolis Police Department who cost the city nearly $2 million in damage awards was fired twice but reinstated both times.[85] In short, external citizen control of police discipline does not always result in appropriate discipline.

The proper role of external oversight is to *heighten* the accountability of police chiefs rather than reduce it. This role includes providing the chief with additional information from nonpolice sources and placing a spotlight on the chief by providing as much information to the public as possible. One important function is to publicize a police chief's consistent failure to discipline officers guilty of misconduct where that pattern exists.

Staff Resources

The effective review of complaints requires adequate staff resources. This is true for police internal affairs units as well as citizen oversight agencies. The ineffective performance of some oversight agencies has been the result of inadequate staffing rather than any inherent flaw in the concept of oversight. For many years, the Cincinnati Office of Municipal Investigations (OMI) had only one staff investigator for a police department with about 1,000 sworn officers.[86] The Berkeley PRC experienced a significant drop in the number of investigators in the 1990s. The Mollen Commission found that the NYCPD's capacity to investigate corruption allegations was completely undermined by inadequate staffing and excessive workloads in the Field Internal Affairs Units (FIAUs) which handle most allegations.[87]

With regard to internal police complaint procedures, the accreditation standards promulgated by the Commission on Accreditation for Law Enforcement Agencies (CALEA) merely require that there be a special unit or person for handling complaints but are silent on the question of the level of staffing.[88] With respect to oversight agencies, neither the International Association for Citizen Oversight of Law Enforcement (IACOLE) nor the National Association for Citizen Oversight of Law Enforcement (NACOLE) has developed sets of standards for the profession.

Some oversight agencies have no staff at all. The Baltimore Complaint Evaluation Board (CEB) and the Omaha Civilian Review Board both have no staff. Partly as a result, the Baltimore CEB has little visibility in the community and a very low complaint caseload, while the Omaha CRB also has no visibility and at one point virtually ceased operating.[89] A 1993 survey by the New York Civil Liberties Union found tremendous variation in the level of staffing of oversight agencies. The ratio of investigators to sworn officers ranged from highs of 1:60 in Berkeley to 1:1,000 in Cincinnati, and 1:1,152 in Washington, D.C.[90] (It might be noted that Berkeley subsequently lost several staff positions, the Washington, D.C., review board was abolished, and the Cincinnati Office of Municipal Investigations was supplanted by a new review board.)

The consequences of inadequate staffing are enormous. The Oakland Citizens' Police Review Board 1997 Annual Report stated bluntly: "With only one investigator the goals mandated by the ordinance for handling individual complaints are not being met and cannot possibly be met."[91] The board recommended the addition of at least one investigator and one clerical support person. An ACLU report on the old Washington, D.C., CCRB concluded that between 1982, when it was founded, and 1992, "it was literally impossible for the CCRB to perform its delegated functions in an efficient and effective manner."[92] With respect to corruption control, the Mollen Commission in New York City found control efforts had collapsed because of inadequate staffing and excessive caseloads in Field Internal Affairs Units (FIAUs), which were responsible for investigating the vast majority of allegations.[93]

Despite the importance of this factor, it is shocking to discover that there are no professional standards for the proper level of staffing of an oversight agency. For that matter, there are no specific standards for staffing police internal affairs units. The CALEA accreditation standards for law enforcement agencies specify only that there be a formal process for handling complaints.[94] A survey of selected internal affairs units found investigator-to-officer ratios range from a high 1:63 to a low of 1:461.[95]

The voters of San Francisco took the first step toward defining the proper level of staffing. A 1995 referendum required that the OCC have one investigator for every 150 sworn officers in the San Francisco Police Department. Most other oversight agencies fall far below the 1:150 standard.[96] Even with the restoration of a second investigator's position, the San Diego County CLERB had an investigator/officer ratio of 1:750, only one-fifth the San Francisco standard.[97] The Portland auditor found that the police department's Internal Affairs Division had only four investigators for a department with 900 sworn officers (or a ratio of 1:225), and recommended the assignment of an additional investigator.[98]

Personnel Standards

Standards for the recruitment and training of complaint investigators has also received almost no attention from professionals in either the law enforcement or citizen oversight communities. With respect to internal police complaint procedures, police departments have very different practices regarding assignment to internal affairs units. In some of these departments it is a discretionary assignment controlled by the chief. And in some it is seen as a preferred assignment and a path to promotion. In others, however, assignments are governed by the seniority system, with the result that the unit must take officers who do not want to be there and whom unit supervisors would not have chosen. Within the police subculture internal affairs investigators have traditionally been regarded as "snitches" who violate the code of officer solidarity. In some departments, in fact, union seniority rules oblige internal affairs units to accept investigators who do not want the assignment. Under such circumstances, it is unlikely that investigations will be of consistently high quality.

Summary

In sum, effectiveness of a complaint review procedure will be heavily affected by a variety of factors related to its powers and resources. It is inappropriate, therefore, to pose the question in simplistic terms as: Does independent review of complaints work? The answer is that it depends. An agency that cannot require officer testimony and obtain all other facts relevant to an alleged incident, that is limited by an unreasonably high standard of proof, that does not have the power to make binding determinations about allegations, that does not have adequate staff resources, and that fails to recruit, train, and supervise its personnel in a professional manner is ultimately doomed to failure. Some of the existing citizen oversight agencies have not been successful precisely because they have been severely limited on one or more of these points. Agencies that do have adequate powers and resources and operate in a professional manner at least have the capacity to be effective.

CONCLUSION

The original goal of citizen oversight of the police was to provide an independent review of citizen complaints. This chapter has found that achieving this goal is far more complex than most of its advocates have realized. Our discussion has raised as many questions as it has answered. One point is very clear, however. Merely creating an oversight agency is no automatic solution to the problem of police misconduct. This is true even when such an agency is structurally independent and appears to be independent of the police department. As this chapter has attempted to demonstrate, the keys to successful independent complaint review are buried in the details of structure and process. Much depends on the formal powers of an agency, the quality of its leadership, the activities it chooses to engage in, and the resources it commands.

As explained in Chapter 1, the focus of this book is on organizational change. The implications of this chapter are that if—and it is a very big if—the necessary conditions exist (that is, structure, leadership, resources, etc.), independent review of complaints could very well help to facilitate positive change in the organizational culture of a police department. But if those necessary conditions do not exist, independent review is not likely to make much of a difference.

With respect to the criteria defined by Perez, we can conclude that a citizen oversight agency that is genuinely independent of the police and has the necessary powers and resources will have integrity. An oversight agency which is perceived as being independent and doing an effective job will have legitimacy. And finally, an oversight agency that uses the complaint process to provide feedback that leads to improvements in policing is a learning organization.

In the broader context, it is important to recognize that independent review of complaints is only one role that citizen oversight can play with respect to the police. It is important not to focus our attention too narrowly on this particular role. The following chapter explores the monitoring role in detail. As will become clear in that chapter, it is likely that the monitoring role may in the long run be more effective in changing police organizations and promoting police accountability.

POSTSCRIPT:
MEDIATING CITIZEN COMPLAINTS

As discussed in this chapter, the investigation of citizen complaints, whether by a police internal affairs units or a citizen oversight agency, defines the complaint process as analogous to the criminal process: a formal procedure for investigating alleged misconduct, determining guilt or innocence, and imposing punishment on those individuals found guilty. Walker and Kreisel call this the criminal trial model of complaint review.[99] As a postscript to the main body of this chapter, it is worth considering an emerging alternative model for handling complaints: mediation.

Mediation has emerged as a popular approach to resolving disputes in other areas of American life, such as divorce and commercial small claims conflicts.[100] In mediation, the complainant and the officer agree to meet face to face with an independent mediator present, discuss the incident that gave rise to the complaint, and attempt to reach some mutual understanding. When a complaint is successfully mediated, both sides sign a statement that the complaint has been resolved. This document contains no details about the alleged incident.

The goals of mediation are appealing. According to the Minneapolis Redesign Team, "it save[s] time and money . . . enhances understanding, raises awareness of other perspectives and increases customer satisfaction."[101] Mediation is also more consistent with the goals of complainants than the traditional adversarial process. The Vera evaluation of the New York City CCRB and a focus group study of citizens in Omaha both found that many complainants want an opportunity to meet face to face with either the officer or a supervisor. Many just want an opportunity to tell their side of the story.[102]

Despite its popularity in other areas of American life, it is rarely used for complaints against the police. Only about sixteen mediation programs existed in 1999, and most of those handled few if any cases.[103] The Minneapolis CRA mediation program, for example, struggled at first, successfully mediating only ten complaints in its first three years. But it mediated fourteen and thirteen cases in 1997 and 1998, respectively.[104] The Portland, Oregon, The PACT program also struggled at first, mediating only three complaints in the first three years, but then succeeded in mediating a total of twenty-eight complaints between 1996 and 1998.[105] Mediation—or *informal resolution,* as it is generally called—is more extensively used by oversight agencies in other countries. In British Columbia, for example, one-third of all cases disposed of by the Police Commission in 1992–93 were informal resolutions.[106]

There are a number of reasons for the infrequent use of mediation. The basic assumptions and approach of mediation are out of step with the highly polarized nature of citizen complaints in the United States and the traditional adversarial, legalistic style of complaint procedures. The basic attitude of police officers seems to be, "You say I did something wrong? Prove it." Mediation asks participants to be open to at least the possibility of acknowledging a mistake.

Mediation appears to be highly successful in those jurisdictions where it is used. A survey of complainants in Queensland, Australia found that 76.2 percent were "very satisfied" or "fairly satisfied" with how the mediation was handled, compared with only 39.8 of those complainants who chose to have their complaint investigated in the traditional manner.[107]

At present, however, very little is known about the mediation of complaints in the United States and it is not possible to draw any conclusions about whether it is a more or less effective approach to the handling of complaints than the traditional criminal trial model approach.

NOTES

1. William A. Westley, *Violence and the Police* (Cambridge: MIT Press, 1970).

2. Christopher Commission, *Report of the Independent Commission on the Los Angeles Police Department* (Los Angeles: Christopher Commission, 1991), p. 168.

3. New York City, Commission to Investigate Allegations of Police Corruption and the Anti-Corruption Procedures of the Police Department [Mollen Commission], *Commission Report* (New York: Mollen Commission, 1994).

4. Richard J. Terrill, "Alternative Perceptions of Independence in Civilian Oversight," *Journal of Police Science and Administration* 17: 2 (1990): 77.

5. Anthony M. Pate and Lorie A. Fridell, *Police Use of Force*, 2 vols. (Washington, DC: The Police Foundation, 1993).

6. Franklin E. Zimring and Gordon J. Hawkins, *Deterrence: The Legal Threat in Crime Control* (Chicago: University of Chicago Press, 1973).

7. Americans for Effective Law Enforcement, *Police Civilian Review Boards* (San Francisco: AELE, 1982), 17.

8. Ibid., 10.

9. Douglas Perez, *Common Sense about Police Review* (Philadelphia: Temple University Press, 1994).

10. AELE, *Police Civilian Review Boards*, 12.

11. This argument was accepted by the American Bar Association, *Standards for Criminal Justice*, 2nd ed. "The Urban Police Function," Standard 5.3 (Boston: Little, Brown, 1980).

12. W. E. Moore, *The Professions: Roles and Rules* (New York, Russell Sage Foundation, 1970); AELE, *Police Civilian Review Boards*, 14.

13. Mollen Commission, *Commission Report;* Christopher Commission, *Report of the Independent Commission*. New York City Public Advocate, *Disciplining Police: Solving the Problem of Police Misconduct* (New York: The Public Advocate, 2000).

14. Susan Watt, "The Future of Civilian Oversight of Policing," *Canadian Journal of Criminology,* 33 (July/October 1991): 8.

15. Walter Gellhorn, *When Americans Complain* (Cambridge: Harvard University Press, 1966); Wayne A. Kerstetter, "Who Disciplines the Police? Who Should?" in W. A. Geller, ed., *Police Leadership in America* (New York: Praeger, 1985), 149–82.

16. James R. Hudson, "Organizational Aspects of Internal and External Review of the Police," *Journal of Criminal Law, Criminology, and Police Science* 63 (September 1972): 427–32.

17. Samuel Walker, Geoffrey P. Alpert, and Dennis J. Kenney, *Responding to the Problem Police Officer: A National Evaluation of Early Warning Systems,* Report to the National Institute of Justice, U.S. Department of Justice (2000).

18. David Bayley, *Police for the Future* (New York: Oxford University Press,

1994); Wesley Skogan and Susan M. Hart-nett, *Community Policing, Chicago Style* (New York: Oxford University Press, 1997).

19. George W. Griesinger, Jeffrey S. Slo-vak, and Joseph J. Molkup, *Civil Service Systems: Their Impact on Police Administra-tion* (Washington, DC: Government Print-ing Office, 1979).

20. Mark Iris, "Police Discipline in Chicago: Arbitration or Arbitrary?" *Journal of Criminal Law and Criminology* 89 (Fall 1998): 215–44.

21. Aogan Mulcahy, "'Headhunter' or 'Real Cop'? Identity in the World of Internal Affairs Officers," *Journal of Con-temporary Ethnography* 24 (April 1995): 106.

22. New York City Council, Committee on Public Safety, *Beyond Community Rela-tions: Addressing Police Brutality Directly* (New York, 1998), 16.

23. Douglas Perez, *Common Sense about Police Review* (Philadelphia: Temple Uni-versity Press, 1994), 65–84.

24. Terrill, "Alternative Perceptions of Independence in Civilian Oversight."

25. These models are described in Samuel Walker and Betsy Wright Kreisel, "Vari-eties of Citizen Review: The Implications of Organizational Features of Complaint Review Procedures for Accountability of the Police," *American Journal of Police* 15:3 (1996): 65–88. Alternative classification schemes, with somewhat different termi-nology, are found in Wayne A. Kerstetter, "Who Disciplines the Police? Who Should?," in Geller, *Police Leadership in America,* 149–82; Andrew Goldsmith, "New Directions in Police Complaints Procedures: Some Conceptual and Com-parative Departures," *Police Studies* 11 (Summer 1988): 60–71; Perez, *Common Sense about Police Review.*

26. Seattle, Citizens Review Panel, *Final Report* (Seattle, 19 August 1999).

27. Walker and Kreisel, "Varieties of Citi-zen Review."

28. Both agencies have the power to con-duct independent investigations of citizen complaints. The CCRB, however, is a board of citizens appointed by the mayor and city council. The New Orleans OMI, on the other hand, consists of a single per-son (with a staff) and with no board. The director of the OMI also has civil service protection and can be removed only for cause.

29. San Diego County Grand Jury 1996–1997, *Civilian Oversight of Law Enforcement: Are We Getting What We Voted For?* (12 June, 1997).

30. Author's term.

31. "City's First Police Watchdog Resigns Post," *Los Angeles Times,* 11 November 1998.

32. Perez, *Common Sense about Police Review,* 138–39; AELE, *Police Civilian Review Boards.* The evidence on this issue is discussed in this book in Chapter 5.

33. Christopher Commission, *Report,* 207. See also The Police Foundation, *The Years of Controversy: The Los Angeles Police Commission 1991–1993* (Washington, DC: The Police Foundation, 1995).

34. Los Angeles Police Department, *Board of Inquiry into the Rampart Area Corruption Incident* (Los Angeles, 1 March 2000), especially chapter 10.

35. City of Milwaukee, *Guide to the Citi-zen Complaint Procedure* (Milwaukee, June 1992).

36. Milwaukee Fire and Police Commis-sion, *1990 Annual Report* (Milwaukee, 1991), 4, 14.

37. U.S. Commission on Civil Rights, *Police Protection of the African American Community in Milwaukee* (Washington, DC: Government Printing Office, 1994), 44.

38. Interview, OMI Director, 1998.

39. This difficult issue is at the heart of Lani Guinier, *The Tyranny of the Majority* (New York: The Free Press, 1994). On the related issue of conflicting notions of community, see Samuel Walker, *The Rights Revolution: Rights and Community in Amer-ica* (New York: Oxford University Press, 1998).

40. Walker and Kreisel, "Varieties of Citi-zen Review."

41. U.S. Commission on Civil Rights, *The Baltimore Police Complaint Evaluation*

Procedure (Washington, DC: Government Printing Office, 1980), 3.

42. Interviews by author.

43. Observations by author, 1998 NACOLE Conference, Indianapolis, Indiana.

44. Observations by author.

45. Samuel Walker, *A Critical History of Police Reform* (Lexington: Lexington Books, 1977).

46. This problem is at the heart of Guinier's proposals for alternative voting procedures; see Guinier, *Tyranny of the Majority.*

47. New York City Council, Committee on Public Safety, *Beyond Community Relations* (New York: City Council, 1998).

48. There is a large and growing body of literature on the Independent Counsel law. For a start, see Terry Eastland, *Ethics, Politics and the Independent Counsel: Executive Power and Executive Vice, 1789–1989* (Washington, DC: National Legal Center for the Public Interest, 1989), along with the Congressional hearings in 1999 on renewal of the law.

49. The history of the PCA and its predecessors is in Mike Maguire, "Complaints against the Police: The British Experience," in Andrew Goldsmith, ed., *Complaints against the Police: The Trend to External Review* (Oxford: Clarendon Press, 1991), 177–209.

50. Goldsmith, *Complaints against the Police.*

51. Walker and Kreisel, "Varieties of Citizen Review."

52. Iowa Citizens' Aide/Ombudsman, *1994 Annual Report* (Des Moines: Ombudsman, 1995).

53. San Diego, Citizens Law Enforcement Review Board, *1997 Annual Report* (San Diego, 1998).

54. Walker and Kreisel, "Varieties of Citizen Review."

55. Walter Gellhorn, *When Americans Complain* (Cambridge: Harvard University Press, 1966), 185.

56. AELE, *Police Civilian Review Boards.*

57. American Bar Association, "The Urban Police Function," *Standards for*

Criminal Justice, 2nd ed. (Boston: Little, Brown, 1980), Standard 5.3.

58. Bureau of Justice Statistics, *Local Police Departments, 1993* (Washington, DC: Government Printing Office, 1996).

59. *Vance v. Ananich,* 378 N.W.2d 616 (Mich. App. 1985).

60. San Diego Grand Jury, 1996–1997 *Citizen Oversight of Law Enforcement.*

61. *Dibb v. County of San Diego,* 12 December 1994.

62. Minneapolis Civilian Review Authority, *Administrative Rules* (Minneapolis: Civilian Review Authority, 1990), 17.

63. Memorandum, Eduardo P. Garcia, Chair, CPRB, to Oakland City Council, 13 December 1994.

64. William A. Westley, *Violence and the Police* (Cambridge: MIT Press, 1970).

65. Minneapolis Civilian Review Authority, *Rules and Regulations* (Minneapolis, 1990).

66. Denver Public Safety Review Commission, *Annual Report 1994* (Denver, 1994), 8.

67. ACLU–National Capitol Area, *Analysis of the District of Columbia's Civilian Complaint Review Board and Recommendations for Its Replacement* (Washington; ACLU-NCA, 1995).

68. Oakland Citizens' Police Review Board, *1997 Annual Report* (Oakland, 20 January 1998), 11.

69. San Diego Citizens Law Enforcement Review Board, *Minutes* (12 May 1998), 2–5.

70. Minneapolis Civilian Review Authority, *1997 Annual Report,* (Minneapolis, 1998), 8.

71. Oakland City Council, Ordinance #11905 Sec. 6(G)(5) (30 July 1996).

72. Berkeley, Police Review Commission, *Regulations,* 14, contained in Berkeley PRC, *Statistical Report, 1997–June 1998* (Berkeley: PRC, 1998).

73. Merrick Bobb, *Five Years Later: A Report to the Los Angeles Police Commission on the Los Angeles Police Department's Implementation of Independent Commission Recommendations* (Los Angeles, 1996), 41.

74. Ibid., 41.

75. Anthony M. Pate and Lorie A. Fridell, *Police Use of Force,* 2 vols. (Washington, DC: The Police Foundation, 1993).

76. John Crew, *Reforming the SFPD Accountability System* (San Francisco: ACLU of Northern California, 1997), 14.

77. San Francisco Office of Citizen Complaints, *Annual Report 1997* (San Francisco: OCC, 1998).

78. Walker and Kreisel, "Varieties of Citizen Review," table 1.

79. Paul Chevigny, *Edge of the Knife: Police Violence in the Americas* (New York: New Press, 1995), 94–95.

80. Griesinger et. al, *Civil Service Systems: Their Impact on Police Administration;* Walker, *Critical History of Police Reform.*

81. Edward Littlejohn, "The Civilian Police Commission: A Deterrent of Police Misconduct," *University of Detroit Journal of Urban Law* 59 (Fall 1981): 5–62.

82. Christopher Commission, *Report of the Independent Commission on the Los Angeles Police Department* (Los Angeles, 1991), 183. It is a matter of some controversy whether the weakness of the Police Commission is a product of the City Charter or self-imposed.

83. Littlejohn, "Civilian Police Commission."

84. Griesinger et al., *Civil Service Systems: Their Impact on Police Administration.*

85. "High Risk Profile," *Minneapolis Star Tribune* (13 May 1994).

86. New York Civil Liberties Union, *Police Abuse: The Need for Civilian Investigation and Oversight* (New York: NYCLU, 1990).

87. Mollen Commission, *Commission Report.*

88. Commission on Accreditation for Law Enforcement Agencies, *Standards for Law Enforcement Agencies,* 3rd ed. (Fairfax, VA: CALEA, 1994).

89. U.S. Civil Rights Commission, *The Baltimore Complaint Evaluation Procedure;* interview, Director, Complaint Evaluation Board, 1997.

90. NYCLU, *Civilian Review of Policing* (1993), 131–45.

91. Oakland Citizens' Police Review Board, *1997 Annual Report* (20 January 1998), 8.

92. ACLU Report, 7.

93. Mollen Commission, *Report.*

94. Commission on Accreditation for Law Enforcement Agencies, *Standards for Law Enforcement Agencies,* 3rd ed. (Fairfax: CALEA, 1994).

95. Patrick Knoll, *A Focus on Internal Affairs: International Perspective* (Calgary: School of Law, 1997), 39. The lowest ratio, however, was reported by the New York City Police Department, which has been severely criticized for the ineffectuality of its handling of both corruption investigations and citizen complaints.

96. New York Civil Liberties Union, *Police Abuse: The Need For Civilian Investigation and Oversight* (New York: NYCLU, 1990).

97. San Diego, Civilian Law Enforcement Review Board, *Minutes* (13 June 1998).

98. Portland PIIAC, *Fourth Quarter Monitoring Report, 1997* (Portland, 1998), 11.

99. On the criminal trial model, see Walker and Kreisel, "Varieties of Citizen Review."

100. See, for example, U.S. Department of Justice, *Community Mediation Programs: Developments and Challenges* (Washington, DC: Government Printing Office, 1997). Police mediation programs are described in Peter Finn, *Citizen Review of Police: Approaches and Implementation* (Washington, DC: Government Printing Office, 2000 forthcoming).

101. Minneapolis Civilian Review Authority, *Redesign Team Report,* (Minneapolis, 1997), 15.

102. Michelle Sviridoff and Jerome E. McElroy, *Processing Complaints* (New York: Vera Institute, 1989); Samuel Walker, "Complaints against the Police: The Results of a Focus Group Study of Citizen Perceptions," *Criminal Justice Review* 22 (Autumn 1997): 207–25.

103. Samuel Walker and Carol Archbold, "Mediating Citizen Complaints Against

the Police: An Exploratory Study," *Journal of Dispute Resolution,* 5:2 (forthcoming).

104. Minneapolis, Civilian Review Authority, *Annual Report 1997,* 7.

105. Julien Minard, *PACT: Police and Citizens Talking: A Police-Citizen Mediation Pilot Program* (Portland: Neighborhood Mediation Center, 1997), 11.

106. British Columbia Police Commission, *Annual Report, 1992/93* (British Columbia: Attorney General, 1993), 13.

107. Robert C. Holland, "Dealing with Complaints against the Police: The Resolution Process Adopted by the Queensland Police Service, Australia," *Police Studies* 19:2 (1996): 45–62.

4

The Monitoring Role

INTRODUCTION

Complaint review is only one of the roles that citizen oversight agencies play, or potentially can play. The other role may be characterized in terms of monitoring the police. This chapter examines the activities related to the monitoring role: community outreach, customer assistance, policy review, auditing the quality of complaint investigations, and changing the police subculture (see Figure 4-1). Some oversight agencies engage in several of these activities, while others confine themselves to complaint review.

This chapter argues that the monitoring role offers the best opportunities for changing police organizations and thereby enhancing accountability and achieving long-term improvements in the quality of policing. While the complaint review process examined in the previous chapter is undeniably important, it inevitably focuses on individual officers and particular incidents. Monitoring role activities, on the other hand, address organizational issues that are more likely to create a self-sustaining culture of accountability within a police department. The potential contributions of the monitoring role was summed by the San Francisco OCC. When it hired a new staff member in 1998, it explained that this person's outreach activities "should help take the OCC beyond an exclusively complaint-driven and discipline centered model of police accountability, by aiming to *prevent* alleged police misconduct through policy innovations, education and proactive problem-solving."[1]

COMMUNITY OUTREACH
　　Informational Materials
　　Special Population Efforts
　　Complaint Intake Locations
　　Community Meetings

CUSTOMER ASSISTANCE
　　Information
　　Assistance
　　Listening

POLICY REVIEW
　　New Policies
　　Revise Old Policies
　　Comprehensive Management Audit
　　Feedback for Training
　　Monitor Risk Management

AUDITING COMPLAINT INVESTIGATIONS
　　Ensuring:
　　　　Openness
　　　　Thoroughness
　　　　Fairness
　　　　Timeliness

CHANGING THE POLICE SUBCULTURE
　　Early Warning System
　　Investigating False and Misleading Testimony

SELF-MONITORING

FIGURE 4-1 Monitoring Activities

It is also important to point out that while this book is primarily about citizen oversight, many if not most of the activities described in this chapter also can be undertaken by police departments themselves. External citizen oversight is one important means of promoting police accountability, but considerable responsibility remains with police departments.

COMMUNITY OUTREACH

Community outreach requires an agency to make a concerted effort to inform the public about the complaint process, explain police department policies, listen to community concerns about the police, and ensure access to the complaint process. The goals of the community outreach program of the Boise (Idaho) Community ombudsman are listed in Figure 4-2.

Community outreach for the Office of Community Ombudsman has three goals:

- To listen to the needs, opinions, and concerns of the community so as to better serve them.
- To familiarize members of the public with the mission and services of the Office of Community Ombudsman.
- To encourage and facilitate greater dialogue and collaboration between the Boise Police Department and the community they serve.

FIGURE 4-2 Community Outreach

SOURCE: Boise Community Ombudsman, *Year End Report 1999* (Boise: Community Ombudsman, 15 February 2000), 12–13.

One of the driving forces behind the oversight movement has been the fact that police departments have been closed, self-protective bureaucracies that resist even accepting complaints. A substantial body of research on the police supports this view. In the 1960s, the U.S. Civil Rights Commission, the President's Crime Commission, and the Kerner Commission documented the fact that many police departments had no formal complaint process at all and often met potential complainants with hostility. Many of the police reforms that have been proposed and attempted over the past thirty years have been designed to overcome the isolation of the police and their hostility to the public. These reforms include police-community relations units, team policing, foot patrol, and community policing.[2] The community outreach function is consistent with the goals of these efforts.

Outreach Activities

Informational Materials Community outreach involves a number of different activities. The first step is to publish and distribute informational brochures explaining how to file a complaint. In some agencies, the brochure includes the complaint form. While this step might seem rather elementary, many police departments (and some oversight agencies) do not do this. Police departments traditionally provided as little specific information as possible about the complaints process. An evaluation of the Albuquerque police department found that while it had a brochure in both English and Spanish versions, copies were not distributed throughout the city and few community leaders were aware of it. Copies were obtained at the Internal Affairs office, but unannounced visits to four police substations found the brochures at only two of them.[3] In 1999, the Washington, D.C. police department had no brochure or informational literature of any sort on the complaint process.[4]

Not providing information about the complaint process has important consequences. Most important, it reduces the number of official complaints received. The Albuquerque police department cited the low number of citizen complaints as evidence that it was doing a good job. The Baltimore Complaint Evaluation Board (CEB) receives slightly more than about 100 complaints per year against Baltimore police officers. This is an astonishingly low figure for a department with about 3,000 sworn officers (1997). San Francisco, with only about 1,800 officers, received 1,126 complaints in 1997.[5] A visit to Baltimore quickly revealed why. The CEB is virtually a secret, with almost no public visibility whatsoever. When this author asked the Maryland ACLU about the CEB, the reply was, "The what?" When the local ACLU does not even know about the oversight agency, it clearly has no public presence at all. In fact, the chairperson of the CEB conceded that it was a "low-cost alternative" to a genuinely independent oversight agency.[6]

Reaching Special Populations Outreach is especially important for connecting with certain segments of the community that may be particularly reluctant to file complaints even when they have legitimate grievances. The San Francisco OCC expressed special concern about reaching "underserved" populations, mainly young Asian-Americans, Filipino-Americans, Pacific Islanders, Native Americans, and Latino/Latina Americans. It noted that all of these groups were underrepresented in OCC complaint data.[7] Nationally, Hispanic Americans are underrepresented in official complaint data, whereas African Americans are overrepresented.[8] Language barriers are certainly a problem for many potential complaints, but many others are probably reluctant to complain because of concern about their immigration status.[9]

To overcome these problems, many oversight agencies publish brochures and other informational pieces in several languages. The Minneapolis CRA, for example, issues brochures in eight languages other than English. In 1999, when it discovered that Minneapolis was the center of immigration from Somalia with an estimated 15,000 Somali in the city, the CRA took steps to have its brochures translated into the appropriate language. The San Francisco OCC complaint forms contain instructions in three languages other than English. The Portland auditor argued in one of its reports that "the complaint system should be as accessible as possible to minority communities" and criticized the Portland police department for not following through on its recommendation that complaint brochures be published in Spanish and possibly other languages.[10]

Facilitating Complaint Intake Facilitating the filing of complaints is another important aspect of outreach. The Mission and Values statement of the New York City CCRB declares that the board's purpose is "to *encourage* members of the community to file complaints when they feel they have been victims of police misconduct" [emphasis added].[11] Not only is police headquarters an intimidating place for many people, but traveling downtown is time consuming and costly for people who have to take time off from work. This can be done by making it possible to file a complaint at locations other than police headquarters. As one retired Milwaukee police officer told the U.S. Civil Rights Commission, going to police headquarters "can be intimidating to a person who is frightened by a badge to begin with."[12]

In many cities and counties it is now possible to file complaints in a variety of different ways: at police headquarters, at the oversight agency, at various other public offices, or by phone or mail. The Police Foundation survey of police use of force found that 80 percent of all municipal police departments accept complaints by mail, 76 percent accept complaints by telephone, and 31 percent have a separate telephone number for complaints.[13] (On a methodological note, however, we should be careful about accepting the findings of this survey at face value. Investigations by scholars have found serious reliability problems with answers to mail surveys to police departments.[14] Surveys by community activists have found that police departments are often not doing what they claim to be doing with respect to complaints.[15])

Several police departments—San Jose and New Orleans, for example— have moved their internal affairs offices to a location separate from police headquarters. This separation is designed to relieve citizen anxiety about going to police headquarters, and it also helps police officers who are often embarrassed about being seen spending time in internal affairs, either as the subject of complaints or as witnesses against other officers. And in another recent development, some police departments have created websites that include information about how to file complaints. In some cities the website includes a complaint form that can be downloaded. Some departments even accept electronically filed complaints.

Community Meetings Neighborhood community meetings are another important outreach activity. On one hand, community meetings create an appearance of openness and responsiveness to the public. On the other, they are an opportunity to convey information to citizens about the police and the complaint process and to hear citizen concerns about the police. Neighborhood meetings of this sort are a basic component of community policing.[16] It is not clear, however, that community policing-related meetings necessarily address citizen complaints since they may have other items on their agenda. An oversight agency has a special responsibility for sponsoring neighborhood meetings in cities where community policing meetings are not held.

Some oversight agencies conduct meetings on a systematic basis. The San Jose Auditor reported meeting with thirty different community and professional groups in late 1993 and 1994.[17] The San Diego CLERB, for example, specifically asked the San Diego Sheriff's Department about holding community meetings in towns that the SDSD serves under contract. According to the New York Civil Liberties Union, the New York CCRB has had an on-again, off-again record of community meetings. The CCRB held a series of public meetings in 1994 and 1995 but abandoned the program in 1996.[18] Probably in response to these criticisms, the program revived, and in fiscal year 1997–98 the CCRB held 115 community meetings.[19]

San Jose offers an example of how community outreach opens channels of communication that can help address police problems. At several meetings the San Jose auditor heard complaints that police officers were not allowing people to observe incidents involving the police and other people, with officers ordering bystanders to leave the scene. This discovery led to a recommendation by the San Jose auditor for an onlookers' policy, specifically instructing officers that bystanders had a right to observe them. The San Jose Police Department subsequently adopted the policy, and several other departments adopted similar ones.[20] The development of the onlookers' policy is an example of the policy review function of oversight, which is examined in detail later in this chapter.

In sum, an active outreach program rests on the assumption that police departments should welcome citizen complaints as indicators of problems that need departmental attention. As Malcolm Sparrow explains, complaints in this framework become *management tools,* serving as indicators of problems that need attention.[21] This is a reversal of the traditional police approach that regards complaints as attacks and threats that should be fended off at all costs. This approach is consistent with the basic philosophy of community policing that emphasizes developing partnerships with community groups and actively seeking input regarding community problems.

CUSTOMER ASSISTANCE

Because the role of citizen oversight has traditionally been defined narrowly in terms of reviewing citizen complaints, little thought has been given to those cases in which someone contacts an oversight agency but does not file a formal complaint. In its first six months of operation, the Boise Community Ombudsman had 327 contacts with citizens, only fifty-five of which resulted in complaints that were investigated.[22] These contacts are generally forgotten because they are regarded as not being part of the agency's official mission. In fact, however, noncomplaint contacts are quite numerous and represent an important part of an oversight agency's role.

More detail on customer assistance activities is available from the Minneapolis Civilian Review Authority. In 1998, 742 people contacted the CRA, either in person or over the telephone. Only 136 (or 18.3 percent) signed a formal complaint that the CRA investigated, however. The CRA staff provided several general kinds of service to those who did not file a complaint.[23] In about 24 percent of these cases, CRA staff members *provided information.* Generally, this involved explaining either the law or police procedure to them. Many people contacting oversight agencies do not understand police procedures, and are upset because they believe they have been mistreated. CRA staff often do nothing more than explain, for example, that the police routinely handcuff people who are under arrest, that this is standard procedure, and that it is entirely legal. This information often satisfies the potential complainants and they leave or hang up the phone, if not happy at least provided with an explanation of what happened to them. Other people do not understand the law. CRA staff members explain that you cannot park in that location, for example, and the police routinely tow away cars that are parked there.[24] (See Figure 4.3)

In about 6 percent of the noncomplaint contacts, CRA staff members provide *direct assistance.* This usually involves a referral to some other government agency. One CRA staff member described how he had taken the person

---

1. Provide Information
      Explain the law
      Explain police procedures

2. Provide Direct Assistance
      Referral to other government agencies

3. Listen
      Provide audience

FIGURE 4-3 Customer Assistance Activities

down the elevator, walked him across the street and pointed out the traffic violations desk in city hall. And in about 11 percent of the cases, the CRA referred the person to the Minneapolis police department or some other government agency to resolve the problem.

CRA staff explain that many contacts involve people who simply want to talk to someone about their grievance. For these contacts, the CRA role might be described as *listening,* or peacekeeping. Some of the citizens in this category just want to rant and rave about real or imagined wrongs that have been done to them. There is nothing tangible that can be done, and in some cases a sounding board is all they really want. As with providing information, the oversight agency performs a useful social function by simply listening and cooling out these contacts.

A few people who contact oversight agencies can be characterized as "repeaters." These are people who, for one reason or another, bring chronic complaints to the police and other government agencies. Many cities have local characters who always attend city council meetings and continually bring up their particular grievance. The San Jose auditor, for example, reported that a small percentage of the people contacting the office "consume a high percentage of time and energy." Some of these people "misunderstand the purposes and results of filing a complaint." Some seemed to feel that filing a complaint would help them with the criminal charges against them. The auditor "routinely explains that the purpose of the complaint process is to address police misconduct, not to prove or disprove factual matters relating to pending criminal cases, appeals, or even civil suits."[25] In Iowa City, meanwhile, half of all complaints received by the new civilian review board were filed by the same person.[26]

It is legitimate to ask whether these activities are a proper part of the role of a citizen oversight agency. An evaluation of the Minneapolis CRA responded to the criticism that the CRA was handling many "trivial" complaints by arguing that "it is important to handle all concerns effectively to build better rapport with the public."[27] Each case involves a situation in which someone is upset (for reasons that may be legitimate or illegitimate) and that person's grievance happens to focus on the police. It seems reasonable, in the interest of maintaining an orderly society, that there be some person or agency who can provide the information that will help to resolve the person's distress. If the oversight agency did not exist, many of these people would go to the police department. In important respects, an oversight agency can be more effective than the police precisely because it is independent of the police department and the explanation will not be automatically seen as self-serving.

The role of an oversight agency in this regard parallels the role of the police on the street. The first field observations of police officers in the 1950s and 1960s discovered that only about 20 to 30 percent of police patrol work involves criminal law enforcement. Most of it involves order maintenance and "peacekeeping." Much of this work involves resolving actual or potential disputes by explaining things, providing assistance, and simply listening. One study characterized the role of the police officer as "philosopher, guide, and friend."[28] Oversight agencies perform, or at least potentially perform, a similar role in helping people who believe they have a problem.

Unfortunately, because the complaint review role has dominated so much thinking about oversight, few agencies document their customer assistance activities or recognize it as an important function. Along with the Minneapolis CRA, the Boise, Idaho, ombudsman is one of the few agencies that documents all citizen contacts, including those that do not result in a formal complaint.[29] In Minneapolis many police officials like having the CRA around because, as one explained, "they handle all the bullshit complaints." In other words, if the CRA did not handle these individuals, the police department would have to, thereby burdening Internal Affairs with more workload. For the cases involving information about police procedures, the explanation of a CRA staff member is inherently more credible, by virtue of being independent of the police department.

POLICY REVIEW

Policy review is a process through which an oversight agency examines a police department's policies and procedures (or the lack thereof) and recommends new or revised policies.[30] The basic goal is preventive: to identify problems or potential problems and to correct them before they result in a major crisis such as a questionable shooting, a lawsuit, or a serious disturbance. More than thirty years ago, the eminent law professor Walter Gellhorn characterized policy review as providing "information feedback" to the police, arguing that it could play a preventive approach that was more likely to be effective in improving policing than simply investigating individual complaints.[31] Douglas Perez refers to this process as the "learning" function of citizen oversight.[32] It is also consistent with William Geller's concept of transforming police departments into "learning organizations."[33] Of all the roles and activities that oversight agencies can play, policy review is the one most likely to produce organizational change and thereby achieve long-term improvements in policing.

As Malcolm Sparrow points out, police internal affairs units have traditionally been defensive in nature; they exist "to satisfy external demands . . . and to

protect the chief by providing evidence of a competent, thorough, and efficient complaints investigation system." The policy review function conceptual-
izes the complaints process in a *proactive* role, as a *management tool for identifying
and correcting problems.*[34] Complaints can provide four different types of potentially valuable information: about individual incidents, problem officers, community concerns, and departmental policies that need revision.

By the mid-1990s, about two-thirds of all oversight mechanisms were
authorized to engage in policy review. While some oversight agencies make
substantial use of it, others engage in it sparingly if at all.[35] In 1993, for example, the San Diego County Citizens' Law Enforcement Review Board issued a
total of eleven policy recommendations.[36] The 1997 Annual Report of the
San Francisco OCC included fourteen separate policy recommendations.[37]
Between 1993 and 1996 the San Jose auditor made a total of forty-two policy
recommendations, thirty-eight of which were adopted, two were rejected,
and two were still pending.[38] A list of the recommendations is presented in
Figure 4.4 (pp. 95–96).

In other agencies, however, there appears to be no policy review activity of
any kind. The annual reports of the Kansas City OCC offer no evidence of
any such efforts. The former director of the New Orleans Office of Municipal Investigations, meanwhile, claimed to engage in a form of policy review
through his practice of sending "corrective action" (CA) letters to agencies,
but in a personal interview he was unable to cite any example of a policy
change in the police department that he had achieved in thirteen years.[39]

The most comprehensive approach to policy review is undertaken by Merrick Bobb, Special Counsel to the Los Angeles County Sheriff's Department.
A quick scan of Bobb's semiannual reports reveals that hardly any aspect of the
sheriff's department's operations escapes his scrutiny. His reports cover use-of-
force policies, high-speed pursuit policies, the use of canines, gender equity
and sexual harassment, issues related to sexual orientation, recruitment and
training issues related to women and minorities, the field training officer program, and the psychological services available to officers.[40]

Policy review activity falls into three basic categories: developing policy on
issues where there is no current policy; reexamining existing policies, in what
is essentially a housecleaning process; and, conducting a comprehensive audit
of management practices. Policy review is not restricted to issues of on-the-
street law enforcement but can also involve a wide range of management issues
related to recruitment, training, assignment, and supervision of officers.

New Policy

One of the best examples of new policy development is the crowd control
policy recommended by the San Francisco Office of Citizens' Complaints
(OCC) and subsequently adopted by the San Francisco Police Department in
1994. Large political demonstrations are a regular part of life in San Francisco,
and a number of those demonstrations have been marked by conflict, including excessive use of force and violations of First Amendment rights. Even

ISSUES RAISED IN	ISSUE	DISPOSITION	RESOLUTION PERIOD
1993 1st Quarter Report	Create a new system for the classification of complaints	Adopted	1st Quarter, 2nd Quarter, and 1994 Year-End Report
	Standardize the definition of procedural and informal complaints	Adopted	*2nd Quarter* and *1994 Year-End Report*
	Apply intervention counseling to all complaints	Adopted	*2nd Quarter* and *1994 Year-End Report*
	Establish procedures to address potential bias within the Internal Affairs Unit	Adopted	*2nd Quarter* and *1994 Year-End Report*
	Enact policy to ensure objectivity of the intake process	Adopted	*2nd Quarter* and *1994 Year-End Report*
1994 3rd Quarter Report	Establish and comply with a timetable regarding the length of time required for complaint classification and investigation	Adopted	*1994 Year-End Report*
	Implement citizen "Onlooker Policy"	Adopted	*1995 Midyear Report*
	Standardize investigation writing format	Adopted	*1994 Year-End Report*
	Provide report writing training for "Drunk in Public" cases	Adopted	*1994 Year-End Report*
	Provide chemical testing for "Drunk in Public" cases	Adopted	*1994 Year-End Report*
	Send minor complaints to BFO to expedite investigators	Adopted	*1994 Year-End Report*
1994 Year-End Report	Establish neutrality in the selection of formal or informal complaint process	Adopted	*1994 Year-End Report*
	Interview complainants and witnesses within three months of complaint initiation	Adopted	*1994 Year-End Report*
	Contact complainants at regular intervals through updates and closing letters	Adopted	*1994 Year-End Report*
	Provide a sample of all SJPD Reports to the Police Auditor	Adopted	*1994 Year-End Report*
	Use of mandatory consent forms for consent searches	Not Adopted	*1995 Year-End Report*
	Enact policy for collecting physical evidence in use of force cases and immediate investigation by supervisor	Adopted	*1995 Year-End Report*
	Write complainant's statement in addition to recording and provide copy to complainant	Adopted	*1994 Year-End Report*
	Handle informal complaints through counseling by field supervisor and contact with complainant (where desired)	Adopted	*1994 Year-End Report*
	Revise letters sent to complainants to include information about the IPA's role	Adopted	*1994 Year-End Report*

(continued)

FIGURE 4-4 Independent Police Auditor's Recommendations

SOURCE: San Jose, Independent Police Auditor, *1999 Year-End Report* (San Jose, IPA, 2000), appendix J.

ISSUES RAISED IN	ISSUE	DISPOSITION	RESOLUTION PERIOD
1995 Midyear Report	Maintain a central log of contacts from potential complainants	Adopted	*1995 Year-End Report*
	Obtain additional office space for PSCU	Adopted	*1997 Year-End Report*
	Police Department should refer complainants to either PSCU or IPA	Adopted	*1995 Year-End Report*
	Implement policy to standardize format for officer's interview	Adopted	*1995 Year-End Report*
	Review off-duty employment practices	Adopted	*1997 Year-End Report*
1996 Midyear Report	Connect IPA to City of San José's internet network	Adopted	*1997 Year-End Report*
	Conduct intake investigation of complaints lacking a signed Boland Admonishment	Adopted	*1996 Midyear Report*
	Retain name of officer where Boland Admonishment is not signed (but need not place in personnel file)	Not Adopted	
	Complaint classification should more appropriately reflect the nature of the complaint	Adopted	*1996 Midyear Report*
	Assist in the implementation and design of new computer system	Adopted	*1996 Midyear Report*
1996 Year-End Report	Implement process for responding to citizen's request for officer identification	Adopted	*1997 Year-End Report*
	Establish Class I and Class II of use of force categories	Adopted	*1996 Year-End Report*
	Complete Class I Use of Force investigations within 180 days	Adopted	*1996 Year-End Report*
	Complete all investigations of citizen complaints within 365 days	Adopted	*1996 Year-End Report*
	Establish IPA's authority to audit relevant DI cases	Adopted	*1997 Year-End Report*
1997 Year-End Report	Establish a procedure for officers to identify themselves to civilians when requested to do so. The identification should be in writing	Adopted	*1998 Year-End Report*
	When forcibly taking a blood specimen from an uncooperative suspect, do so in an accepted medical environment, according to accepted medical practices and without the use of excessive force	Adopted	*1998 Year-End Report*
	All complaints not covered under a Cardoza exception should be investigated by the PSCU and reviewed by the Chain of Command within 10 months, allowing the IPA enough time to request additional investigation, if needed	Adopted	*1998 Year-End Report*
	Time limits and reliable tracking system should be set for every bureau and department involved with the complaint process	Adopted	*1998 Year-End Report*
1998 Year-End Report	Review of officer-involved shootings	Adopted	*1999 Year-End Report*

FIGURE 4-4 Independent Police Auditor's Recommendations *(continued)*

within the parameters of the First Amendment, there are occasions when the police need to order people to disperse. In many cases, however, the police have simply yelled "disperse" and then waded into the crowd with billy clubs.

Working closely with John Crew of the ACLU, the OCC drafted a crowd control policy that was subsequently adopted by the San Francisco Police Department. The policy opens with a clear declaration about protecting the First Amendment rights of citizens advise officers that "Crowds shall not be dispersed or ordered to move unless there are reasonable and articulable factors justifying the order in accordance with law." A separate 53-page Crowd Control Manual defines the permissible uses of force and, among other things, specifies that horses, fire hoses, motorcycles, and canines are not to be used for crowd control.[41]

The significance of the San Francisco crowd control policy lies in the fact that it fills a void that existed for decades. Despite recurring controversies over police handling of demonstrations, no one in either the police department or the city law department had seen fit to develop a policy giving police officers informed guidance on the handling of a difficult category of situations. The policy review function of the OCC provided an orderly mechanism for filling this policy void.

The onlookers' policy recommended by the San Jose auditor offers another example of policy review. The auditor learned from a number of complainants that San Jose police officers were preventing them from observing police actions involving other persons. Neighbors who come out of their homes, for example, were "told by the police to reenter their homes," or people coming upon the scene of a police-citizen encounter were ordered to leave. Worse, people who attempted to make video or audio recordings reported being threatened by the police and in some instances having their equipment confiscated. The auditor found only a small number of these kinds of allegations in the official complaint files but heard a number of stories at community meetings.[42]

The San Jose auditor recommended, and the police department subsequently adopted, an Onlookers' Policy that states: "Onlookers shall be permitted to observe and overhear conversations in detention or arrest situations in public areas when it is reasonable to do so." The only exception is that onlookers not "interfere with the officers' duties or create a safety concern for the officer, person detained, or onlooker." If an officer believes that an onlooker is creating a disturbance, he or she is to call a supervisor "to resolve and document this incident."[43] San Francisco followed suit and adopted its own onlookers' policy that is more elaborate and adds several important specifics. An officer can bar an onlooker from overhearing a conversation if the suspect requests it or if there is some specific reason for keeping the conversation confidential. Even more significant, it explicitly allows onlookers to inquire about the suspect's name and whether the suspect "wishes a witness." In such instances, the onlooker is not required to give his or her name to the officer.[44]

A controversy in Portland illustrates how an oversight agency can use complaints to identify a new problem, investigate it, and initiate corrective action. The Portland auditor heard reports of police officers using so-called "distraction techniques" in physical force incidents. Upon investigation, it found that officers would hit or a kick a suspect to distract his attention and take him into custody. The auditor also found that the technique was not authorized by the police department and had apparently been developed informally by officers on their own. The auditor's investigation brought the issue to public attention and succeeded in having it officially forbidden by the police department.[45]

Review of Existing Policies

Policy review can also serve as a form of housekeeping, helping to revise outdated policies. Perhaps the most astonishing policy recommendation by the San Francisco OCC was one in 1997 to abolish the police department's Form 25. Last revised in July 1978, Form 25 used the designations "Negro" and "Mexican" and asked officers to identify a citizen's speech as "Broken English," "Dumb," or "Brooklyn Accent."[46] While hardly as serious as on-the-street brutality, Form 25 was nonetheless offensive and certainly communicated inappropriate messages to police officers. Most important, it was symptomatic of managerial neglect. Apparently, no one in the police department noticed or thought it objectionable.

Comprehensive Management Audit

Merrick Bobb's work as special counsel to the Los Angeles Sheriff's Department is the best example of how policy review can serve as a comprehensive, ongoing audit of management practices. One of Bobb's most significant contributions was an investigation of a high number of shootings by officers assigned to the department's Century Station. The shooting rate by officers assigned to this station was three times as high as the rate in the contiguous and comparable Southeast Station of the Los Angeles Police Department. An internal LASD study had focused narrowly on the individual shooting incidents. His five-month investigation included a review of all relevant documents, interviews with LASD personnel, ride-alongs with officers, and a helicopter fly-along. He found that certain aspects of the station were "exemplary" and that despite the high number of shootings it was "not at 'war' with the community." A number of "chronic serious problems existed, however." Most important, the problems did not involve the proverbial "rotten apples" but were the product a poor management practices.[47]

The Century Station was marked by a serious "mismatch" between the experience level of the officers, the level of supervision they received, and the demands placed on the officers in this high-crime area of South Central Los Angeles County. Noting that a significant number of shootings occurred in foot and automobile pursuits, Bobb recommended that the LASD tighten the standards for pursuits. He also found that one-third of all shootings involved trainees. The Century Station had the youngest group of deputies in the entire department and the second lowest experience level (an average of about three years of street experience).

Most of these problems were well known to the department, and Bobb found that "Supervisors at Century Station readily confirmed that the deputies under their command were too young and inexperienced."[48] The fact that some of the problems at the Century Station were well known highlights one of the endemic problems in American police management and the potential value of policy review. It is often the case that officials knew about problems in a department. Historically, other officers have known about their "problem" colleagues who receive multiple citizen complaints and use excessive force frequently. But until the recent development of early warning systems, police departments have done nothing about dealing with these officers.[49]

Although the LASD had a good field training program, the field training officers (FTOs) in the Century Station were themselves extremely young. Some had been on the job only a year and a half. When asked about certain departmental policies, some gave incorrect answers. Bobb also found that community residents were aware that Century Station served essentially as a training area for new officers and that this was a source of community "dissatisfaction." Bobb recommended that the burden of training new officers be more evenly spread across all stations and that to this end the field training program be centralized within the department.[50]

The problem of inexperience was compounded by an informal stigma of working at Century Station. Officers sought to transfer out quickly and felt tainted if they stayed there very long. There was also a high turnover among sergeants, with a resulting serious shortage of supervisors. At times the officer-sergeant ratio was 20:1 or even 25:1, despite a departmental goal of an 8:1 ratio.[51] Along the same lines, random audits by the New York City City Council found that only an occasional precinct met the department's own 8:1 ratio and the majority had ratios higher than 14:1.[52]

On this and other issues, Bobb's investigation dramatized the extent to which street-level problems, such as shootings or citizen complaints about excessive force, cannot be separated from the full range of personnel and management practices in a department. If oversight agencies confine themselves to the review of individual complaints and refuse to address the underlying causes, their overall impact on policing will be marginal at best. Rank-and-file officers have opposed citizen oversight in part because they feel they are being made the scapegoats for larger societal problems. To the extent that they are made the scapegoats for police department management problems, they have a valid point.[53] The policy review function attempts to overcome this problem by examining policies rather than individual officers. After a "dramatic drop" in shootings in the first half of 1998, Bobb suggested optimistically "that management focus and attention can impact on the number of shootings."[54]

In San Jose, meanwhile, the Independent Police Auditor's 1995 *Year-End Report* brought to light an explosive issue related to the off-duty employment of San Jose police officers. Auditor Teresa Guerrero-Daley found potentially serious conflicts of interest arising from the fact that some police officers were hiring their department supervisors on their off-duty jobs. She noted that in some cases "sergeants may find themselves having to discipline the same officer who hires him/her off-duty for on-duty conduct" and concluded that in these situations, officers' concern about their off-duty jobs "is in direct conflict with their duties as police officers."[55] A similar situation was also discovered in New Orleans, a department that already had serious discipline problems at the time.[56]

A major part of the problem was that the San Jose Police Department (SJDP) did not adequately supervise off-duty employment and secure proper documentation regarding places of employment, number of hours worked, the use of SJPD uniforms, and the impact of off-duty employment on officer stress and fatigue. The auditor recommended "an in-depth study" by the police department including a full review of departmental policies.[57] The auditor, in short, brought to light a previously hidden personnel practice that did not relate directly to citizen complaints but threatened the larger system of discipline system within the police department.

Training

The policy review function can also provide input into police training, identifying either general areas where additional training is needed or individual officers who need to be retrained. One of the great failures of police complaint procedures has been the lack of feedback from either the internal affairs unit or the oversight agency to the police department about areas where new or refresher training appears necessary. Complaints are treated as isolated events, an unpleasantness to be disposed of as quickly as possible. A KPMG audit of the Charlotte-Mecklenburg Police Department complaints process recommended that the department's internal affairs division play "a more formal role in providing input to training programs and setting policies and procedures" for the department.[58]

In 1998 alone, the San Francisco OCC issued four policy recommendations related to training: one recommending that the department determine which officers had not been trained in the use of pepper spray and the handling of persons exposed to pepper spray; another recommending that officers receive updated training on the handling of persons requiring medical treatment; a third on the proper procedures for changing citations when an officer receives new information about a criminal incident; and a fourth on enforcement of taxi cab regulations.[59] Each of these recommendations arose out of a specific citizen complaint. In effect, the recommendations represent a form of housekeeping: spotting small problems that need attention and bringing to the attention of both the responsible authorities and the public. Auditor systems of oversight monitor the handling of complaints by internal affairs units, and in that capacity they are able to spot investigators who need to be retrained. The Portland auditor, for example, identified cases where investigators were asking leading questions of police officers and recommended retraining.[60]

Risk Management

Policy review can also be used to control the cost of civil litigation against a department. One of the notable failures of both police departments and other city officials has been their neglect of modern concepts of risk management and in particular their refusal to examine incidents that result in litigation and seek to correct the underlying problems. In some cities and counties, such payments have soared and are a significant financial burden. New York City paid out $177 million between 1994 and 2000 in cases involving police misconduct.[61] The city of Albuquerque was paying out an average of about $2 million a year in police misconduct cases, an enormous sum for a department with only about 900 sworn officers. Other cities, on the other hand, control these costs very effectively. Seattle, for example, paid out $336,883 in 1993 and only $180,000 in 1995.[62]

The high cost of civil litigation can be the result of several factors. On one hand, it may be the result of frequent misconduct by officers on the street. On the other, civil rights attorneys believe that some jurisdictions are "easy touches" and readily settle misconduct suits in amounts that make litigation worth the effort. Portland and Charlotte have low civil litigation costs in part because they make a concerted effort to not settle easily and to keep litigation costs down.[63]

The principal reason for creating the position of Special Counsel to the Los Angeles Sheriff's Department, in fact, was to reduce the cost of civil litigation. The 1992 Kolts Report found that the department had paid out $15.5 million in excessive force cases in three and a half years between 1989 and mid-1992.[64] As already noted, Special Counsel Merrick Bobb takes a broad view of his role and has not hesitated to examine aspects the department with some indirect impact on misconduct and litigation. In 1999, he reported that the docket of excessive force-related cases had been reduced from 381 cases in fiscal year 1992–93 to 70 in FY 1998–99. The combined total of judgments and settlements, meanwhile, had been reduced to an average of about $2 million a year, less than half the total before the Kolts report.[65]

In New York City, a 1998 City Council report recommended that the New York City Police Department "should do more to monitor officers who are the subject of civil suits." Specifically, it recommended that cross-reference civil litigation with citizen complaints, disciplinary records, "and all other relevant data sources to develop accurate profiles of police officers and to detect any patterns of misconduct."

Two years later the Public Advocate found that the New York City Police Department had disciplined only one of 40 officers involved in the 25 most costly civil suits in the previous six years.[66] Along the same lines, the early warning systems in some police departments include involvement in civil litigation as an indicator that an officer is having problems on the street.

Policy Review and Problem-Oriented Policing

The policy review function parallels one of the most important new developments in policing over the past twenty years: problem-oriented policing (POP). As developed by Herman Goldstein, POP holds that the police need to disaggregate the general categories of "crime" and "disorder" into specific problems such as graffiti, chronic alcoholics on the street, homeless people, and so on.[67] Whereas traditional policing treats individual calls for service as isolated events, the POP approach looks for patterns of recurring problems and attempts to develop solutions specifically tailored to each problem.[68]

STEPS	APPLICATION
1. Scanning	Review Citizen Complaints

2. Analysis	Identify
	    Problem Officers,
	    Policy Change Needs,
	    Training Needs

3. Response	Counsel Officers
	    Develop New Policies
	    Provide In-Service Training

4. Assessment	Review Citizen Complaints Review Problem Officer Records

FIGURE 4-5 The SARA Process

POP has been conceptualized in terms of a process known as SARA: scanning, analysis, response, and adaptation (Figure 4-5). Applied to the policy review function, oversight agencies can scan citizen complaints, identify recurring problems (analysis), and then develop policy recommendations (response) designed to reduce or even prevent these problems. Bobb's analysis of shootings at the Century Station of the LASD is an excellent example of this problem-solving approach. Under the SARA approach, complaints become a management tool, a potentially valuable source of information about problems that need attention.

Recommended vs. Mandated Policies

As currently practiced, policy review involves recommendations for policy changes. With the exceptions explained here, oversight agencies do not have the power to dictate policy. Some oversight advocates argue that oversight agencies should have such power and that without it they are powerless and therefore useless. Police chiefs, on the other hand, fear that giving oversight agencies policy-making authority would undermine their managerial authority and render them powerless.

Several comments on this issue are in order. First, even where a police chief rejects or substantially modifies a recommendation, the policy review process provides a mechanism for citizen input and orderly debate over police practices. The process opens a window into the police department, the thinking of the police chief, and the activities of the oversight agency.

A few examples from San Diego County illustrate the policy review process. In 1996, the Citizens' Law Enforcement Review Board (CLERB) made six policy recommendations. Four were declined, one was adopted, and another was still in the process of being adopted.[69] In one case, CLERB recommended that when an inmate is remanded to another agency, the sheriff's department require the transporting officers "to maintain custody of the inmate's property." Apparently, there had been allegations that inmate property was lost or stolen in transit. The sheriff rejected the recommendation on the grounds that the department has no jurisdiction over the agencies or contracting agents who transport inmates and concluded: "We cannot implement this policy recommendation." In another instance, CLERB recommended a new policy for inventorying inmate property to discourage staff theft. The sheriff replied that no evidence had been presented regarding staff theft and therefore he would make no policy change at this time.[70]

The give and take between the CLERB and the sheriff on these issues represents an orderly debate. It promotes the spirit of accountability by forcing the sheriff to respond in a formal way to specific recommendations for change. Publication of the recommendations and the sheriff's responses in the CLERB minutes informs the public about the issue. The process also represents a constructive alternative to the traditional practice of resolving policy disputes through litigation. One can envision, for example, a suit that resulted in a court-imposed crowd control policy on the San Francisco police department. Not only is litigation expensive and time consuming, but it requires waiting for some major harm to be done.

A second response to the idea of mandated policy changes reiterates the point made earlier about the power to discipline officers. In the long run, it is extremely unwise to undermine the authority of police chief executives. Policy review advances the general principle of accountability by opening up the process, informing the public, and spotlighting the responsibility of the chief executive to take some action on the issue at hand. The policy review function promotes accountability in this respect by creating a procedure through which the chief executive has to answer to the public and explain his or her position.

The question of who controls police policy deserves an additional comment. In important respects, the police department objections to policy review are without foundation for the simple reason that outside agencies have always controlled police policies. When a city council or state legislature enacts a law on domestic violence arrests or high-speed pursuits, it is dictating police department policy. The courts have also imposed policies covering the nitty-gritty aspects of police work—with the famous *Mapp* and *Miranda* decisions being the most obvious examples. Civil service systems control personnel standards and much of the recruitment and testing procedures for most law enforcement agencies. The question is not whether outside agencies should prescribe police policies, but how an oversight agency can use information about complaints to play a constructive role in improving policing.

It also needs to be pointed out that in a number of cities, citizen oversight agencies already have extensive policy-making authority. As already noted, the police departments in Detroit, Los Angeles, San Francisco, Milwaukee, and several other cities are governed by police commissions consisting of politically appointed citizens. These commissions have authority over all aspects of the police department.[71] This governance structure was quite common during the nineteenth century, as part of a long political struggle over control of the police, but with the exception of the cities noted was eliminated in the twentieth century.[72] Unfortunately, many of these commissions have failed to make full use of their authority to examine citizen complaints and contribute to the development of better police policies.[73]

Summary

The policy review role is potentially one of the most important roles that citizen oversight can play. Properly conducted, with a broad vision and a commitment to examining the underlying causes of police problems on the street, it can serve a preventive function and lead to improved policing. It directs attention away from individual officers, who often become scapegoats, and focuses on the responsibilities of top police management. In the long run, this is a more effective approach to achieving police accountability than focusing narrowly on complaint review.

AUDITING THE QUALITY
OF COMPLAINT INVESTIGATIONS

One of the basic criticisms of police internal affairs units has been their failure to investigate citizen complaints thoroughly and fairly. The 1973 Metcalfe Report on police brutality in Chicago found that in the Chicago police department, "there are no guidelines for the thoroughness of an investigation, with the result that only cursory investigations are made in many cases. For example, no efforts are usually made to interview witnesses at their homes; instead registered letters are sent telling them to come to Police Headquarters."[74]

Oversight agencies can play an important role in ensuring the quality of complaint investigations by police departments. The exact nature of this role varies according to the structure of the oversight agency. In Class IV auditor systems it represents their primary role. In Class I systems, which have primary responsibility for investigating complaints, the challenge is to develop self-monitoring procedures to ensure the quality of their own investigations. Auditing the quality of complaint investigations can involve a number of different activities. The complaint investigation process consists of a number of different stages, each of which needs to be examined separately for quality.

Complaint Intake

The first stage of the complaint process is *complaint intake*. Important parts of this stage are closely related to community outreach activities discussed earlier. An oversight agency can help ensure that the complaint process is as open and accessible as possible. This includes making sure that the appropriate informational materials exist, are available in all the appropriate languages, and are widely distributed throughout the community. It is also important that complaints can be received at convenient locations other than police headquarters and over the phone. In addition, all police officers in the department need to be well informed about the complaint process, have informational material with them, and be instructed to give citizens accurate and polite responses to inquiries about how to make complaints.

Complaint intake procedures have been audited by community activist groups. A 1996 investigation by the ACLU of Northern California and PUEBLO, another community organization, found a shocking level of ignorance about the complaint process among Oakland police officers. Through a series of telephone calls and in-person visits to particular police offices, they found that "a staggering 95% [of officers] failed to mention or acknowledge the existence of the independent Citizens Police Review Board" as a place where someone could file a complaint. Only 36.8 percent correctly answered that a person could file a complaint by telephone. It was not clear whether the officers' responses resulted from a genuine lack of information, which would indicate a training failure, or a willful effort not to provide accurate information, which would suggest a hostile police subculture.[75]

Screening Complaints

One of the most important issues in the handling of complaints involves early screening. Many potential complaints are indeed without merit, because of ignorance, misunderstanding, or delusion on the part of the complainant. There are legitimate reasons for screening out genuinely frivolous complaints at a very early stage. Screening is also necessary for the efficient operation of a complaint process. The demise of the old Washington, D.C., CCRB resulted in part from the fact that it became hopelessly bogged down because it did not have a procedure for prioritizing cases and focusing its resources on the legitimate and serious cases.[76] The danger, of course, is that early screening will be used to dismiss legitimate complaints. The Christopher Commission found that potential complainants who went to precinct stations were harassed or even threatened, with the result that their complaints were never formally filed.[77]

The San Jose auditor noted that certain people file frequent complaints against the police and that police officers showed a natural tendency "to dismiss such complaints." The auditor advised that "each complaint must be treated with a uniform and consistent degree of seriousness and objectivity." Some formal procedures are needed to ensure that the early dismissal of complaints is not abused. At a minimum, an oversight agency needs to recognize the potential for abuse, to develop some minimal standards for early screening, and to conduct regular audits of the handling of potential complainants to ensure that staff members are complying with official policy. The challenge is to balance the need for efficiency with the requirement that the process have integrity.

Recording, Classifying, and Reporting Complaints

The second stage of the complaint process is *recording, classifying, and reporting complaints*. Many agencies have two-part classification systems to distinguish between the serious and less serious complaints. The Boise ombudsman, for example, fully investigates all serious Class I complaints but may, at its discretion, refer less serious Class II complaints to the police department for investigation.[78] While important for reasons of efficiency, such a system can be abused. The San Jose auditor found that the San Jose Police Department was improperly classifying many apparently serious complaints as minor administrative complaints. This practice kept them "off the books" and created the appearance of a low annual complaint rate. At the auditor's recommendation, the recording and classification procedures were changed, with the result that the official number of reported complaints increased. Similarly, the work of the Inspector General in Los Angeles brought about changes in the recording, classification, and reporting of complaints against the LAPD. One result was a tenfold increase in the official number of complaints between 1997 and 1998.[79]

Investigative Effort, Thoroughness, and Fairness

The relevant issues for quality of investigations are the level of investigative effort expended on each case and the thoroughness and fairness of investigations. The traditional argument by civil rights groups that police departments whitewash police misconduct basically rests on the belief that the police do not expend much investigative effort.

The level of investigative effort may be determined by examining the documentation in complaint files. This documentation includes, or should include, the investigator's notes on the incident that generated the complaint, notes of interviews with complainants, officers, and witnesses, tape recordings of interviews, and a log of investigative steps taken, including attempts to identify and contact witnesses. If there is little or no documentation, it suggests that investigators are not doing thorough jobs, conduct sloppy investigations, and are poorly supervised.

In its first months of operation, the San Jose auditor found that the complaint files often contained handwritten notes that were difficult to read. Upon the auditor's recommendation, the police department's Professional Standards and Conduct Unit created a standard form on which all notes could be typewritten and entered into a computerized database system. Investigators were provided laptop computers to ensure that their notes were legible.[80] Auditors in Portland, meanwhile, have found some complaint files that were incomplete, had illegible reports, and lacked the required tape recordings of interviews. These audits led to recommendations for corrective action.[81]

An investigation by a mayoral task force in Seattle found that as a result of provisions of the police union contract, police department internal affairs investigators did not routinely conduct face-to-face interviews with officers accused of misconduct. Investigators were required to submit questions in writing in advance to the officers. Moreover, if additional misconduct came to light, investigators would have to again provide notice and submit the relevant questions in advance.[82] Clearly, such a procedure inhibits thorough complaint investigations. In passing, it might be noted that over the course of several years, the Seattle police auditor never addressed these and other problems with the Seattle police complaint process.[83] In New York City, meanwhile, the police union contract prevents officers suspected of criminal conduct from being interrogated by department investigators for 48 hours. Many believe that the "48-hour rule" gives officers a chance to coordinate their stories and minimally creates the impression that officers receive protection that ordinary citizens do not enjoy.[84]

In another corrective action, the San Jose auditor recommended, and the San Jose police department adopted, a formal policy in 1995 on the proper method of documenting alleged force incidents. In any case of reported "injury to a citizen or police officer that requires medical treatment," supervisors have an "affirmative duty to respond to the scene and ensure that a complete investigation is completed." The investigation should include obtaining (and taping) statements from persons involved, "conducting a canvas for independent witnesses," and collecting physical evidence.[85]

This recommendation is particularly significant because most police departments provide little if any training specifically related to complaint investigations. At best, they select officers with prior criminal investigation experience, apparently on the assumption that their investigative skills will transfer to complaint investigations. There is good reason for questioning this assumption. Citizen complaints involve allegations against fellow officers and place investigators in an awkward position in relation to their colleagues. Also, it is not clear that departments place the same priority on citizen complaints that they do on crimes against citizens. As a result, investigators may not make a full effort in terms of gathering evidence, searching for witnesses, and so on.

Perhaps the most important auditing technique that has emerged is the practice of reviewing the audiotape recording of interviews with complainants and police officers. Tape recording interviews is now standard practice in the more professional police departments. Review of these tapes can identify instances where the investigator asks hostile questions of complainants, fails to ask obvious follow-up questions, or helps to provide an answer for the police officer. The Portland auditor, for example, found cases where police investigators felt uncomfortable when an officer was unable to answer a question and suggested an answer themselves.[86] Such tactics represent biased investigations. Another problem involves investigators who fail to ask obvious follow-up questions. The Portland auditor pointed out these problems to the police department, recommended corrective training, and eventually found that the quality of investigations improved.

In another move to ensure unbiased investigations, the San Jose auditor recommended that investigators with "significant prior contact" with a complainant not be assigned to new complaints.[87] In a later report, the auditor recommended the adoption of a formal policy to prevent conflicts of interest in situations where the investigator had prior contact with the subject officer as well as the complainant.[88]

Timely Disposition of Complaints

One of the chronic and pervasive problems with complaint procedures, including both police internal affairs units and citizen oversight agencies, is delay in completing investigations. In 1995, the New York Civil Liberties Union concluded: "The single most serious systemic problem facing the new CCRB is its backlog of cases." At the end of 1994, it had a backlog of 3,312 cases that were more than four months old. Of these, 1,305 were a year old.[89] In the most notorious instance, the old Washington, D.C., CCRB was successfully sued because it failed to comply with its own guidelines for timely disposition of complaints. Some complaints languished for as long as three years without a final disposition.[90] Less serious but nonetheless unacceptable delays appear to be a chronic problem in even some of the better-run complaint procedures.

Several citizen oversight agencies monitor the *timely completion* of complaint investigations. The San Jose auditor found in 1993–94 that 25 percent of investigations were taking more than a year to complete. Some, in fact, were not even being classified until six months after they were initially received. In response, the auditor established a set of formal timelines. All complaints were to be classified within thirty days; 75 percent of investigations were to be completed within 120 days; and all investigations were to be completed within 300 days. In an initial audit for 1993–94, it found that the San Jose police department met the first goal in 71 percent of all cases, but met the 120-days-to-completion goal in only 28 percent of the cases. And only 53 percent of the investigations were completed within the prescribed 300 days.[91] Subsequent reports by the auditor found significant improvements. By 1996, for example, 86 percent of all investigations were completed within one year.[92]

Summary

As the preceding discussion should make clear, the quality of complaint investigations depends upon a series of small administrative details. A structurally independent oversight agency can easily become ineffective because of inattention to these details. The experience of the San Jose auditor illustrates the range of issues that need to be addressed. In its first *Year-End Report,* the auditor published a table listing a total of twenty-four changes in the complaints process that it had helped to effect during the first year and a half of operation. By the end of 1998, it cited a total of forty recommendations, thirty-eight of which had been adopted (see Figure 4-5). To a great extent, these recommendations represent another dimension of the policy review role described earlier in this chapter. The significance of the various San Jose auditor recommendations lies not in any one single change, but in the comprehensive nature of the set of recommendations, which hopefully contributes to lasting organizational change.

One important aspect of this list is the subtle impact on the organizational culture of a police department. Officers assigned to the internal affairs have the experience of someone looking over their shoulders and making an endless series of suggestions for improvement on a regular basis. This experience represents what we really mean by accountability. Findings to date suggest that while police departments initially resent and resist this form of oversight by outsiders, with time they come to accept it (at least in some, but not necessarily all, police departments).

SELF-MONITORING

One of the problems in the history of the oversight movement is that agencies established as alternatives to inadequate police complaint investigations have not taken sufficient steps to ensure the quality of their own work. The old adage: Who is guarding the guardians? has acquired a corollary: Who is guarding the guardians of the guardians?

An exception to this rule is the Quality Service Audit (QSA) developed by the Minneapolis Civilian Review Authority (CRA) in 1998. The program involves a simple customer feedback survey that allows both complainants and police officers to evaluate their experience with the CRA. (In the interests of disclosure, it should be noted that the author of this book helped to develop the program under contract with the CRA.) The questions are designed to distinguish between satisfaction with the outcome of the case and satisfaction with the complaint investigation process. The most important aspect of the CRA program is that it is an institutionalized self-monitoring process, providing continuing feedback from clients. This process is better than the one-time assessment typical of traditional evaluations.[93] Following the lead of Minneapolis, the San Francisco Office of Citizen Complaints began initiating its own Customer Satisfaction Survey in 1999.[94]

The Office of the Kansas City Auditor, after finding inadequacies with the complaint intake process of both the police department and the Office of Citizen Complaints, recommended periodic testing of the intake process.[95] Citizen oversight agencies should arrange for the testing and evaluation of their own procedures by independent investigators on a regular basis.

CHANGING THE POLICE SUBCULTURE

Virtually all experts on policing agree that the single greatest obstacle to achieving accountability is the police subculture, and in particular the "code of silence."

A national survey of police officers by the Police Foundation in 1998 found that slightly more than half (52.4 percent) agreed that "It is not unusual

for a police officer to turn a blind eye to improper conduct by other officers."[96] With respect to citizen complaints, the testimony of officers is often
the most critical evidence for the simple reason that other officers often
witness the incidents. In terms of promoting accountability, the crucial question is how to transform the police subculture from one that is primarily self-
protective to one that is self-policing. Oversight agencies can contribute to
that transformation through two specific programs: early warning systems for
"problem officers," and investigations targeting officers who give false and misleading testimony in complaint investigations.

Early Warning Systems

Early warning (EW) systems are a relatively new management strategy for
identifying "problem" officers, defined as those who receive an abnormally
high number of citizen complaints or have other indicators of problematic
performance. EW systems then provide some kind of intervention, in the
form of counseling or training, designed to correct the officers' behavior. EW
systems are informal in the sense that they are not punishment, with no formal
record of discipline in an officer's personnel file, and are designed to help officers. If the policy review function is designed to identify and correct problem
situations, EW systems focus on problem *officers.*

There is substantial evidence indicating that in every police department a
small group of officers receive a disproportionate number of citizen complaints.
Typically, these officers are also involved in a high number of use of force and
resisting arrest incidents. The Christopher Commission identified forty-four
problem officers among the then 8,500-officer Los Angeles Police Department.
These officers averaged more than twelve times as many complaints as all other
officers.[97] A similar pattern has been found in other police departments. In
Kansas City, 2 percent of the officers were responsible for half of all citizen
complaints.[98] In Boston, 11 percent of the officers generated 62 percent of all
complaints.[99] It is now part of the folklore of police management that, as one
chief lamented, 10 percent of your officers cause 90 percent of your headaches.

The phenomenon of the problem officer has been a dirty secret within
policing for a long time. More than twenty years ago, Herman Goldstein
pointed out that officers with chronic performance problems are generally well
known within their departments. The Christopher Commission noted that the
problem officers in the LAPD were "readily identifiable" on the basis of available
records.[100] Until recently, however, departments did nothing about these officers, either to correct their behavior or to remove them from sensitive assignments. Research in the 1960s found that some police departments knowingly
dumped their incompetent officers on African-American neighborhoods.[101]

The U.S. Civil Rights Commission recommended the development of
early warning in its 1981 report, *Who Is Guarding the Guardians?*[102] Few police
departments responded to the Commission's recommendation, however. The
Miami-Dade Police Department established its EW system in 1979 but the
concept did not really begin to spread until the 1990s. About one-third of all
municipal police departments claimed to have an early warning system in place

or in development by 1998.[103] An evaluation of EW systems in three police departments found that they were effective in significantly reducing complaints among those officers who were subject to intervention. A report by the Vera Institute found that in two NYPD precincts in the Bronx precinct commanders successfully reduced the total number of complaints and repeat complaints against particular officers through proactive supervisory action. Both commanders talked personally to officers with repeat complaints and in some cases reassigned them to other duties or did not recommend them for promotion. In short, the commanders took citizen complaints seriously, used complaint data as a management tool, and took decisive action with "problem" officers.[104]

Although the power to implement an EW system—that is, to provide the counseling or training—lies with the police department, an oversight agency can play an important role in developing a system. An oversight agency can take the lead in recommending the development of an EW system. By virtue of reviewing citizen complaints, oversight officials are in a position to notice that certain officers' names keep reappearing. In the case of Class I systems that receive citizen complaints, the oversight agency will have a more complete picture of complaint patterns than the police department itself. The oversight agency can also publish information about complaint patterns—indicating, for example, the number of officers with three or more complaints in the previous year. This does not involve publishing the names of the officers, since doing that might violate either civil service law or the police union contract or both. The San Jose auditor publishes summary data.[105]

Investigating False and Misleading Testimony

The "code of silence" is a particularly difficult problem to solve. The most persuasive evidence that an officer has lied would come from other officers, but obviously where the code is strong, no other officers will come forward with the truth. Historically, police departments have done little to break the code of silence. In additional to the difficulty of the problem, it is embarrassing for departments to publicly expose lying by its own officers.

Recently, some oversight agencies have attempted to attack the problem. The former Los Angeles Inspector General Katherine Mader undertook an audit of code of silence violations as one of her office's first activities. Her approach used allegations of false and misleading testimony that had come to the attention of the department, most of which were identified on the basis of testimony that was contradicted by other evidence, or was inconsistent with previous testimony, or was simply not credible given the facts of the case. Between 1993 and 1996, there were 137 such cases. Of these, the IG determined that 19 percent were code of silence violations where the officer did not "provide adverse information against a fellow officer." Only four of these cases involved incidents where an officer was alleged to have used excessive force against a citizen. Of the fifty-three officers involved in these cases, thirty-five (or 66%) were disciplined. The number of code of silence allegations declined significantly between 1993 and 1996, reaching zero by 1996.

The IG stated that it was not possible to reach any definitive conclusions about the LAPD's efforts to root out code of silence violations. The downward trend could reflect less aggressive enforcement rather than a decline in violations.[106] Nonetheless, the significant aspect of the IG's inquiry is that it brought the issue to public attention, provided facts that had not previously been available, and presumably helped to strengthen the department's efforts to eradicate officer lying. In short, at least an initial first step was taken. Unfortunately, IG Mader became embroiled in a controversy over the extent of her authority in late 1998 and eventually resigned. The future of the IG's efforts to identify false and misleading testimony is therefore uncertain.

Along similar lines, the New York City Commission to Combat Police Corruption, created in the wake of the Mollen Commission investigation, audited New York City's efforts to investigate police officer perjury. The audit found that most of the cases adjudicated by the NYCP did not involve corruption but rather were "routine" false statements. Many involved protecting misconduct by the officers themselves or by other officers. As with the LA Inspector General's audit, this investigation only involved cases where the police department had some information and brought formal charges against a police officer. The full extent of the problem is not known. The audit determined that the punishments imposed on those caught and found guilty were incredibly light. Many officers suffered only loss of vacation days. The commission made a number of recommendations designed to strengthen the NYCPD's efforts against police lying.[107]

Meanwhile, the Civilian Complaint Review Board (CCRB) in New York City identified officers it believed had made false statements during complaint investigations, reported them to the NYPD, and recommended that they be disciplined. The NYPD responded by claiming that the CCRB had no legal authority to investigate this problem and make such recommendations. It suggested that the CCRB forward the names of officers to internal affairs for investigation. The CCRB rejected this recommendation. In short, the CCRB made a good-faith effort to eradicate officer perjury but was met by resistance from the police department itself.[108]

The efforts by the L.A. Inspector General and the NYC anti-corruption commission are pioneering attempts to eradicate one of the greatest obstacles to police accountability. It is too early to make a determination about the effectiveness of these efforts. Nonetheless, it is extremely significant that something was done. Both efforts represent a proactive role by an oversight agency in addressing a serious police problem and provide a model for other oversight agencies in this area.

CONCLUSION

Citizen oversight agencies do, or at least can do, far more than investigate complaints. This chapter has described six different areas where oversight agencies can monitor the police and the complaints process, including their own procedures: Community outreach, customer assistance, policy review, auditing complaint investigations, cultivating a culture of professionalism, and self-monitoring. Although investigating allegations of misconduct and punishing guilty officers is extremely important, this chapter argues that in the long run the monitoring role is more likely to promote police accountability, help change the police organization, and lead to a higher quality of police service.

NOTES

1. San Francisco, Office of Citizen Complaints, *Annual Report 1997* (San Francisco; OCC, 1998), 10.

2. Samuel Walker, *The Police in America: An Introduction,* 3rd ed. (New York: McGraw-Hill, 1999).

3. Samuel Walker and Eileen Luna, *A Report on the Oversight Mechanisms of the Albuquerque Police Department* (Albuquerque: City Council, 1997).

4. Personal observation, author. Outreach activities are described in Peter Finn, *Citizen Review of Police: Approaches and Implementation* (Washington, DC: Government Printing Office, 2000 forthcoming), 5-2-5-9.

5. San Francisco Office of Citizen Complaints, *1997 Annual Report* (San Francisco: OCC, 1998), 5.

6. Interview, director, ACLU-Maryland, 1997; interview, chair, Law Enforcement Board, 1997.

7. San Francisco Office of Citizen Complaints, *Annual Report, 1996* (San Francisco: OCC, 1997), 12–13.

8. Anthony M. Pate and Lorie A. Fridell, *Police Use of Force,* 2 vols. (Washington, DC: The Police Foundation, 1993).

9. A series of focus groups found high levels of fear and lack of understanding about the complaints process among Spanish-speaking Latinos (but not among English-speaking Latino students): Samuel Walker, "Complaints against the Police: A Focus Group Study of Citizen Perceptions, Goals, and Expectations," *Criminal Justice Review* 22 (Autumn 1997): 207–25.

10. Portland Police Internal Investigations Auditing Committee [PIIAC], *First Quarter Monitoring Report, 1998* (Portland: PPIIAC, 1998), 6.

11. New York City Civilian Complaint Review Board, *Semiannual Status Report, January–June, 1999* (New York, 1999), iii.

12. U.S. Commission on Civil Rights, *Police Protection of the African American Community in Milwaukee* (Washington, DC: Government Printing Office, 1994), 44.

13. Pate and Fridell, *Police Use of Force,* 2: table B17.1.

14. Samuel Walker and Charles M. Katz, "Less than Meets the Eye: Police Department Bias Crimes Units," *American Journal of Police* 14:1 (1995): 29–48.

15. ACLU of Southern California, *The Call for Change Goes Unanswered* (Los Angeles: ACLU-SC, 1992); ACLU of Northern California, *Failing the Test: Oakland's Police Complaint Process in Crisis* (San Francisco: ACLU-NC, 1996).

16. Wesley Skogan and Susan M. Hartnett, *Community Policing, Chicago Style* (New York: Oxford University Press, 1997).

17. San Jose, Independent Police Auditor, *Year-End Report,* September 1991–December 1994 (San Jose: IPA, 1995), 33.

18. New York Civil Liberties Union, *Third Anniversary Overview of the Civilian Complaint Review Board* (New York: NYCLU, 1996), 19.

19. New York City Civilian Complaint Review Board, *Semiannual Status Report, January–June, 1998* (New York, 1998), 12.

20. San Jose, Independent Police Auditor, *Third Quarterly Report* (San Jose: IPA, June 1994), 23–24.

21. Malcolm K. Sparrow, "Complaints against Police and Departmental Management: Making the Connection," *Police Chief* (August 1992): 65–73.

22. Boise Community Ombudsman, *Year End Report 1999,* 4.

23. Minneapolis, Civilian Review Authority, *1998 Annual Report* (Minneapolis, 1999), Exhibit A, p. 2; interviews, CRA staff members, 1998.

24. The former ombudsman in Louisville, Kentucky spent a lot of time on similar activities. Interview, ombudsman, 12 October, 1998.

25. San Jose, Independent Police Auditor, *First Quarterly Report* (San Jose: IPA, 1993), 17–18.

26. Interview, assistant to the board, 1998.

27. Minneapolis Civilian Review Authority, *Minneapolis Redesign Team Report* (Minneapolis: CRA, 1997), 14.

28. Elaine Cumming, Ian Cumming, and Laura Edel, "The Policeman as Philosopher, Guide, and Friend," *Social Problems* 12:3 (1965): 276–86.

29. Minneapolis Civilian Review Authority, *1997 Annual Report* (Minneapolis: CRA, 1998), exhibit A; Boise, Ombudsman, *Policies and Procedures* (Boise, 1999), chap. 2, 7.

30. Samuel Walker and Betsy Wright Kreisel, "Varieties of Citizen Review: The Implications of Organizational Features of Complaint Review Procedures for Accountability of the Police," *American Journal of Police* 15:3 (1996): 65–88; Peter Finn, *Citizen Review of the Police: Approaches and Implementation* (Washington, DC: Government Printing Office, 2000 forthcoming), 3-2–3-7.

31. Walter Gellhorn, *When Americans Complain* (Cambridge: Harvard University Press, 1966), 191; Algernon Black, *The People and the Police* (New York: McGraw-Hill, 1968).

32. Perez, *Common Sense about Police Review,* 76–81.

33. Geller, "Learning Organizations."

34. Malcolm Sparrow, "Complaints against Police and Departmental Management: Making the Connection," *Police Chief* (August 1992): 65, 71–72.

35. Walker and Kreisel, "Varieties of Citizen Review."

36. San Diego Citizens Law Enforcement Review Board, *1993 Annual Report* (San Diego, 1994) 8–9.

37. San Francisco Office of Citizen Complaints, *Annual Report 1997* (San Francisco: OCC, 1998), 43–62.

38. San Jose, Independent Police Auditor, *Year-End Report 1999* (San Jose: IPA, 2000), Appendix J.

39. Interview, director, Office of Municipal Investigations, 1998.

40. Merrick Bobb, Special Counsel to the Los Angeles Sheriff's Department, *11th Semiannual Report* (Los Angeles, 1999), and previous reports, 1993–1999.

41. San Francisco Police Department, General Order 803 (3 August, 1994); San Francisco Police Department, *Crowd Control Manual* (n.d.); John Crew, interview.

42. San Jose, Independent Police Auditor, *Third Quarterly Report* (San Jose: IPA, June 1994), 23–24.

43. San Jose, Independent Police Auditor, *Year-End Report 1994,* 57, and appendix 6.

44. San Francisco Police Department, General Order 5.07, "Rights of Onlookers," 17 May, 1994.

45. Portland PIIAC, *First Quarter Monitoring Report, 1996* (1996), 5–6.

46. San Francisco Office of Citizen Complaints, *Annual Report 1997* (San Francisco: OCC, 1998), 46–47.

47. Special Counsel to the Los Angeles Sheriff's Department, *9th Semiannual Report* (Los Angeles, June 1998), 9–10.

48. Ibid., 17–18.

49. In one police department, problem officers are taken off patrol duty and assigned to a desk job In another department, however, sergeants are said to know about problem officers but do not have the flexibility of removing officers from patrol cars and have no support from the administration in developing other alternatives.

50. Special Counsel, 9th Semiannual Report, 19.

51. Ibid., 21–23.

52. New York City Council, Committee on Public Safety, *Beyond Community Relations: Addressing Police Brutality Directly* (New York: NYCC, 1998), 25–26.

53. George L. Kelling and Robert B. Kleismet, "Civilian Review of Police: The Way to Establish Accountability?," *Police Union News,* 1 (January 1991): 1–3.

54. Ibid., 7, 9, 15–17.

55. San Jose, Independent Police Auditor, *Year-End Report 1995* (San Jose: IPA, 1996), 9–10.

56. "The Thinnest Blue Line," *New York Times Magazine,* 31 March 1996, 32ff.

57. San Jose, Independent Police Auditor, *Year-End Report 1996* (San Jose: IPA, 1997), 10.

58. KPMG, *Report on Complaint and Use of Force Review Policies and Procedures of the Charlotte-Mecklenburg Police Department* (Washington, DC: KPMG, 1997), 20.

59. San Francisco Office of Citizen Complaints, *1998 Annual Report,* appendix.

60. Portland PIIAC, *Fourth Quarter Monitoring Report, 1995* (Portland: PPIIAC, 1996), 12.

61. New York City Public Advocate, *Disciplining Police: Solving the Problem of Police Misconduct* (New York: The Public Advocate, 2000), 2.

62. Walker and Luna, *A Report on the Oversight Mechanisms of the Albuquerque Police Department.*

63. Interviews.

64. James Kolts, *The Los Angeles County Sheriff's Department* (Los Angeles: Los Angeles County, 1992), 26.

65. Special Counsel, *11th Semiannual Report* (Los Angeles, 1999), 85–86.

66. New York City Council, *Beyond Community Relations: Addressing Police Brutality Directly* (New York: NYCC, 1998), 11. New York City Public Advocate, *Disciplining Police,* 2.

67. Herman Goldstein, "Improving Policing: A Problem-Oriented Approach," *Crime and Delinquency,* 25 (1979): 236–58.

68. See the contributions in Tara O'Connor Shelley and Anne C. Grant, eds., *Problem-Oriented Policing* (Washington, DC: PERF, 1998).

69. San Diego Citizens Law Enforcement Review Board, *Annual Report 1997* (San Diego, 1998), 13.

70. Memo, Sheriff to Citizens Law Enforcement Review Board, San Diego Citizens Law Enforcement Review Board, *Minutes,* 11 February, 1997

71. Edward Littlejohn, "The Civilian Police Commission: A Deterrent of Police Misconduct," *University of Detroit Journal of Urban Law* 59 (Fall 1981): 5–62.

72. Samuel Walker, *A Critical History of Police Reform* (Lexington: Lexington Books, 1977). Walker argues that the commission form of governance failed because reformers in the nineteenth century had no clear vision of how to change on-the-street policing, apart from appointing their own people as police officers. Thus, struggles over police commissions were little more than partisan contests for control with no substantive program at issue.

73. On the Los Angeles Police Commission, see Christopher Commission, *Report of the Independent Commission,* 185–87.

74. Metcalfe Report, *The Misuse of Police Authority in Chicago* (Chicago, 1972), 35.

75. ACLU of Northern California and PUEBLO, *Failing the Test: Oakland's Police Complaint Process in Crisis* (San Francisco: ACLU-NC, 1996).

76. ACLU–National Capital Area, *Analysis of the District of Columbia's Civilian Complaint Review Board and Recommendations For its Replacement* (Washington, DC: ACLU–NCA, 1995).

77. Christopher Commission, *Report of the Independent Commission on the Los Angeles Police Department* (Los Angeles, 1991), 158–59.

78. Boise, Ombudsman, *Policies and Procedures* (Boise, 1999), chap. 2, 2.

79. "New LAPD Complaint Logging System Makes Mark," *Los Angeles Times,* 25 February 1998.

80. San Jose, Independent Police Auditor, *Year-End Report 1994,* 16.

81. Portland PIIAC, *Fourth Quarter 1995 Monitoring Report* (Portland: PPIIAC, 1996), 10.

82. Seattle, Citizens Review Panel, *Final Report* (Seattle, 1999), 18.

83. Seattle, Internal Investigations Auditor, annual reports.

84. New York City Council, Committee on Public Safety, *Beyond Community Relations: Addressing Police Brutality Directly* (New York: NYCC, 1998), 17.

85. San Jose, Independent Police Auditor, *Year-End Report 1994,* 42–49. Teresa Guerrero-Daley, "Collecting Physical Evidence Following a Use of Force, *Policing by Consent* (December 1995): 16–17.

86. Portland PIIAC, *Fourth Quarter 1995 Monitoring Report* (Portland: PPIIAC, April 1996), 10.

87. San Jose, Independent Police Auditor, *First Quarterly Report* (San Jose: IPA, December 1993), 15.

88. San Jose, Independent Police Auditor, *Second Quarterly Report* (San Jose: IPA, March 1994), 12.

89. New York Civil Liberties Union, *Second Anniversary Overview of the Civilian Complaint Review Board* (New York: NYCLU, 1995), 3–4.

90. ACLU–National Capital Area, *Analysis of the District of Columbia's Civilian Complaint Review Board and Recommendations for its Replacement* (Washington, DC: ACLU–NCA, 1995).

91. San Jose, Independent Police Auditor, *1995 Year-End Report,* 16–17.

92. San Jose, Independent Police Auditor, *Year-End Report 1996,* 14.

93. Samuel Walker, ""Setting the Standards: The Efforts and Impacts of Blue Ribbon Commissions on the Police," in W A. Geller, ed., *Police Leadership in America: Crisis and Opportunity* (New York: Praeger, 1985), 354–70.

94. San Francisco, Office of Citizen Complaints, *Third Quarter Statistical Report, 1999* (San Francisco: OCC, 1999), 5.

95. Kansas City Office of the City Auditor, *Performance Audit: Police Citizen Complaint Procedure* (Kansas City: OCA, March 2000), 14.

96. David Weisburd and Rosann Greenspan, with Edwin E. Hamilton, Hubert Williams, and Kellie A. Bryant, *Police Attitudes Toward Abuse of Authority: Findings From a National Study* (Washing-ton, DC: Government Printing Office, 2000). William A. Westley, *Violence and the Police* (Cambridge: MIT Press, 1970).

97. Christopher Commission *Report of the Independent Commission on the Los Angeles Police Department,* 32–47.

98. "Kansas City Police Go after Their 'Bad Boys'," *New York Times* (10 September 1991), 1.

99. "Wave of Abuse Laid to a Few Officers," *Boston Globe* (4 October, 1992).

100. Christopher Commission, *Report of the Independent Commission.*

101. Albert Reiss, *The Police and the Public* (New Haven: Yale University Press, 1971), 168.

102. US. Commission on Civil Rights, *Who Is Guarding the Guardians?* (Washington, DC: Government Printing Office, 1981), 81–86.

103. Samuel Walker, Geoffrey Alpert, and Dennis Kenney, *Responding to the Problem Police Officer: A National Evaluation of Early Warning Systems,* Final Report, National Institute of Justice (2000).

104. Vera Institute of Justice, *Respectful and Effective Policing: Two Examples in the South Bronx* (New York: Vera Institute, 1999), 13.

105. San Jose, Independent Police Auditor, *Year-End Report 1997,* 32–33.

106. Office of the Inspector General, *Six-Month Report* (Los Angeles: Los Angeles Board of Police Commissioners, January 1997).

107. Commission to Combat Police Corruption, *The New York City Police Department's Disciplinary System: How the Department Disciplines its Members Who Make False Statements* (New York, 12 December 1996).

108. "Police Officials Ask Panel Not to Cite Officer for Lying," *New York Times,* 18 November, 1999. New York City Public Advocate, *Disciplining Police: Solving the Problem of Police Misconduct* (New York: The Public Advocate, 2000), 31–36.

❖

PART III

Evaluating
the Effectiveness
of Citizen Oversight

5

❖

Evaluating the Effectiveness of Complaint Investigations

INTRODUCTION

I s the independent investigation of complaints effective? Does it succeed in achieving the goals discussed in Chapter 3: providing more thorough and more fair investigations, sustaining more complaints and disciplining more officers, deterring police misconduct, improving public opinion about the police, and promoting police professionalism? This chapter examines the effectiveness of complaint review procedures. It should be noted, of course, that the evidence on these questions apply with equal relevance to both external oversight agencies and internal police complaint procedures. It is important to know, for example, whether investigations conducted by internal affairs units are fair and thorough, deter misconduct, and so on.

Evaluating the effectiveness of complaint review procedures, whether external or internal, is extremely difficult. As Chapter 3 also points out, there is little research on most of these issues. Consequently, much of this chapter is devoted to a discussion of what kinds of data we need and research strategies for developing the necessary data.

In evaluating the effectiveness of complaint procedures, we can apply Douglas Perez's three criteria: integrity, legitimacy, and learning.[1] *Integrity* refers primarily to the thoroughness and fairness of a complaint process. *Legitimacy* refers to how a complaint process is perceived by its various clients and audiences, including complainants, officers who are subject to complaints, the community at large, the police department, and elected officials ultimately responsible for the process. *Learning* refers to the extent to which a process provides meaningful feedback to responsible officials in such a way that allows them to make improvements in both the complaint process and the police department.

THE MISGUIDED FOCUS
ON THE SUSTAIN RATE

To an unfortunate degree, the debate over the effectiveness of complaint review has focused very narrowly on the sustain rate—the percentage of complaints sustained in the complainant's favor.[2] Sustain rates are consistently very low in all complaint review procedures. The Police Foundation, for example, found that municipal police departments sustain only about 10 percent of all citizen complaints.[3] Civil rights activists cite these figures as evidence of the need for external citizen oversight. The fact that the police officer "wins" 90 percent of the time is offered as proof that police internal affairs investigations are a whitewash for police abuse.[4] For their part, the police cite low sustain rates as evidence that most complaints are without merit and that they are doing a professional job of policing.

Citizen oversight agencies also have low sustain rates, however, and generally sustain an average of about 12 or 13 percent of all complaints. The Minneapolis Civilian Review Authority finds probable cause in about 10 percent of the complaints it accepts and sustains about half of those that reach a formal hearing.[5] Moreover, low sustain rates are not unique to the United States. In the United Kingdom, only 4.2 percent of all complaints against police officer filed between 1979 and 1989 were sustained.[6]

In short, low sustain rates appear to be a universal phenomenon common to all complaint procedures. This chapter argues that low sustain rates are an inherent aspect of citizen complaints against the police, that it is unreasonable to expect high rates even in the best of circumstances, and that the evaluation of complaint procedures should utilize other measures.

Problems with the Sustain Rate

Before proceeding to a detailed discussion, we should briefly indicate three basic problems with the sustain rate as a performance measure. First, there are enormous problems with the data that are used to compute the sustain rate. In the next section this chapter examines the data and the problems associated with them. That examination illuminates a number of important issues related to policing, how both police departments and citizen oversight agencies operate, and the difficulties in attempting to measure what they do.

The second problem with the sustain rate is that no one has developed a standard for an acceptable rate. Should it be 30 percent, 50 percent, or some higher figure? Critics of the police who believe the prevailing 10 percent sustain rate is unacceptable imply that the rate should be higher. They do not, however, specify what an acceptable rate should be. In baseball we know that a batting average of .300 represents excellent performance. In professional football, however, a 30 percent pass completion rate for a quarterback is unacceptable, and the best quarterbacks complete 55 percent or more of their passes. We have developed these standards only after years of experience. No one has defined an acceptable sustain rate for citizen complaints against the police, however,

Third, as Chapter 3 indicates, the investigation of complaints is only one of several functions of oversight. To focus only on this function is analogous to evaluating the police solely on the basis of the crime rate. Police experts have long recognized that the police have many roles and responsibilities, only one of which is criminal law enforcement.[7] It is inappropriate to evaluate the police solely on the basis of only one part of their role and to ignore their other responsibilities. Only recently, and largely in response to the community policing movement, have police experts begun to explore performance measures appropriate to what police actually do.[8] A similar challenge arises with respect to oversight agencies. At present there are no generally accepted performance measures that encompass the full range of roles and responsibilities as described in Chapters 3 and 4.

A Formal complaint is a serious misconduct on the part of a member of the San Jose Police Department (SJPD). The complaint alleged a serious violation of the City policy, the Department policy or the law by an officer. A Formal complaint may be citizen-initiated (CI) or department-initiated (DI), which is a complaint initiated by the Chief of Police. The findings available for a Formal complaint are:

1. **Sustained:** The investigation disclosed sufficient evidence to clearly prove the allegation made in the complaint.

2. **Not Sustained:** The investigation failed to disclose sufficient evidence to clearly prove the allegation made in the complaint or to conclusively disprove the allegation.

3. **Exonerated:** The acts which provided the basis for the complaint or allegation occurred; however, the investigation revealed that they were justified, lawful and proper.

4. **Unfounded:** The investigation conclusively proved that the act or acts complained of did not occur. This finding also applies when the individual member(s) or employee(s) named were not involved in the act or acts which may have occurred.

5. **No Finding:** The complaint failed to disclose promised information to further the investigation. The investigation revealed that another agency was involved and the complaint or complainant has been referred to that agency. The complainant wishes to withdraw the complaint. The complainant is no longer available for clarification(s). Additional reasons may include: lack of signature on the Boland Admonishment; officer resigned from the SJPD before the investigation was closed; or the identity of the officer could not be determined.

FIGURE 5-1 Formal Complaint Categories, San Jose Police Department

SOURCE: San Jose, Independent Police Auditor, *1999 Year-End Report* (San Jose: IPA, 2000), 83.

OFFICIAL DATA
ON CITIZEN COMPLAINTS

The problems with the sustain rate become evident when we examine the data that are used to compute it. The sustain rate is expressed as a simple percentage of complaints sustained or resolved in favor of the complainant. Complaint review procedures, both external and internal, generally use four different categories of disposition. A complaint is *unfounded* when the investigation determines that actions alleged by the complainant did not occur. A disposition of *exonerated* is reached when the investigation determines that the police officer did act as alleged but that the actions were justified given the circumstances of the case. A complaint is *not sustained* when the investigation determines that the officer may have acted as alleged but that the evidence is not sufficient to find the police officer guilty of misconduct. A complaint is *sustained* when the investigation determines that the officer did engage in the alleged misconduct. Figure 5-1 presents the categories used in San Jose.

The number of officially recorded complaints can be converted into an official complaint rate, expressed either as complaints per 1,000 population or per 100 officers.[9] The Police Foundation's report on the Big Six police departments found complaint rates that ranged from a high of 36.9 per 100 officers in Houston to a low of 5.5 per 100 in Philadelphia.[10] Data for 1998 indicate a complaint rate of 53.6 per 100 officers in San Francisco and 13 per 100 in New York City (see Figure 5-2).

Most police experts recognize that variations of this magnitude probably do not reflect real differences in the quality of police officer behavior. No one

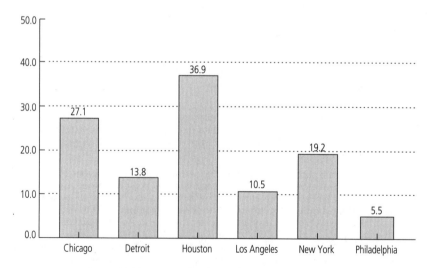

FIGURE 5-2 Complaints Against Police, per 100 sworn officers, 1986

SOURCE: The Police Foundation, *The Big Six* (Washington, DC: The Police Foundation, 1991), 144.

seriously believes that San Francisco police officers are four times worse than New York City officers. Rather, variations in complaint rates reflect social and administrative factors that influence the creation of official data.

Like most official government data (e.g., the crime rate, the unemployment rate) the data are not reliable indicators of the phenomena they purport to measure. They represent only *officially recorded* phenomena. The FBI's official crime rate represents only crimes that are *reported* by citizens and *recorded* by the police. Similarly, the official unemployment rate records only those people who register with a government employment agency as seeking employment. In both cases the official data are the end result of complex bureaucratic procedures that are in turn influenced by many factors. Factors influencing complaints against the police include the tendency of people to file complaints, the formal structure of complaint procedures, and a series of discretionary decisions related to the acceptance, recording, and classification of complaints.

A low complaint rate may reflect not good policing but a complaint procedure that is not well publicized or is even hostile to complainants. In New York City, for example, the number of complaints rose tenfold from the mid-1960s to the mid-1970s: from about 300 to 3,000 per year. No one seriously suggests that this increase was the result of a tenfold deterioration in the performance of New York City police officers. To the contrary, it appears that the increase was the result of administrative changes that increased public awareness of the complaints process, facilitated the filing of complaints, and professionalized the recording of complaints.[11]

The fact that citizen oversight agencies do not necessarily sustain a higher rate of complaints than internal police complaint procedures does not mean that oversight makes no valuable contribution. One consequence of creating an oversight agency is that the number of complaints rises significantly, in large part because the complaint process is perceived as being more open. Thus, if the number of complaints received by a police department rises from 300 to 450 a year, and the sustain rate remains stable at 10 percent, the net result is a 50 percent increase in sustained complaints (45 vs. 30), or to put it another way, a 50 percent increase in the department-wide *discipline rate*. In this respect a stable sustain rate masks the positive impact of citizen oversight with respect to the number of complaints filed.

Let us now examine in detail each of the factors related to the development of official complaint data.

The Reporting of Police Misconduct

The first problem with official complaint data is that police misconduct is an extremely underreported phenomenon. Most people who feel that they have some reason to complain about a police officer do not do so. Data from the Police Services Study (PSS) in the 1970s found that only 36 percent of the people who felt they had some reason to complain took *any* kind of action, and most of those actions involved contacting some person or agency other than the police. Many people contacted a friend, for example. (Because of the design of the PSS survey, it is not possible to determine how many of those responses involved filing a formal complaint with a police department).[12]

It is extremely difficult to measure the rate of nonreporting because police use of force (along with other kinds of improper behavior) is a rare phenomenon. Attempting to measure it through conventional social survey techniques requires an extremely large sample—to the point where the cost becomes prohibitive. The Justice Department's 1996 study of police use of force surveyed 6,421 citizens and found that police were alleged to have used force in only 1 percent of all police–citizen interactions. None of the citizens in this survey, moreover, filed a complaint against a police officer.[13] (It should be noted that other research has found that police officers use force in only about one percent of all encounters with citizens.)[14]

Why do people not file complaints even though they are unhappy with how they were treated by the police? Although there is little research on the subject, it is reasonable to assume that the reasons closely parallel the reasons that crime victims do not report crimes to the police. The National Criminal Victimization Survey (NCVS) reports that only 38 percent of crime victims report the crime to the police. Among victims of personal crimes of violence, 19.5 percent indicate that it was a private or personal matter, while about 10 percent say that either the police would not want to be bothered or that they were ineffective or biased.[15] In short, even though something bad has happened to them, most crime victims do not report the crime.

Similar considerations undoubtedly shape citizens' response to mistreatment by the police. A series of focus groups in Omaha, Nebraska, found widespread belief that filing a complaint would do no good.[16] The ACLU of Southern California contacted seventy-seven individuals who had reported misconduct by a Los Angeles police officer to a hotline operated by Police Watch, a police monitoring group. Over half (57 percent) said they had decided not to file a formal complaint with the LAPD. Twenty percent of that group said that complaining would be futile, and 13 percent said they feared retaliation.[17] Many people simply do not want any further contact with the police; some may be involved in criminal activity; others may be worried about their immigration status; and still others may just want to be left alone.

Fear of reprisal is probably a more important factor in the nonreporting of complaints than in the nonreporting of crime. Fear of reprisal represents only 3.8 percent of the reasons why people do not report crimes against persons, and less than one percent of the reasons for not reporting property crimes, according to the NCVS.[18] The Christopher Commission found that people in Los Angeles fear what might happen to them if they do go to a police station.[19] The ACLU affiliate in Washington, D.C. found a special problem with respect to Hispanic/Latino citizens, concluding that "some members of the Latino community may not file complaints, as they are fearful of police retaliation," a fear based on the history of police retaliation in Latin American countries.[20]

Fear of police retaliation is not wholly unfounded. A special provision of California law, which was declared unconstitutional in 1999, allowed police officers to bring defamation suits against citizens who criticize them, a right that was specifically denied other government officials.[21] In New York City, one person who filed but then withdrew a complaint told the Vera Institute that the officer called him at home and said, "You're a dead mother fucker."[22] And in one of the most shocking incidents, New Orleans police officer Len Davis ordered the murder of a woman who had filed a complaint against him.[23]

Data on the age of complainants suggests one major area of nonreporting. Young people file very few complaints. In Minneapolis, 42 percent of all people filing complaints with the Civilian Review Authority (CRA) are over the age of thirty-five. Only 27 percent are under the age of twenty.[24] Yet young people and young males in particular have the highest rate of problematic contacts with the police. They are more likely to be involved in crime, to be targeted for stops and frisks, and to express disrespect for the police. The typical victim of police use of force is a young, low-income male regardless of race or ethnicity.[25] A survey of young people in Chicago found that 71 percent had been stopped by the police, and of those who were given a reason why they were stopped, 53 percent did not believe what the police told them.[26] Yet young people are significantly underrepresented in official complaint data.

The most plausible explanation for the low rate of filing complaints by young people is that they live "in the moment." When something bad happens to them (e.g., a police officer calls them a name) they are likely to just "blow it off" and move on to the next moment. The middle-aged person, on the other hand, is more likely to think in terms of his or her social status as a person deserving respectful treatment by public officials and also to think in terms of a social obligation to report official misconduct if it occurs. A number of the middle-aged participants in the Omaha focus groups indicated that they would file a complaint not because they wanted the officer punished, but because they felt they had an obligation to inform the department about officer misconduct, with some participants indicating their expectation that this would help prevent future misconduct.[27] Citizen oversight officials report that a number of complaints involving minors are in fact filed by their parents, with the result that the official data lists an adult as the complainant.

Some opponents of citizen oversight argue that citizen complaints are used by criminals in an effort to inhibit prosecution and deflect attention away from their behavior and to the police officer. Official complaint data do not support this argument, however. In New York City, for example, only about 10 percent of all complaints in 1993 arose from an incident involving the arrest or citation of the complainant.[28] As the Minneapolis data suggest, the typical complainant is not a young criminal but a middle-aged person who feels that a police officer's behavior was improper. The vast majority of these complaints involve discourtesy, rudeness, or a failure to provide adequate service and are not related to a criminal incident.

Issues for Evaluation Given the low rate at which complaints are filed and the enormous variations that exist across jurisdictions, the official complaint rate

---

1. Availability of Informational Material
   - Determine that the agency has produced the relevant material.
   - Site visits to offices of government agencies and private social service organizations to determine if materials are available.

2. Site visits to police department and/or citizen oversight offices.
   - Determine that informational materials are available and provided on request.
   - Determine that persons making inquiries about the complaint process are treated in a polite and respectful fashion.

3. General community surveys
   - Include questions related to (a) knowledge of and (b) perception of the complaint process.

4. Surveys of persons having contact with the complaint process
   - Regular customer feedback survey provided to complainants.
   - Recontact survey of persons having contact with the complaint process.

FIGURE 5-3 Research Strategies for Evaluating the Openness of a Complaint Procedure

cannot be used as a performance indicator of either the quality of police service or the complaint process. A low complaint rate, for example, could mean that the police are doing an excellent job or that the complaint process is perceived as closed and hostile to citizens. Conversely, a high volume of complaints could mean that there is a lot of police misconduct or that the complaint process is perceived to be very open and responsive.[29]

The variations in complaint rates do, however, suggest a number of issues for research. Why is the complaint rate four times higher in San Francisco than in New York City? To what extent is it a function of the quality of policing as opposed to perceptions of the complaint process.

Several research strategies can be used to investigate the openness and accessibility of complaint procedures (see Figure 5-3). First, it can easily be determined whether informational material about the complaint process exists, is widely distributed throughout the community, and is available in the appropriate languages. Second, site visits can determine whether or not there are multiple and convenient locations for filing complaints. In the largest metropolitan areas, and for state law enforcement agencies, toll-free telephone numbers are appropriate. Third, systematic community surveys can determine the level of community awareness of and confidence in the complaint process. Kerstetter and Rasinski, for example, found that citizens were aware of changes in the complaint process in Minneapolis in the 1980s and that these perceptions affected their assessment of the fairness of the system.[30] Surveys can also investigate perceptions of and experience with specific aspects of the complaint process (e.g., location of places where complaints can be filed).

Fourth, people who have contact with the police can be contacted and interviewed. Some police departments have already experimented with callbacks to people who have called 911.[31] Fifth, it is possible to include additional questions to the ADAM survey of arrestees investigating whether they are aware of the complaint process.

Complaint Intake

Assuming that a person attempts to file a complaint by personally visiting a police station or an oversight agency or by making a telephone call, a formal complaint will not necessarily be accepted and recorded.

A recurring problem across the country is that people attempting to file complaints are discouraged from doing so. Human Rights Watch concluded that "Filing a complaint is unnecessarily difficult and often intimidating."[32] An investigation by the Office of the City Auditor in Kansas City found that in sixteen test visits citizens were allowed to take the complaint form with them in only seven instances. And in several instances testers were given misinformation about how to file complaints.[33] The Christopher Commission found that people seeking to file complaints against Los Angeles police officers "face significant hurdles." Citizens told the Commission of being forced to wait for long periods of time, or being threatened with defamation suits, or in the case of Latino citizens being referred to Immigration and Naturalization Service. One audit of the LAPD "confirmed systematic failures to fill out the Form 1.81," the official citizen complaint form. Allegations were written down on a yellow legal pad ("yellow sheeting") and converted into an official complaint only when a citizen made a second visit to the police station and demanded such action.[34]

Not recording a citizen complaint is analogous to police officers' practice of unfounding—not formally recording—crimes.[35] In many instances, a citizen reports a crime but the responding police officer decides that no crime actually occurred and does not complete a crime report. This action has the effect of lowering the official crime rate. By the same token, not recording a complaint lowers the official complaint rate.

Issues for Evaluation How an agency receives complaints is an important issue for evaluation. The integrity of a complaint procedure, in Perez's terms, requires that it be open and responsive to citizens and record complaints in a fair and consistent manner. By the same token, a closed and unresponsive procedure loses legitimacy in the eyes of citizens.

A number of research strategies can be used to investigate these issues. First, actual complainants can be surveyed. The Christopher Commission contacted a sample of people who had filed complaints against the LAPD and found that about one-third described the process as "not hospitable."[36] This evaluation strategy, however, did not permit surveying those who had in fact been discouraged from filing a complaint. The Minneapolis Civilian Review Authority's Quality Service Audit (QSA) program solicits feedback from complainants and officers about the CRA process. Included are the large number of people who contact the CRA but do not file a formal complaint. This survey is designed to identify any pattern of complainants feeling they were turned away by the CRA or were otherwise discouraged from filing a complaint.[37]

Second, the nature of a complaint intake process can be investigated through simple observation or testing. The director of one oversight agency periodically makes unannounced visits to the lobby of police headquarters, where she sits and observes how citizens are treated at the front desk. In the past, many people were treated very brusquely ("What do you want?") instead of in a friendly manner. (Most of these citizens were not there to file a complaint.) Under the leadership of a new chief, however, a more friendly atmosphere began to emerge.[38] In 1997 and 1998, meanwhile, NBC *Dateline,* working with the Police Complaints Center, sent an African-American male with a concealed video camera into thirty New York City precinct stations to ask for a complaint form. He received disrespectful treatment and was not given the form in about half of the precinct stations. By any reasonable standard, this would not be a passing grade. In one station house, the officer at the desk eventually ordered the tester to "get out of my station." It should be noted that the person was merely asking for the complaint form and that half of the station house visits occurred *after* New York City Police Commissioner assured NBC that all officers had been retrained on this matter.[39]

Testing of this sort is not without precedent in policing. The New York City Commission to Combat Police Corruption initiated a Random Integrity Testing Program to root out corruption. The program involved creating situations where an officer has an opportunity to commit a corrupt act (e.g., posing as an intoxicated citizen in possession of a large amount of money) In 1995, the NYPD conducted 565 tests, involving 1,222 officers, compared with only about 100 in 1994.[40] Under Superintendent Richard Pennington, the New Orleans Police Department began a similar integrity testing (or "sting") program to identify corruption. [41]

The ACLU placed phone calls to police officials in both Los Angeles and Oakland to determine whether police officers respond promptly and politely to citizen inquiries and provide accurate information. Both police departments failed these tests. In Los Angeles, only 4.8 percent of the callers were promptly and correctly informed about the LAPD's new 800 toll-free telephone number for filing complaints. Most were put on hold, given incorrect information, or told that no such number existed.[42] A systematic set of phone calls to the Oakland police department, meanwhile, found that officers in a variety of units were unable to give correct information about how to file a complaint.[43]

The tests cited here have been directed at police department complaint procedures. Similar tests can be developed for citizen oversight agencies. Moreover, in cities where complaints can be received at either the police department or the oversight agency (and in some cities, other public agencies), a properly designed evaluation strategy can determine which office provides the most open and receptive response.

Classifying Complaints

Once a complaint has been officially recorded, it must be properly classified according to the nature of the allegation(s). The person taking the complaint may not record the incident as it was reported by the complainant. This practice is analogous to police officers who record a crime in a category different from what the citizen reports: for example, recording an alleged attempted rape as a simple assault. A citizen allegation about use of force by a police officer, for example, might be recorded as an allegation of discourtesy. The Christopher Commission cited one case where the complaint file contained photographs of the complainant with apparent evidence of having been beaten but the official classification by the commanding officer made no mention of excessive force (and the complaint ultimately was not sustained).[44]

Typically, police departments classify complaints into two general categories, representing the more serious and the less serious complaints. Figure 5-4 indicates the categories used in Kansas City.

In one of its first actions, the San Jose Independent Police Auditor (IPA) found that the San Jose Police Department was recording a number of officer misconduct allegations in the lower category of "procedural" complaints, which meant that they did not appear in the official records as "citizen complaints." Auditor Teresa Guerrero-Daley recommended and got the department to adopt a new classification procedure ensuring that all serious allegations were recorded as official complaints. As a result, the number of official citizen complaints jumped from 173 in 1992–93 to 243 in the following twelve-month period.[45] The change achieved by the IPA is one of the ways in which citizen oversight can contribute to the professionalization of a police department and ensure quality control of the complaint process.

There are other examples of how changes in complaint classification procedures radically alter the number of official complaints. In Portland, the number of complaints fell by 50 percent in 1981–82 compared with previous years because a change in classification procedures demoted "minor" complaints to a lesser category.[46] In Los Angeles, a change in the procedures for recording complaints produced a tenfold increase in the number of complaints from 1997 to 1998—from about 800 to 8,000 a year.[47]

Additional Problems with Official Complaint Data

There are a number of other problems with official complaint data. Two of the more important are discussed in the next section.

Complaints vs. Allegations Another problem with official complaint data is the lack of a standard definition of a complaint. A single complaint may consist of several different *allegations*. The allegations, moreover, may involve more than one officer. The citizen, for example, may allege that one officer used excessive physical force and also used an abusive racial epithet and that another officer used only a racial epithet. The net result is one complaint with three

Category I

Unauthorized Use of Force. Those instances where the amount of force used is more than needed to effect the arrest or apprehension of a suspect, to restrain a prisoner, or to subdue a belligerent party.

Abuse of Authority. Those instances when a sworn officer used his authority in a manner not outlined by law or his professional duties in which he gains access to buildings, materials, or information not specifically delegated to him. This category also includes orders issued by a sworn officer not in accordance with established department policy or procedure, or not in accordance with the city ordinances or state and federal law.

Discourtesy. The excessive use of rude and/or belligerent language or behavior during arrest. Also includes profanity. The use of threats and the use of language which casts aspersions upon a person's parentage, physical make-up, occupation, mental capabilities, etc.

Inappropriate Slurs. Language, conduct, or behavior, which is derogatory of a person's race, religion, creed, or nationality.

Category II

Missing Property. The taking of a suspect/prisoner's property which is unlawful, unwarranted, or unrecorded during an arrest, detention or investigation. This category also includes items removed from a vehicle during towing and while impounded.

Harassment. Unnecessary or excessive contact between a sworn officer and a citizen without real or good cause. This category may include threats of imprisonment without notification of arrest.

Violation of Department Procedures. A breach of departmental guidelines or operating procedures. Includes improper search and seizure, not advising an arrest of the Miranda warnings, etc.

Improper Police Conduct. Unnecessary or unprofessional language or actions by an officer in the discharge of duties, including traffic enforcement, general arrests, other police service and off duty employment. More serious breaches of conduct are coded as discourtesy.

Lack of Police Service. Instances where officers are either extremely slow in responding or do not respond to a scene where police intervention is deemed necessary. Includes officer's refusal to take a report where required.

FIGURE 5-4 Complaint Classifications, Kansas City

SOURCE: Kansas City Office of the City Auditor, *Performance Audit: Police Citizen Complaint Process* (Kansas City: OCA, March 2000), 21.

allegations involving two officers. In the first six months of 1998, for example, the New York City CCRB received 2649 complaints involving 3,816 separate allegations.[48]

The lack of standard definitions and a uniform classification system—that is, something equivalent to the FBI's Uniform Crime Reports (UCR) system for reported crime—means that official complaint data cannot be used to compare different police departments. One example illustrates some of the problems. Let us say that two departments each report one complaint. But in one department the complaint involved an allegation of a racial slur against one officer, while in the other department the complaint involved allegations of excessive force and a racial slur against one officer and an allegation of offensive language against a second officer. Although the official data will indicate that both departments received one complaint, the conduct of the officers in the second department is in fact much worse.

The distinction between complaints and allegations also has important ramifications for the sustain rate. In the case of one complaint with three allegations against two officers, what is the official sustain rate if only one of the allegations is sustained? Is it 33 percent (one out of three allegations), or 100 percent (one complaint with at least one allegation sustained), or 50 percent (one of the two officers receiving a sustained complaint)?

Until there are professional standards for the recording and classification of complaint data that are used by all agencies (something equivalent to the UCR), official complaint data cannot be used for purpose of comparing different agencies.

The Distribution of Types of Complaints Even taken on its own terms, the total number of officially recorded complaints masks important distinctions. One issue is the relative percentage of different types of complaints. All complaints are not equally serious. Force complaints are far more serious than discourtesy complaints. The official crime rate suffers from an analogous problem. By giving equal weight to homicides and larcenies, it can mask important variations in violent crimes between jurisdictions. In New York City, use of force complaints represent 40 percent or more of the total. In San Francisco, however, force complaints are between 10 and 15 percent of the total. Part of the explanation lies in the fact that, as noted earlier, the official complaint rate in San Francisco (53.6 per 100 officers) is four times higher than in New York City (13 per 100).[49] And as previously mentioned, San Francisco probably receives more complaints because the OCC is perceived as a more open and responsive agency than the New York City CCRB, which has been heavily criticized for its lack of responsiveness, even by the NYCLU, the strongest advocate of oversight.[50]

A higher overall volume of complaints probably means that citizens are bringing forward more complaints on less serious matters (e.g., routine discourtesy). When the police department and/or the oversight agency is perceived as being unresponsive, a higher percentage of potential complainants will feel that there is no point in filing a complaint over a relatively minor issue. By the same token, it is reasonable to speculate that as a police department improves, there will be a shift in the distribution, with an increase in the percentage of the less serious complaints, for rudeness or discourtesy, and a decrease in the relative percentage of use of force complaints. This change would reflect not a change in police performance but a change in public expectations, with more people filing minor discourtesy complaints.

Issues for Evaluation The classification of complaints raises a number of issues for evaluation. First, a review of official documents can determine whether or not the agency has a set of formal policies on the handling of complaints and whether staff members are familiar with these policies. Second, an audit of complaint files can determine whether complaints are recorded in categories consistent with complainants' versions of incidents. Third, callbacks to a sample of complainants can determine whether official complaint records accurately reflect what they initially reported.

The Problem of Controlling Discretion in Complaint Processing

Controlling the discretion of officials who process citizen complaint data is one of the major problems related to the integrity of the data and the complaint process. A basic question is whether the process should be centralized or decentralized.

The exceedingly low number of complaints under the old system in Los Angeles was the result of a highly decentralized and disorganized process. First, as already noted, many complaints were not accepted, with complainants threatened or discouraged at division stations. Second, many complaints were received and recorded by someone in the LAPD but did not enter into a centralized data system. The Los Angeles Inspector General found that the official departmental figure included only those that reached the level of a formal personnel action within the department. This did not include other citizen complaints that had come to the department's attention, such as letters sent to IAD, phone calls, walk-ins to division offices, complaints recorded in a "Sergeant's Log" or a "Watch Commander's Log," complaints related to civil suits against officers, "Comment Cards" maintained at an officer's division, or "Miscellaneous Memorandums." The Inspector General concluded that the LAPD's records were so varied and unsystematic that "it is not possible to accurately determine how many public complaints are received by LAPD in a given year."[51]

The Los Angeles experience supports the argument in favor of a centralized bureaucratic process. Other evidence also supports this approach. The reform of policing since the turn of the century has emphasized centralized control primarily through administrative rule making.[52] Recent successes in controlling police use of deadly force and high-speed pursuits adopt this approach. With respect to citizen complaints, a succession of administrative reforms in New York in the 1950s and 1960s that involved centralized record-keeping also produced a tenfold increase in the number of complaints.[53]

One possible solution to the problem of unrecorded complaints is to abolish the practice of leaving the handling of complaints to the discretion of officials. The consent decree in the U.S. Justice Department's suit against the Pittsburgh Police Department took this approach. The Supreme Court directed the Office of Municipal Investigations (OMI) to accept all complaints, specifically ordering that "there shall be no discretion by any OMI staff to not accept a complaint."[54] The Los Angeles Sheriff's Department, meanwhile, adopted a policy "to record and investigate every citizen's complaint, however trivial or inherently unbelievable."[55]

Requiring that all complaints be accepted and recorded is complicated by two factors. First, some allegations are clearly without merit. The individual may be delusional and the allegation obviously reflecting some psychological disorder. Second, some complainants quickly withdraw their complaints for personal reasons that are not known. As already noted, a certain number of people go to a police office with the intent of filing a complaint but in the end do not do so. They may be satisfied with the explanation they receive or they may be intimidated out of filing a complaint by the police. Others file a complaint but subsequently withdraw it. Interviews with individuals who filed but subsequently withdrew complaints with the New York City CCRB revealed a wide range of motives for withdrawing: They had received an apology from the officer; they did not want to hurt the officer's career; some who had filed on behalf of another person withdrew the complaint at that person's request; they aspired to become police officers and did not want to hurt their chances; they feared retaliation; they thought it would take too much time; they felt nothing good would result; and so on.[56]

The New York CCRB records withdrawn cases as "administratively truncated." There are several problems with this category, however. We do not know whether some of those people were intimidated into withdrawing, or, discouraged by the lack of response they received. In short, the decision to withdraw a complaint may be influenced by improper action on the part of the agency.

Attractive though it might appear, the idea of abolishing all discretion with respect to complaint intake is not a cure-all. First, long experience with other aspects of the criminal justice system clearly suggests that "abolishing" discretion is neither desirable nor likely to be effective. With respect to police discretion, bail, plea bargaining, sentencing and other key decisions, knowledgeable experts long ago abandoned abolition as a reform strategy.[57] The problem is that some procedure for early screening of complaints is necessary. A certain number of complaints are in fact without merit and can be readily identified as such. The staff of the Minneapolis CRA, for example, have experience with both chronic "repeaters" and individuals who are delusional or otherwise without a valid complaint.

Purely from the standpoint of maintaining an efficient complaint process, it would be a good idea to screen out obviously meritless cases at an early point and to make distinctions between serious and less serious cases. The Boise ombudsman, for example, conducts a full investigation of all Class I complaints. At its discretion, it may refer less serious Class II complaints to the police department for investigation, thereby conserving its resources for the more serious Class I cases.[58]

Recording *all* citizen contacts and informal inquiries is an important means of documenting the activity of a complaint procedure. Both the Minneapolis Civilian Review Authority (CRA) and the Boise ombudsman record and report all contacts.

A fully decentralized complaint process, where complaints are heard and resolved at the precinct or neighborhood basis, has some merit, at least in theory. Citizens would have a chance to talk directly with someone in authority (e.g., a precinct commander with supervisory authority over the accused officer), and the process could be speedy and informal as opposed to time consuming and bureaucratic. The historical evidence, however, weighs strongly in favor of centralization and formal recordkeeping.

Sustained Complaints

To this point we have addressed problems with the number of complaints—the denominator in the sustain rate equation. There are additional problems with the number of complaints officially sustained—the numerator in the sustain rate equation. As discussed previously, there are no professional standards as to whether the official sustain rate should be based on complaints or individual allegations. If one out of three allegations in one complaint is sustained, is the sustain rate 33 percent or 100 percent?

One of the major issues regarding the disposition of complaints is whether the disposition (e.g., not sustained, exonerated, etc.) is reasonably related to the facts of the case. One of the persistent problems with internal police investigations is that complaints are not sustained when the facts reasonably suggest that the officer did engage in the alleged misconduct. This issue is at the heart of the longstanding criticism that internal police department investigations are whitewashes that systematically excuse police misconduct. There is, unfortunately, no easy solution to this problem. Incidents that give rise to complaints often involve matters of perception. What appears to be unreasonable use of force by a police officer to one person will appear to be reasonable and justifiable to another person. What appears to be threatening behavior by a citizen to one person will appear to be nonthreatening to another.

A crucial aspect of this issue is the quality of complaint investigations. A disposition may be reasonably related to the evidence in the complaint file, but the important question is whether the investigation was thorough and succeeded in gathering all possible evidence. The subject of the quality of complaint investigations, including the standards for thoroughness and fairness, are examined in detail in Chapter 6.

Issues for Evaluation The issue of whether complaints are properly disposed of can be investigated through an audit of complaint files. Police consultant Lou Reiter's manual on internal investigations recommends that police chiefs conduct an annual audit of departmental investigative files. These audits should focus on three particular issues: a lack of consistency in investigations, failure to follow department policies and procedures, and "inappropriate adjudications and recommendations."[59] Audits should not just focus on particular cases where the investigation may have been inadequate but also look for general patterns of inappropriate dispositions. There will always be cases where reasonable and fair-minded people will disagree. This is particularly true with complaints against the police, which so often involve ambiguous facts and conflicting testimony and call for difficult judgments. Identifying patterns of inappropriate dispositions should point toward needed corrective action, such as retraining for one or more investigators, the dismissal of particularly bad investigators, or the development of investigative guidelines. These possibilities are discussed in more detail in Chapter 6.

Feedback to Complainants and Officers

One of the greatest sources of discontent among complainants is the lack of feedback about the status of their complaints. Citizens claim that they file complaints but then never hear anything from the police department. Complainants not only want information about the status of the investigation (completed, not completed), but also details about the disposition and the reasons a particular decision was made. Lack of information about the status of investigations is aggravated by the pervasive problem of long delays in reaching final dispositions.

Typically, police departments provide no updates about the status of investigations. Additionally, final disposition letters usually provide little detail, simply stating that the complaint was or was not sustained. In the case of complaints not sustained, no explanation is provided for the reasons for that decision. In the case of sustained complaints, no explanation is given of what disciplinary action was taken against the officer or officers involved. In many departments, the release of information about disciplinary actions is severely restricted by the police union contract. From a procedural justice standpoint, the lack of information is probably a greater source of discontent than the actual outcome of cases.[60] Complainants often feel that their complaint was simply not taken seriously by the police department.

At the same time, police officers are often equally upset about the lack of feedback about the status of complaints against them. The Portland auditor, for example, found the case of one officer who was frustrated over the fact that a complaint against him was still unresolved after nine months and where the investigation did not even begin until four months after the incident.[61] Although as members of the department they may have access to informal channels of information, internal affairs units are often regarded as unresponsive. As with complainants, this problem is aggravated by the chronic delays in completing complaint investigations. In 1999, the commander of the internal affairs unit in the Portland Police Bureau began the practice of not only providing complainants with detailed explanations of why a disposition was made, but also of sending copies of the letter to the officer who was the subject of the complaint. The officers greatly appreciated the feedback and the practice apparently had a very positive effect on morale.[62]

Issues for Evaluation   The feedback process involves a number of issues for evaluation. An audit of the complaint process can determine an agency's official policy on notifying complainants and police officers. Such an audit should also determine the extent to which the feedback is in fact provided in accordance with official policy. Surveys of complainants and officers can determine whether they are satisfied with the timeliness and quality of the feedback they receive.

Resources and Staffing

As noted in Chapter 3, the effectiveness of a complaint review procedure depends on the level of resources and the quality of the staff. And as also noted, there are no professional standards in either the law enforcement or the citizen oversight professions on minimum standards. The only existing standard is the San Francisco policy requiring one investigator for every 150 sworn officers. There are no published standards related to qualifications or training of staff, however.

Issues for Evaluation In the absence of any other standards, the San Francisco 1:150 investigator to sworn officer ratio can be used to evaluate the level of staffing in a complaint agency. This is an extremely high standard. The Minneapolis Civilian Review Authority has only about half that level of staffing. Other oversight agencies, however, are even less adequately staffed.

On the subject of the selection and training of investigators, there are some different standards that apply to police departments as opposed to citizen oversight agencies. Oversight agencies have a broader pool of potential job candidates to draw from. Police departments are limited to those individuals who are already sworn officers. For the police, the relevant questions include whether or not the chief has full discretion in selecting internal affairs investigators. In some departments, the chief can select whomever he or she wishes. In others, however, appointments are bound by a rigid seniority system and a chief is often forced to appoint officers who do not want this assignment and whom the chief would not otherwise pick. Such a situation does not seem likely to guarantee high standards of accountability.

The basic issue for evaluation of training is whether the complaint agency provides training that is specifically related to investigating citizen complaints. The common practice in police departments appears to be to select for internal affairs units officers who have criminal investigation experience. There is good reason to assume, however, that citizen complaints are different from criminal cases in important ways. The crucial difference is that an officer is investigating fellow officers. This factor suggests that special training for complaint investigators is warranted.

A final issue for evaluation involves the nature of supervision and performance evaluation provided for investigators. Obviously, there should be regular review of complaint investigations by supervisors. Such reviews are meaningful, however, only if there are clearly established performance standards related to the thoroughness and fairness of investigations. These issues are discussed in Chapter 6. Unfortunately, little attention has been given to these issues, by either the law enforcement or citizen oversight professions.

Summary The preceding discussion highlights the need for the development of professional standards related to the staffing of complaint investigations. We cannot at present evaluate complaint procedures because we have no generally accepted standards by which to judge them. This subject should be high on the agenda of professional associations in law enforcement—the Police Executive Research Forum (PERF), the International Association of Chiefs of Police (IACP), the National Sheriffs Association (NSA)—and citizen oversight associations—the National Association for Citizen Oversight of Law Enforcement (NACOLE) and the International Association for Citizen Oversight of Law Enforcement (IACOLE).

Cost Effectiveness

In *Common Sense about Police Review,* Douglas Perez raises serious questions about the cost effectiveness of citizen oversight. The only serious attempt to do a cost-effectiveness analysis was done by the Minneapolis Redesign Team in 1997. It found that the CRA spent $3,649 per case investigated, compared with $6,278 per case for the police department's IAD unit. It then asked the relevant question of what would the cost to the city be if the CRA were eliminated (the Redesign Team evaluation was prompted, in part, because some officials in the city wanted to abolish it). Assuming that all CRA cases would be handled by IAD and that IAD investigators would maintain the same caseloads, the result would be a net cost increase of about $77,000 to the city.[63] Minneapolis was substantially more cost effective than the Berkeley Police Review Commission ($8,571 per case), but less than the Pittsburgh Office of Municipal Investigations (OMI) ($872 per case). The consent decree in the federal civil rights suit against the Pittsburgh Police Department that year, however, suggested that the OMI was not a model of complaint review.[64]

At present, there are no well-defined criteria for cost effectiveness in the area of complaint investigation. This is another item that needs to be developed as part of a set of professional standards for complaint investigations, along with recommended caseloads and personnel standards.

Summary Nothing is more likely to guarantee an ineffective complaint procedure than a lack of resources. Ensuring adequate resources and properly trained and supervised staff members is essential to the integrity of a complaint procedure.

COMPARING INTERNAL AND EXTERNAL COMPLAINT PROCEDURES

One of the main issues in the political debate over citizen oversight has been the question of whether it results in more sustained complaints than police internal complaint investigations. As we argued earlier in this chapter, this debate is misguided because the many problems with official complaint data render the sustain rate an invalid performance measure. Nonetheless, it is important to examine the evidence that is commonly cited in the debate over comparative sustain rates because that evidence has been seriously misinterpreted.

The original evidence in this debate is James Hudson's evaluation of the Philadelphia Police Advisory Board (PAB) in the late 1950s and 1960s.[65] Hudson compared the disposition of citizen complaints handled by the PAB with a set of cases handled by the police department's internal Police Board of Inquiry (PBI). The PBI cases included complaints filed by departmental personnel as well as by citizens. At first glance, the data suggested that the PBI was tougher on discipline than the PAB. Only 15 percent of the PAB cases resulted in a suspension or dismissal, compared with 66 percent of the citizen-generated PBI cases and 81 percent of the department-generated PBI cases.[66]

Hudson quickly warned, however, that the data were "far from conclusive." The PAB and the PBI had very different mandates and as a result handled very different kinds of cases. The PAB accepted virtually any kind of complaint for review. The police department, on the other hand, forwarded to the PBI only those cases where there was reasonably good evidence to support the allegation, screening out the weak cases. The result is that the PBI's sustain rate is based only on those most likely to be sustained. This is analogous to a prosecutor dismissing weak cases and basing the conviction rate only on the remaining strong cases.[67]

Moreover, relatively few of the PBI cases involved accusations of excessive force, whereas two-thirds of the PAB cases involved allegations of either brutality or harassment. As most experts on this subject recognize, force and harassment allegations are the most difficult to sustain. The facts are often ambiguous, with no physical evidence or witnesses that clearly support either side. The PBI, meanwhile, primarily handled allegations related to neglect of duty, disobedience of orders, and intoxication. Such allegations are the most clear-cut and easiest to resolve (e.g., the officer was or was not drunk on duty or failed to respond to a call). Thus, the PBI (and by extension other internal complaint procedures) has a natural advantage with respect to its official sustain rate—an advantage that is independent of the quality of its investigations.[68]

Because of these factors, Hudson concluded that it was not possible "to conclude whether [the PBI or the PAB] is the better method of resolving police-citizen altercations."[69] Critics of citizen oversight have blatantly ignored this explicit stricture and, citing Hudson either explicitly or implicitly, continue to argue that police internal affairs units are tougher on discipline than oversight agencies.[70] In passing, it is also important to note that Hudson's study was published in 1972 and is based on data from the late 1950s and early 1960s. In short, it represents the "stone age" of citizen oversight and should not have an undue influence on contemporary policy debates.

Additional Considerations

Apart from Hudson's study, there remains the question of whether complaint officials who are not police officers are more lenient than police themselves. One aspect of this matter involves discipline cases that are appealed outside the police department. Such appeals are heard by civil service boards or arbitrators, depending upon the jurisdiction. In many jurisdictions there appears to be a pattern of outside decision makers who significantly mitigate the punishments handed out by police chiefs. In Chicago, for example, arbitrators fully reversed about 40 percent of all suspensions (in the 1 to 30 day range), fully upheld about 40 percent, and rendered split decisions in the remaining 20 percent.[71] And, it should be noted, these cases included only those where the department believed it had sufficient evidence to make discipline stick. The weak evidence cases were screened out earlier. In short, officers who are in fact disciplined by their departments have—at least in some jurisdictions—a very good chance of having the decision overturned if they take an appeal to nonpolice decision makers. Police chiefs complain bitterly over the fact that officers they fire are occasionally returned to the department as the result of an appeal.

The success that officers have in appealing discipline to nonpolice decision makers has not been adequately researched, and the actual dynamics of these decisions are not known. One important factor involves the quality of legal representation. On appeal, police officers are generally represented by police union attorneys, who, as a general rule, are experienced and aggressive. Renewal of their retainer, moreover, depends in part on a good record in such disciplinary appeals. The police department, meanwhile, is generally represented by lawyers from the city attorney's office, who generally have civil service protection and, in some jurisdictions at least, owe their jobs to their political connections. In short, there is some question about the relative quality of the legal representation in police discipline appeal cases.

INHERENT PROBLEMS IN INVESTIGATING CITIZEN COMPLAINTS

One of the basic assumptions underlying citizen oversight is that it will sustain more complaints than internal police review procedures. Advocates of oversight are often shocked and disillusioned to discover that the sustain rate of a newly created oversight agency is not much different than the old internal affairs unit's sustain rate. The overriding fact, however, is that citizen complaints against police officers are *inherently* difficult to sustain. This is a result of the nature of police work and citizen complaints about misconduct, and it poses problems for all forms of investigation, internal and external alike.

First, most police patrol work involves officers working alone or in pairs, with no other officers or citizen witnesses present. The Police Services Study (PSS) found no bystanders in half (52.3 percent) of the 5,688 police-citizen encounters.[72] As a result, there are often no independent witnesses to the incident that gave rise to a complaint. The witnesses who are present, moreover, are often presumptively biased toward one side or the other. They include either friends of the complainant or fellow police officers. And because of the "code of silence" among officers, the other officers cannot be presumed to be independent sources of information, willing to provide testimony against other officers. As a result, many complaints become the proverbial "swearing contest" between the complainant and the officer.

Second, the typical complaint does not involve any physical evidence of police abuse. The typical complaint is not a Rodney King–style beating but rather an incident of discourtesy, abusive language, racial or ethnic slurs or a relatively low level of police use of force—a push or a blow that leaves no bruise or other evidence. Relatively few complaints involve a level of force that requires medical attention. The New York City CCRB found injuries in only 8 percent of all complaints and in only 11.5 percent of all use-of-force complaints.[73] It is also important to note that "force" is a very broad category, and in some jurisdictions it includes any physical restraint of a person and use of handcuffs (the Miami-Dade Police Department, for example, uses the very broad category "control of person"). In short, few complaints leave any forensic evidence that investigators can use to support an allegation.

Third, and closely related to the absence of physical evidence, is the fact that most complaint-related incidents are ambiguous. That is to say, it is simply not clear what happened, who did what, or whose behavior initiated the conflict. The officer may in fact have used force but it is often not provable that the force was unjustified. In many cases, both the officer and the citizen used some kind of force, but it is impossible to reconstruct the scenario and determine whether the officer's actions were provoked by a threatening action by the citizen or whether the citizen's actions were in response to an unprovoked use of force by the officer.

Fourth, the ambiguity of incidents is compounded by the fact that police officers have an inherent justification for using force. By law, they are empowered to use force to effect an arrest, overcome resistance to arrest, bring a threatening situation under control, or for their own protection. In the absence of clear evidence that the officer's use of force was excessive or unjustified, the law is on the side of the officer. (The issue of "the tie goes to the officer" is discussed in Chapter 3, pp. 74–75.) This is an inherent aspect of police work that affects all complaint investigations, whether they are conducted by internal or outside investigators.

Two aspects of this point deserve comment. It must be said that the fact that the law inherently favors them has encouraged officers to stretch the truth in complaint investigations and to describe the events in ways that justify their actions. The simplest approach is to claim that the citizen attacked or threatened the officer. Officers soon learn that authorities—complaint investigators, judges, juries—generally give them the benefit of the doubt in any ambiguous situation. This point is at the heart of the critical issue of police perjury. The historic "code of silence" developed because officers learned that there was no risk of punishment for backing up fellow officers, no matter how incredible the tale.

At the same time, the fact that the law inherently favors officers provides important justification for independent investigation of complaints. The ambiguity of complaint incidents can be overcome primarily by corroborating evidence. Finding this evidence requires thorough investigations that actively seek out potential witnesses or physical evidence. Ambiguity can also be overcome by unbiased investigations, including primarily interviews that probe and challenge weaknesses in officer testimony. The great failure of internal police investigations is that officers' testimony is too often taken at face value or that officers are asked leading questions by investigators.

Because of widespread public misunderstanding about the subject of "police brutality," it is important to explain further the relatively low incidence of serious physical abuse. Serious beatings of citizens by police officers dominate the public image of this issue. For many citizens, the phrase "police brutality" conjures up images of the Rodney King beating or the grotesque abuse of Abner Louima in New York City. Such cases, however, are comparatively rare. They are classic examples of the "celebrated case," the kind of case that dominates the news and shapes public consciousness but is atypical of most cases (which, of course, is why they make the news).[74] The typical citizen complaint against a police officer involves relatively minor abuse: discourtesy, name calling, racial or ethnic slur, or a shove that leaves no injury. "Minor," in this context, does not mean justified or excusable abuse. It means minor relative to a serious beating that results in injuries requiring medical attention.

A similar gap between image and reality exists with respect to hate crimes, or offenses motivated by racial, religious, or sexual orientation bias. When the term "hate crime" arises, most people conjure up images of a Ku Klux Klan lynching or the brutal murder of a gay student in 1998. The reality is that most hate crimes are low-level misdemeanor assaults, often involving an attack by a group of juveniles against a single person of another racial or ethnic group. These relatively minor assaults are also difficult to document.[75]

The fact that most complaints are relatively minor has other important ramifications. Many community activists discuss complaint procedures in the same breath with civil suits and criminal prosecution of police officers. The fact is, however, that the typical complaint does not raise the possibility of either action. The harm in most cases is, by the prevailing standards of tort actions, of such a low level that it would not produce any meaningful monetary damage award. And, as already mentioned, the lack of physical evidence would make proving it difficult at best. Additionally, prosecution of an officer requires proof of criminal intent. This is an extremely high standard that is difficult to meet even in the most extreme cases, as the Rodney King case illustrated. Police officers can always claim that their actions were justified by the circumstances, usually that the person was threatening the officer or resisting arrest. In short, criminal prosecution is relevant as a remedy for only a very small number of complaint incidents.[76]

For all of these reasons—lack of witnesses, forensic evidence, or sufficient seriousness to warrant civil litigation—citizen complaints are inherently difficult to investigate and even harder to sustain. The important point is that this problem arises for *both citizen oversight procedures and police internal affairs units.* Investigators with citizen oversight agencies face the same problem of documenting a complaint as do internal affairs units, and it is unreasonable to expect that these agencies will have significantly higher sustain rates than police internal affairs units.[77]

CONCLUSION

Is independent review of complaints against the police effective? As this chapter has argued, there is no simple answer to this question. Complaint procedures have many different aspects, and several of them are extremely difficult to evaluate in the best of circumstances. There are many problems with the official data on complaints, and obtaining the data necessary to answer a number of important questions is both difficult and expensive. One point is clear, however: The traditional focus on the sustain rate is an inappropriate way to measure the effectiveness of any complaint procedure.

The three criteria defined by Perez provide a useful framework for evaluating complaint procedures. A complaint procedure has *integrity* if it is thorough and fair. This chapter has covered several aspects of complaint procedures that affect integrity. A complaint procedure has integrity if it is open and accessible to the public and if it receives, records, and classifies complaints in a reasonable and consistent fashion; investigates complaints in a thorough and fair manner; and reaches dispositions that are reasonably related to the facts of the case.

A complaint procedure has *legitimacy* if it is perceived to have integrity by the relevant clients, stakeholders, and audiences. Specifically, is the process perceived to be open and accessible by the public, and is it perceived to be fair and legitimate by both complainants and police officers, and by other members of the community?

Finally, a complaint procedure meets the criterion of *learning* if it provides meaningful feedback to responsible officials in a way that allows them to make improvements in both the complaint procedure and the police department. Learning-related activities of citizen oversight of the police are covered in greater detail in the following chapter on the monitoring role of oversight.

NOTES

1. Douglas Perez, *Common Sense about Police Review* (Philadelphia: Temple University Press, 1994).

2. Human Rights Watch, *Shielded from Justice* (New York: Human Rights Watch, 1998), 59–60.

3. Anthony M. Pate and Lorie A. Fridell, *Police Use of Force,* (Washington, DC: The Police Foundation, 1993), 1:114.

4. Aryeh Neier, "Civilian Review Boards —Another View," *Criminal Law Bulletin* 2:8 (1966): 10–18.

5. This estimate is based on a review of oversight agency annual reports in the author's files. Minneapolis Civilian

Review Authority, *Annual Report 1999* (Minneapolis: MCRA, 2000).

6. Maguire in Andrew Goldsmith, ed., *Complaints against the Police: The Trend to External Review* (Oxford: Clarendon Press, 1991), 188.

7. Herman Goldstein, *Policing a Free Society* (Cambridge: Ballinger, 1977).

8. Geoffrey Alpert and Mark H. Moore, "Measuring Police Performance in the New Paradigm of Policing," in Bureau of Justice Statistics, *Performance Measures for the Criminal Justice System* (Washington, DC: Government Printing Office, 1993), 109–42; Goldstein, *Policing a Free Society.*

9. Anthony M. Pate and Edwin E. Hamilton, *The Big Six* (Washington, DC: The Police Foundation, 1991).

10. Ibid., 144. The Police Foundation's later study of police use of force reports data for different types of law enforcement agencies and for different size agencies, but the data involve only complaints related to use of force: Pate and Fridell, *Police Use of Force.*

11. Ronald Kahn, "Urban Reform and Police Accountability in New York City, 1950–1974," in R. Lineberry and L. Masotti, eds., *Urban Problems and Public Policy* (Lexington: Lexington Books, 1975), 107–27.

12. Samuel Walker and Nanette Graham, "Citizen Complaints in Response to Police Misconduct: The Results of a Victimization Survey," *Police Quarterly,* 1:1 (1998): 65–89.

13. Bureau of Justice Statistics, *Police Use of Force: Collection of National Data* (Washington, DC: Government Printing Office, 1997).

14. Kenneth Adams, "Measuring the Prevalence of Police Abuse of Force," in William A. Geller and Hans Toch, *And Justice For All: Understanding and Controlling Police Abuse of Force* (Washington, DC: Police Executive Research Forum, 1995), 61–97.

15. Bureau of Justice Statistics, *Criminal Victimization in the United States, 1994* (Washington, DC: Government Printing Office, 1997), 94–95.

16. Many of the participants in a series of focus groups expressed fatalism about filing complaints against the police: Samuel Walker, "Complaints against the Police: A Focus Group Study of Citizen Perceptions, Goals, and Expectations," *Criminal Justice Review* 22 (Autumn 1997): 207–25.

17. ACLU of Southern California, *The Call for Change Goes Unanswered* (Los Angeles: ACLU-SC, 1992), 29.

18. Bureau of Justice Statistics, *Criminal Victimization in the United States, 1994* (Washington, DC: Government Printing Office, 1997), 94–95.

19. Christopher Commission, *Report of the Independent Commission to Investigate the Los Angeles Police Department* (Los Angeles: Christopher Commission, 1991).

20. ACLU–National Capital Area, *Analysis of the District of Columbia's Civilian Complaint Review Board and Recommendations For its Replacement* (Washington, DC: ACLU-NCA, 1995), 37.

21. "ACLU Challenges Statute," *San Diego Union-Tribune,* 15 November 1998; Michael S. Vaughn, "Police Civil Liability and the First Amendment: Retaliation Against Citizens Who Criticize and Challenge the Police, *Crime and Delinquency* 42 (January 1996): 50–75.

22. Michele Sviridoff and Jerome E. McElroy, *Processing Complaints against Police: The Complainant's Perspective* (New York: Vera Institute, 1989), 77.

23. "Officer Linked to Killing, Shocking Jaded City," *New York Times* 19 December 1994, A8.

24. Minneapolis Civilian Review Authority, *1997 Annual Report,* exhibit C, 2. The Police Foundation survey collected data on gender, race, and ethnicity, but not on the age of complainants: Pate and Fridell, *Police Use of Force.*

25. Albert Reiss, *The Police and the Public* (New Haven: Yale University Press, 1971).

26. Warren Friedman and Marsha Hott, *Young People and the Police: Respect, Fear and the Future of Community Policing in Chicago* (Chicago: Chicago Alliance for Neighborhood Safety, 1995).

27. Walker, "Complaint against the Police."

28. New York City, Civilian Complaint Review Board, *Status Report, July-December 1993* (New York: CCRB, 1993), 43. Unfortunately, more recent reports by the CCRB do not include data on this subject.

29. Samuel Walker, "A Primer on Police Complaint Data," *Subject to Debate* 12 (January/February 1998): 6–7. A good discussion of the ambiguous nature of official complaint data is found in Vera Institute, *Respectful and Effective Policing: Two Examples in the South Bronx* (New York: Vera Institute, 1999).

30. Wayne A. Kerstetter and Kenneth A. Rasinski. "Opening a Window into Police

Internal Affairs: Impact of Procedural Justice Reform on Third-Party Attitudes." *Social Justice Research,* 7 (1944, No. 2): 107–27.

31. Stephen Mastrofski, "Surveying Clients to Assess Police Performance: Focusing on the Police-Citizen Encounter," in Gordon P. Whitaker, ed., *Understanding Police Agency Performance* (Washington, DC: Government Printing Office, 1984), 111–20. Bureau of Justice Assistance, *A Police Guide to Surveying Citizens and Their Environment* (Washington, DC: Government Printing Office, 1993).

32. Human Rights Watch, *Shielded from Justice,* 50.

33. Kansas City Office of the City Auditor, *Performance Audit: Police Citizen Complaint Process* (Kansas City: Office of the City Auditor, March 2000), 13.

34. Christopher Commission, *Report of the Independent Commission on the Los Angeles Police Department* (Los Angeles: Christopher Commission, 1991), 158–59.

35. Donald Black, *The Manners and Customs of the Police* (New York: Academic Press, 1980).

36. Ibid., 159.

37. This author helped design the Minneapolis CRA Quality Service Audit program.

38. Interview, director (anonymity requested).

39. NBC *Dateline,* August 18 1998.

40. KPMG, *The New York City Police Department Random Integrity Testing Program* (New York: KPMG, 1996); Commission to Combat Police Corruption, *First Report of the Commission* (New York: The City of New York, 1996), 66.

41. New Orleans Police Department, Public Integrity Division, Memorandum, Integrity Tests, 1997.

42. ACLU–Southern California, *The Call for Change Goes Unanswered* (Los Angeles: ACLU-SC, 1992), 2, 20–27.

43. ACLU–Northern California, *Failing the Test: Oakland's Police Complaint Process in Crisis* (San Francisco: ACLU-NC, 1996).

44. Ibid., 163–64.

45. San Jose, Independent Police Auditor, *First Quarterly Report,* (San Jose, December 1993), 10; San Jose, Independent Police Auditor, *Year-End Report* (San Jose, December 1994), 9.

46. Annette I. Jolin and Don C. Gibbons, "Policing the Police: The Portland Experience," *Journal of Police Science and Administration* 12 (September 1984): 320.

47. "New LAPD Complaint-Logging System Makes Mark," *Los Angeles Times* 25 February 1998; see also Pate and Hamilton, *The Big Six,* 257–62.

48. New York City, Civilian Complaint Review Board, *Semiannual Status Report, January–June 1998* (New York: CCRB, 1998), 31.

49. San Francisco, Office of Citizen Complaints, *1997 Annual Report;* New York CCRB, *Semiannual Status Report, January–June 1998.*

50. New York Civil Liberties Union, *Third Anniversary Overview of the Civilian Complaint Review Board* (New York: NYCLU, 1996).

51. Inspector General, *Sixth Month Report, 1997* (Los Angeles: The Police Commission, 1997), 13–15.

52. Walker, *Taming the System; A Critical History of Police Reform* (Lexington: Lexington Books, 1977).

53. Ronald Kahn, "Urban Reform and Police Accountability in New York City: 1950-1974," in R. Lineberry and L. Masotti, eds., *Urban Problems and Public Policy* (Lexington: Lexington Books, 1975), 107–27.

54. *United States v. City of Pittsburgh* (1997).

55. Special Counsel to the Los Angeles Sheriff's Department, *6th Semiannual Report* (Los Angeles, September 1996), 44.

56. Sviridoff and McElroy, *Processing Complaints against the Police,* 76–79.

57. Samuel Walker, *Taming the System* (New York: Oxford University Press, 1994).

58. Boise, Ombudsman, *Policies and Procedures* (Boise, 1999), chap. 2, 2.

59. Lou Reiter, *Law Enforcement Administrative Investigations,* 2nd ed. (Tallahassee: Lou Reiter and Associates, 1998) 15.1.

60. E. Allen Lind and Tom R. Tyler, *The Social Psychology of Procedural Justice* (New York: Plenum, 1988).

61. Portland PIIAC, *First Quarter Monitoring Report, 1998* (Portland, 1998), 7.

62. Interview, Commander, Internal Affairs Unit, Portland Police Bureau, 2000.

63. Minneapolis Civilian Review Authority, *Redesign Team Report* (Minneapolis: MCRA, 1997), 18–19.

64. Ibid., 20.

65. James R. Hudson, "Organizational Aspects of Internal and External Review of the Police," *Journal of Criminal Law, Criminology and Police Science* 63 (September 1972): 427–33.

66. For similar patterns, see Minneapolis Civilian Review Authority, *Redesign Team Report,* 18.

67. Bureau of Justice Statistics, *The Prosecution of Felony Arrests, 1988* (Washington, DC: Government Printing Office, 1992); Samuel Walker, *Sense and Nonsense about Crime,* 4th ed. (Belmont, CA: Wadsworth, 1998).

68. See, for example, the different caseloads in the department studied in Kim Michelle Lersch and Tom Mieczkowski, "An Examination of the Convergence and Divergence of Internal and External Allegations of Misconduct Filed Against Police Officers," *Policing: An International Journal of Police Strategies and Management* 23:1 (2000): 54–68.

69. Hudson, "Organizational Aspects of Internal and External Review of the Police."

70. Perez, *Common Sense about Police Review,* 138–39.

71. Mark Iris, "Police Discipline in Chicago: Arbitration or Arbitrary?" *Journal of Criminal Law and Criminology* 89 (Fall 1998): 215–44.

72. Robert Worden, "The Causes of Police Brutality," in W. A. Geller and H. Toch, eds., *And Justice for All* (Washington, DC: PERF, 1995), 43. The most recent and most comprehensive observational study of police found that one officer was present in about half of all encounters and two officers present in another one-third, for a combined total of over 80 percent: Stephen D. Mastrofski, Roger B. Parks, Albert J. Reiss, Jr., Robert E. Worden, Christina DeJong, Jeffrey B. Snipes, and William Terrill, *Systematic Observation of Public Police: Applying Field Research Methods to Policy Issues* (Washington, DC: Government Printing Office, 1998), 25.

73. New York Civilian Complaint Review Board, *Annual Report 1990* (New York: CCRB, 1990), 15.

74. Walker, *Sense and Nonsense about Crime,* 30–32.

75. James Garofalo, "Racially Motivated Crimes in New York City," M. J. Lynch and E. B. Patterson, eds., *Race and Criminal Justice* (New York: Harrow and Heston, 1991), 161–74.

76. On criminal prosecution as a remedy for misconduct, see Human Rights Watch, *Shielded from Justice,* 85–103.

77. Gellhorn, *When Americans Complain.*

6

Evaluating the Effectiveness of the Monitoring Role

INTRODUCTION

As Chapter 4 explains, monitoring the police and the complaints process is one of the principal roles of oversight agencies. Monitoring activities include community outreach, customer assistance, policy review, enhancing public satisfaction with the complaints process, auditing the quality of complaint investigations, and cultivating a culture of professionalism in law enforcement agencies. This chapter examines the issues associated with evaluating the effectiveness of these activities. As in Chapter 5, most of the issues discussed here are equally relevant to both external citizen oversight agencies and internal police complaint procedures.

Criteria for Evaluation

As in the preceding chapter, the various aspects of the monitoring role discussed in this chapter will be considered from the perspective of Perez's three criteria for evaluation: integrity, legitimacy, and learning.[1] At the same time, a distinction will be made between process evaluation and outcome evaluation. A process evaluation considers whether or not an agency is doing what it claims to be doing. An outcome evaluation considers the impact of the activity in question.

COMMUNITY OUTREACH

The first issue in community outreach is whether an agency has any program at all. The obvious first step is to examine an agency's official documents and to interview key individuals. The annual reports of the Kansas City Office of Citizen Complaints, for example, provide no evidence of any outreach program.[2] The 1998 *Annual Report* of the San Francisco Office of Citizen Complaints, on the other hand, clearly indicates that its outreach program is a high priority item.[3]

Informational Materials

Providing information about the complaint process is the basic element of an outreach program. The first step in an evaluation strategy would be to determine whether or not any effort to provide information is being made. Are there brochures explaining the complaint process and the role of the oversight agency? Are these brochures readily available throughout the community (e.g., at public libraries, from private community groups, etc.)? In 1999, for example, the Washington, D.C. police department had no brochures or other informational material.[4] In Albuquerque, brochures existed in 1997 but were not readily available throughout the community.[5] Are these brochures available in different languages? Unannounced visits to public community centers, private social service agencies, and conversations with community leaders can readily answer these questions.

Reaching Special Populations

It is relatively simple to determine whether or not informational materials are available in languages appropriate to the local community. One of the functions of oversight agencies is to see that police departments make such information available. The Minneapolis CRA publishes brochures in eight languages, while the Portland PIIAC had to prod the Portland Police Bureau into having the complaints brochure translated into different languages.[6] Where the oversight agency is responsible for complaint intake and investigation, the question is whether the oversight agency itself has developed these materials.

In addition to assessing the availability of printed material, an evaluation would also seek to determine whether efforts are being made to reach special populations, meaning either communities where English is not spoken, or groups that are known to have had a history of conflict with the police. Have there been community meetings with such groups or special meetings with community leaders? For individual complainants, are translators available to take the initial complaint and to conduct investigations?

Community Meetings

Community meetings are one major component of the community outreach role. The Boise ombudsman reported a total of sixty meetings with community groups in its first year of operation (1999), along with forty-two meetings with law enforcement agencies.[7] A process evaluation would attempt to determine the number of meetings per year, where they are held, the average number of people attending, and the subjects discussed. An evaluation of community policing in Chicago used this approach to assess the implementation of the program.[8]

A number of questions can be asked about the frequency and location of the meetings. Is there a regular series of meetings, or do they occur randomly and on an ad hoc basis? Are there a series of meetings one year and few the next? Such an irregular pattern, for example, has characterized the New York City Civilian Complaint Review Board.[9] Are meetings held with all relevant segments of the community? In particular, is there an apparent effort to reach racial and ethnic minority communities that have a history of conflict with the police? Are meetings held in convenient community locations, or are they held in inconvenient and potentially unfriendly locations downtown?

Direct observation can be used to assess the content of community outreach meetings. What issues are discussed? Do they appear to be issues that engage the interest of those in attendance? Do meetings appear to be perfunctory and without much energy, or is there a lively discussion of relevant issues? Is there broad-based participation in meetings, or does one community member dominate the meeting and distort the agenda in an unhelpful manner? Or, conversely, does the oversight agency staff dominate? The evaluation of community policing in Chicago, for example, found that police officers tended to dominate meetings, contrary to the goals of the program.[10] With that in mind, do outreach meetings include police officers? What is the nature of their participation? Is there a meaningful dialogue with the public, or is there an apparent attempt to intimidate citizens by their presence? One evaluation strategy would be to provide a standard evaluation form to those in attendance to obtain their assessment of meetings and whether they plan to attend future ones.

Access to the Complaint Process

In terms of access to the complaint process, an evaluation would seek to determine if there are convenient alternatives for filing complaints. Can complaints be filed at police precinct stations, community centers, over the telephone, or by mail? Because they cover such large geographic areas and several different telephone area codes, New York City and Los Angeles established toll-free 800 numbers for the filing of complaints. Do other large metropolitan areas have similar toll-free numbers?

It is relatively easy to test the openness and accessibility of the complaint process. Tests similar to those used to investigate possible housing discrimination can be used. NBC *Dateline,* using a hidden video camera, encountered a hostile reception in half of the thirty precinct stations tested. The ACLU of Southern California placed a series of calls to precinct stations inquiring about a new toll-free 800 number established for filing complaints against the Los Angeles police. Only 4.8 percent of the callers were promptly given the correct number.[11] Callers were told the number did not exist or were placed on hold for long periods of time. The ACLU of Northern California conducted a similar set of phone calls to various police department offices in Oakland and found that few police officers gave accurate information about the complaints process.[12]

An outcome evaluation of community outreach programs is a relatively simple undertaking. The basic question is whether people are aware of the various aspects of the complaint procedure. The U.S. Civil Rights Commission report on the Baltimore Complaint Evaluation Board (CEB) recommended a community survey "to evaluate public awareness of the complaint procedure."[13] A survey of New York state residents in the 1980s found that only about 40% of all respondents were aware of the procedures for filing complaints.[14]

An important question is: Who should conduct such surveys? The City Auditor's office in Portland, Oregon, routinely surveys the public on their assessment of various city agencies and services.[15] In other cities, regular public opinion surveys are conducted under contract with local university research centers or private research firms. It would be relatively simple to include questions about the police complaint process in such surveys.

Using the criteria defined by Perez, a complaint procedure that has an active and effective community outreach program achieves integrity and as a consequence citizens are likely to perceive it as legitimate.

CUSTOMER ASSISTANCE

Evaluating the customer assistance function is relatively simple. The first issue is whether the agency documents all of its contacts with the public and publishes the totals in its annual report. Such documentation should be a minimal requirement for any government agency. Then oversight agencies should record the nature of each citizen's inquiry and the service that was rendered. Finally, following the example of the Minneapolis Quality Service Audit (QSA) program, the agency should provide everyone contacting it with an opportunity to evaluate the quality of the service rendered.[16]

A complaint procedure that attends to customer assistance, in terms of taking it seriously and documenting its activities, achieves integrity and is likely to score very high in terms of legitimacy.

POLICY REVIEW

The policy review function, as Chapter 4 argues, is potentially the most important role that citizen oversight can play, particularly in terms of identifying management problems that are often the underlying causes of police officer misconduct. Evaluating the effectiveness of a policy review program is very difficult, however. By definition, the outcomes are general and lie in the future. Policy review is designed to prevent problems and produce an overall improvement in the quality of police service. A process evaluation of the policy review function is relatively easy to conduct, while an outcome evaluation presents serious difficulties.

Process Evaluation of Policy Review

The first and most obvious step is simply to determine whether or not an oversight agency engages in policy review. If we assume that it is an important role for oversight, we can give a failing grade to one that does not engage in it. The Kansas City Office of Citizen Complaints (OCC), on the evidence of its annual reports, has no policy review activity.[17]

For those oversight agencies that do engage in policy review, the next step in a process evaluation would involve simply counting the number of policy recommendations made each year. Thus, for example, we would rate the San Jose Independent Police Auditor highly because it made a total of 40 policy recommendations between 1993 and the end of 1998, 38 of which were adopted (see the list in Chapter 4, p. 108).[18]

The next step would involve making qualitative judgments about the policy review process based on the nature of the issues involved. One might, for example, give a high rating to the San Francisco crowd control policy by virtue of the seriousness of the potential problems that it seeks to avert, measured in terms of the number of people likely to be involved, the First Amendment issues involved, the potential for excessive force incidents, the potential for litigation, and so on.[19] Other policy review issues might be deemed less important. The 1997 OCC policy recommendation cleaning up the language of SFPD Form #25 (see Chapter 4, p. 96), by comparison, is a housekeeping issue, with far less potential for harming people.[20]

The policy review activities of the New York City CCRB present a more difficult challenge for evaluation. The CCRB is authorized by ordinance to engage in policy review. A 1998 report by the New York Civil Liberties Union (NYCLU), however, gave these activities a mixed review. On the positive side, the CCRB issued a report on police use of pepper spray recommending greater controls over its use and succeeded in having the recommendation adopted by the NYCPD. Excessive force complaints dropped, but the decrease began in 1997 before the pepper spray report was adopted in early 1998. On the other hand, the CCRB studied the issue of hollow-point bullets and issued a report recommending their use. The NYCLU disagreed and accused the CCRB of "abdication of its oversight responsibilities," calling the report "a startlingly superficial piece of work." Based on these two reports, the NYCLU concluded that the CCRB's policy review efforts represented oversight "at its best, and worst."[21]

The NYCLU criticisms represent a substantive disagreement over the question of hollow-point bullets. A more serious problem with the CCRB's policy review role is its limited scope. It appears to be confined to a small number of high-profile issues (pepper spray and hollow-point bullets). This contrasts sharply with the policy review activities of other oversight agencies, which delve deeply into a wide range of administrative matters, such as the complaint intake process, how complaint data are recorded, and various routine on-the-street police activities.

We should not diminish the importance of such issues as pepper spray or hollow-point bullets, but a good argument can be made that in the long run the quality of policing is shaped by attention to small administrative details such as those addressed by the San Jose and Portland auditors and the Los Angeles County Special Counsel.

Another issue to be investigated is the percentage of recommendations accepted by the police department. This area also requires making some difficult qualitative assessments. The fact that a police department rejects all or most of the policy recommendations made by an oversight agency could be a commentary on the police department rather than the oversight agency. A qualitative assessment of rejected policy recommendations could help determine whether (1) the police department was being recalcitrant, or (2) the oversight agency was simply making inappropriate recommendations. The acceptance/rejection rates provide some indications of the nature of the relationship between the oversight agency and the police department. If the basic goal is a *culture of accountability*, we should look for evidence of a positive working relationship between the two agencies. This would not necessarily involve acceptance of every recommendation, but at least an atmosphere of mutual respect and a process of give and take on both sides.

Interviews with past and present officials can be used to assess the quality of the working relationship. It should be readily apparent, for example, if representatives from different agencies speak of each other with respect or, conversely, disparage their organizations and efforts. Such interviews, in fact, can provide a good assessment of the quality of a police department, in ways that go far beyond the narrow issue of policy review. Do officials exhibit an openness and responsiveness? Do they appear to be aware of the most important developments around the country? The San Francisco OCC reported in 1998, for example, that it had a very positive working relationship with the lieutenant in the legal department of the San Francisco Police Department regarding the implementation of OCC policy recommendations.[22]

The Chief of Police in Minneapolis, along with several other high-ranking officials, have spoken respectfully and favorably about the activities of the Minneapolis CRA.[23] Officials with the New York City CCRB, on the other hand, report enormous difficulties in getting routine information from the New York City Police Department.[24] Similarly, police department officials in Pittsburgh were extremely uncooperative toward the new civilian review board in its first year of operation. While hardly systematic, such reports clearly indicate very different levels of trust and cooperation between oversight agencies and their respective police departments.

The Compliance Problem

The extent to which a police department implements a policy recommendation can be conceptualized in terms of the compliance problem. Too often, official policies are nothing more than pieces of paper in the department's Standard Operating Procedure (SOP) manual. The important question is whether a policy enters into the day-to-day working world of police officers and actually affects their behavior. The compliance problem is a fundamental issue facing virtually all efforts to change police behavior. Do police officers, for example, give *Miranda* warnings as mandated by the Supreme Court?[25] Does the exclusionary rule deter illegal searches?[26] Do police officers act any differently under community policing than they did beforehand?[27] Do officers make arrests in felonious domestic violence assaults as mandated by department policy and/or state law?[28] Do police departments make a systematic effort to advise and train officers about important new court rulings? Do they make an effort to ensure that officers are knowledgeable about current law and that their performance conforms to it? These questions are both important and very difficult to answer.

Courts and legislatures may rule, but the implementation of the law is left to officers on the street. Discretion is a basic and inescapable part of policing, and while the exercise of discretion often reflects sound judgment, it also often represents an unacceptable deviation from the law.[29] The effective implementation of a policy—whether a statute, court decision, or department policy arising from an oversight agency recommendation—requires that a department make a serious effort to see that it is in fact implemented.

The auditor monitoring the Pittsburgh Police Department's compliance with the consent decree in the class action suit on excessive force developed a useful three-part definition of compliance. *Primary compliance* involves the development of a formal policy, procedure, or regulation. In short, the department has published a piece of paper stating its official policy. *Secondary compliance* involves "training, supervision, audit and inspection, and discipline to ensure that a specific policy is being implemented as designed." Finally, *operational compliance* means that "by matter of evidence" a particular policy is being implemented on a day-to-day basis.[30] Clearly, achieving and independently ensuring full operational compliance with any new policy is an enormous challenge.

John Crew, director of the Northern California ACLU Police Practices Project, cites one disturbing example of the failure of officers to comply with a new policy. One of his major achievements was the development of an "onlookers'" policy in San Jose under which police officers are instructed that bystanders have a right to observe police at work and police officers cannot order them to leave or arrest them for failing to do so. A few years after the policy was adopted, however, Crew himself was involved in an incident in which he reminded a San Jose police officer about the policy only to have the officer reply, "The what?"[31]

Outcome Evaluation of Policy Review

Evaluating the outcomes of policy recommendations is extremely difficult. The reasons for this involve the nature of policing itself. These problems, moreover, affect attempts to evaluate any and all innovative programs in policing and are not unique to the issue of citizen complaints. There are at least three distinct issues related to the implementation and impact of new policies. The first is whether the department makes a good faith effort to implement a new policy. The second is whether officers on the street comply with the policy in routine police work. The third is whether a new policy makes a difference in the quality of police services received by the public.

Measuring Changes in Police Performance

Evaluating the impact of policy review requires having systematic longitudinal data on police officer performance. Such data is necessary for identifying changes in officer behavior, such as a decline in use of excessive force, and determining whether those changes are the result of changes in departmental policy. The data, for example, might indicate fewer problems with police handling of homeless people following the implementation of a new policy on that issue. Similar data are necessary to determine the deterrent effect of any aspect of citizen oversight.

Unfortunately, no systematic data on police officer performance are available. The 1994 Violent Crime Control Act directed the U.S. Attorney General to issue an annual report on police use of force. No such reports, at least as intended by Congress and many civil rights activists, have been issued. As a 1999 Bureau of Justice Statistics report indicates, the issue of force is extremely complicated (to say nothing about other aspects of police performance) and reliable, systematic data do not exist.[32]

Several different sets of data on police performance do exist, but they are not useful for our purposes here. Most departments require officers to fill out reports on particular incidents and/or maintain a log of their activities. Such documents, however, are self-generated and presumptively self-justifying. At best, they represent the officer's definition of the situation and not the citizen's perspective. Official data on complaints are not a reliable measure of police performance, for all the reasons explained in Chapter 5.

One of the contributions of the community policing movement has been to stimulate recognition of the fact that traditional police data do not adequately measure what police do or the quality of the service that they render to the public. It is increasingly recognized that new performance measures are needed, but the development of such measures is still in its infancy.[33]

The obvious solution to the problem of inadequate data is to conduct systematic observational studies of policing. Scholars have used this technique for many years, and the proper methods are now well established. Unfortunately, research of this type is both extremely expensive and methodologically challenging. It requires systematic observation of a large sample of officers over a sufficiently representative period of time. Because of the cost, it is simply not feasible as a routine evaluation process on the part of individual agencies.[34]

Even if systematic data on routine police behavior were available for a particular department, it would not always be easy to establish a causal relationship between police behavior and the activity of an oversight agency (including policy review and other functions). In some limited cases, ascertaining the causal relationship is relatively easy. For example, it would be possible to determine the impact of a policy change related to dealing with homeless people and use-of-force incidents or citizen complaints involving the homeless. With respect to routine use of force and discourtesy complaints among the general population, however, establishing a causal link between policy change and police behavior would be far more difficult. Many factors influence police officer on-the-street behavior: changes in recruitment and training, new forms of supervision, including the training and assignment of supervisors, changes in patterns of discipline that might have some general deterrent effect. In practice, police departments are in constant states of flux (new recruits, changes in training, etc.). Assuming it were possible to ascertain a reduction in the level of discourtesy, for example, it would be difficult, if not impossible, to associate that change with some activity on the part of a citizen oversight agency.

In short, evaluating the impact of the policy review function is extremely difficult for the simple reason that police work is inherently difficult to evaluate. The problem here is fundamental to all efforts to improve policing and not limited to the issue of citizen oversight. Efforts to evaluate the impact of community policing for example, face the same problem. The proper response to this problem is not to throw up our hands and toss out the baby (in this case, oversight) with the bathwater (in this case, our inability to measure its impact on routine police behavior). The proper response is to recognize the limits of what we can measure and to explore other measures for the effectiveness of citizen oversight.

A Note on Special vs. General Deterrence

One of the goals of oversight is to deter police misconduct. Deterrence consists of two dimensions: special deterrence directed toward specific individuals (e.g., convicted offenders) and general deterrence directed toward the general population. If it is difficult to specify any general deterrent effect of citizen oversight on police officers in general, there are programs directed toward specific officers where the impact is measurable.

One of the most important developments in recent years has been the emergence of early warning (EW) systems. As described in Chapter 4, EW systems are administrative programs designed to identify officers who receive a high number of complaints and then to subject them to some form of intervention (counseling, training) designed to correct their behavior.[35]

Evaluating the impact of an EW system on officers who are subject to the program is relatively manageable. At the simplest level, it is a matter of comparing their performance records before and after the intervention. The basic question is whether their performance improved as indicated by a reduction in citizen complaints. The matter is complicated by the need to control for officers' assignment. It is possible that an officer received fewer complaints because he or she was reassigned either to a low-activity patrol area or to a nonpatrol duty. It is possible that the reassignment represented an informal strategy to remove the officer from conflict situations. The officer's record will likely indicate a reduction in the number of citizen complaints, but that will result from the reassignment and not the EW intervention. At the same time, it is important to examine an officer's record for positive performance indicators. The number of arrests might be one such indicator. The question is whether the EW intervention has the effect of causing the officer to reduce his or her level of effort altogether, with the result that there are both fewer complaints and less desirable activity.

Determining the general deterrent effect of any one change in policing is far more difficult, however. As already noted, many different factors influence police officer behavior and it is difficult to specify the impact of one factor on the performance of all officers in one department. EW systems are generally adopted as one part of a larger effort to raise standards of accountability in a department. It is difficult to isolate the impact of the EW system from other improvements in supervision and discipline that are occurring.

Civil Litigation as a Performance Measure

Civil litigation against a police department is at best an imperfect measure of officer performance. The potential indicators are the number of civil suits involving police misconduct and the amount of money paid each year to settle such suits. The reduction of civil litigation costs was one of the main reasons for the creation of the Special Counsel to the Los Angeles Sheriff's Department. Between 1992–93 and 1998–99, the litigation docket of active use-of-force cases fell from 381 to 70, while the costs of judgments and settlements dropped by half.[36] The special counsel himself argues that this improvement was the result of policy changes resulting from his investigations and recommendations. In New York City, however, a city council report found that the police department's computer system was not tied to the comptroller's computer, and as a result the department could not efficiently track officer involvement in civil suits.[37]

Civil litigation data must be interpreted with care. On the positive side, the money paid out in police misconduct litigation is a crude indicator of tangible costs to taxpayers. This is a legitimate concern of public officials and policymakers.[38]

On the negative side, however, civil litigation costs are influenced by a variety of different factors. First, there are no standards for an acceptable or "normal" level of litigation costs. All we do know is that the costs that have been reported for such cities as New York City, Detroit, Los Angeles, and Albuquerque seem extraordinarily high by any reasonable standard, and particularly so when compared with the relatively low figures for Seattle and Charlotte (Seattle, for example, paid out $180,000 in police-related cases in

1995, a figure far below that of other cities).[39] At some point in the future, it is hoped, experts on risk management may develop some rough guidelines for what a city or county should aim for in terms of civil litigation. These guidelines should be based on the number of sworn officers and could include general categories such as "unacceptable," "high," "acceptable," and "low."

Second, the volume of litigation is affected by factors unrelated to police behavior. A lawsuit represents the transformation of a *problem* into a *dispute*.[40] Individual lawyers and public interest groups play an important role in mediating that process. The rate of police misconduct litigation is probably heavily affected by the number and skills of the local civil rights bar. One particularly skilled and aggressive attorney could make an enormous difference. Attorneys willing to take on local law enforcement are undoubtedly far less available in small cities and towns, for a host of social and political reasons. Thus, small law enforcement agencies may well escape litigation altogether while cities with aggressive civil rights bars may experience a high volume of cases. Another factor is the attitude of city and county officials toward police misconduct litigation. Informal accounts indicate that some cities are "easy touches," in the sense that they readily settle out of court. Other cities, however, are reportedly aggressive in defending themselves against suits. Being an easy touch only serves to encourage litigation in cases that would probably have no chance of a settlement in another jurisdiction. Finally, litigation is undoubtedly influenced by the posture of the local courts. With respect to the criminal process, an informal but nonetheless powerful "going rate" defines the norms of prosecution and plea bargaining.[41] It may be that a similar "going rate" exists in some jurisdictions for police misconduct litigation. In short, in some jurisdictions, winning a case against the police may be next to impossible, with the result that few cases are even filed except in the most egregious instances.

A third problem with civil litigation data is that once a police department brings serious misconduct under control to the point where there are few cases, it is no longer a useful performance measure. It is a useful indicator only for the very bad departments where there is a large number of suits.

One final comment on civil litigation is appropriate at this point. A recent law review article suggests that government entities increase their potential financial exposure if they fail to develop effective complaint review procedures. Ignoring the problem of complaints may expose them to claims of deliberate indifference.[42] This exposure is likely to rise in the future, as an increasing number of cities and counties have adopted many of the complaint review activities described in this book. There is, in short, no excuse for officials not to be aware of the problem of police misconduct and the new remedies that have emerged.

Summary

As we suggested in Chapter 4, the policy review function is potentially the most important activity that oversight can undertake. It represents the best way of fulfilling the learning criterion defined by Perez and turning police departments into "learning organizations" as defined by Geller. From the perspective of this book, policy review appears to be the most effective way to bring about change in police organizations and thereby reduce the police officer behavior that leads to citizen complaints. As this section illustrates, however, evaluating the impact of policy review poses a number of serious problems. The task requires us to have systematic data on routine police behavior so that we can identify any changes that occur over time and then specify the causes of those changes. We do not have such data at present, and, as should be clear, collecting it is enormously difficult and expensive. This is not simply a problem for evaluating the effectiveness of citizen oversight. It is a problem facing attempts to evaluate community policing or any other innovation in policing.

PUBLIC ATTITUDES ABOUT THE POLICE

The goals of citizen oversight include providing satisfaction to individual complainants and enhancing public confidence in the police generally (see Chapter 3, pp. 55–56). The complaint process also needs to be satisfactory to police officers who are subject to complaints, to witnesses, and to higher-ranking police officials who are responsible for the disciplinary process. A complaint process that alienates any of these stakeholders cannot be deemed effective.

Evaluating the impact of oversight agencies on citizen satisfaction is relatively manageable. It is necessary at the outset to distinguish between two different audiences. The first group includes those people directly involved in the complaint process: individual complainants, subject police officers, and witnesses. The second group includes the general population.

Complainant Goals

The question of complainant satisfaction immediately raises an important issue that has not received sufficient attention and which has enormous implications. Satisfaction is a function of one's goals and expectations. What do people want when they file complaints against the police? What do they expect to get out of the process? The few studies that do exist on this issue raise important questions about the structure of complaint procedures.

The Vera Institute surveyed complainant goals as part of a larger evaluation of the New York City CCRB. Vera surveyed 371 complainants on their experience and perceptions of the CCRB process. With respect to their goals in filing complaints, only 20 percent had "serious" goals, defined as seeking to have the officer punished. The majority, 61 percent, had "moderate" goals, defined as seeking to have the officer reprimanded or spoken to. Finally, 19 percent had "mild" goals, defined as just having the incident reported.[43]

The Vera study concluded that the punishment-oriented procedures of the CCRB do not represent a good "fit" with complainant goals. In fact, it concluded that CCRB procedures prevent rather than facilitate serving complainant goals. One of those goals is for a face-to-face meeting with the police officer. Except for the few cases that are mediated, "CCRB investigative procedures preclude face-to-face contact between complainants and subject officers."[44] Based on his knowledge about police complaints in the United Kingdom, Mike Maguire concludes that "what complainants are seeking in most cases is not something akin to a trial and punishment of the officer concerned, but a full explanation, an apology, some pointed remarks to the officer from somebody in a senior position, and/or a clear assurance that steps will be taken to see that 'it does not happen again.'"[45]

A series of focus groups in Omaha found an even more complex mixture of goals and expectations. Participants were presented with a hypothetical incident involving a relatively low level of police misconduct and asked to discuss how they would respond to it. Many participants indicated that they would not bother to file a complaint. Among those who would file a complaint, very few said they would want the officer punished. Most indicated they wanted a chance to talk to someone and to tell their side of the story. Some indicated they wanted to meet with the officer, while others wanted to meet with a supervisor or someone else in authority. Most said they wanted either an explanation of the incident or an apology.[46]

Another group of participants in the Omaha focus groups said their goal was to have the incident documented on the officer's record. Several clearly expected that the record of their incident would be used to discipline the officer in the future if the bad behavior persisted. We might call this goal the "good citizen" response. In effect, they were saying, "I don't want anything for myself, but this behavior is unacceptable and I want to see that it does not happen again."

The Omaha study revealed important differences between groups in terms of their perception of the police, differences that have important implications for complaint procedures. Spanish-speaking Hispanic/Latino adults were clearly uninformed about the complaints process, with many apparently believing it is a criminal rather than an administrative process. Members of this group indicated tremendous reluctance to file complaints in large part because of fear of creating problems related to their jobs and immigration status. Latino college students, however, were more like their African-American counterparts: fluent in English, assimilated into American culture, alienated from the police, but not fearful of filing complaints. These responses highlighted the need for an active community outreach program directed toward immigrants and non–English-speaking persons.

Members of a gay and lesbian group expressed high levels of suspicion of harassment by the police based on sexual orientation even though no one had actually experienced police abuse.[47] Members of this group were the most adamant about wanting a personal meeting with the offending police officer and an opportunity to speak their minds. These responses suggest the need for an outreach program directed toward the gay and lesbian community as well as the need for programs such as mediation that allow for face-to-face meetings.

The Vera and Omaha studies suggest that most complaint procedures, both external and internal, are not well suited to meet complainant goals. Most represent a criminal trial model of dispute resolution that is designed to identify wrongdoing and punish the guilty.[48] With the exception of the few mediation programs that have emerged in recent years, they do not provide face-to-face encounters or facilitate explanations or apologies from officers. As for the "good citizen" goal of documenting misconduct for future reference, it is not clear that, apart from recently developed early warning systems, police departments use officers' complaint history in any systematic fashion. And, in fact, both the Christopher Commission and the Mollen Commission found cases where egregious misconduct was ignored by supervisors.[49]

Complainant and Officer Satisfaction

Surveys of complainants and police officers find widely varying levels of satisfaction with complaint procedures. Doug Perez's initial study compared the experience of complainants with several oversight agencies and both the internal and external procedures in Berkeley, California. The number of subjects in each city was very small, however, and the findings need to be regarded with some caution. (There was a low of only seven responses about the Berkeley internal affairs unit and a high of twenty-two in San Jose). The vast majority of most complainants were dissatisfied with the outcome (18 out of 22 in San Jose, for example). Nonetheless, levels of satisfaction were higher for the Police Review Commission (PRC) in Berkeley than for the police internal affairs units.[50]

The Vera Institute study of the New York City CCRB surveyed complainants and police officers. Both groups believed the process was biased against them. About two-thirds (64%) of the complainants were not satisfied with their experience. Even more ominously, people were more dissatisfied the further they went through the process. Of those who had their complaints fully investigated, 84 percent were dissatisfied, compared with only 38 percent of those who withdrew their complaints.[51]

Vera also conducted focus groups with twenty-two officers. The project had a very difficult time obtaining subjects, and its findings are based on a very unrepresentative sample of the more than 30,000 officers employed at that time by the NYPD. Not surprisingly, the officers were highly critical of the CCRB. As one explained, the process is biased against them: "You're wrong once you walk in the door." Most felt they had been treated badly by CCRB investigators, either as witnesses or subject officers. Many felt that it accepted "frivolous" complaints for investigation and that most complaints did not involve improper behavior by officers. Most were aware that the odds of having a complaint sustained were small, but they felt the investigation process was biased against them. Many officers felt they were kept in the dark about complaints until the last minute. The study also supported the idea of a "blue curtain" of silence among police officers, as several officers conceded that they would not be entirely truthful in a complaint investigation.

Most officers felt that the NYPD's increased sensitivity to citizen complaints had a negative impact on their work, creating morale problems and

encouraging less activity. Many expressed resentment that the police department did not back them up in situations where their actions were controversial
but nonetheless legal. Only one officer indicated that a new procedure for
reporting complaints, including unsubstantiated ones, had a positive effect on
his behavior. He explained that he had "learned to think like a lawyer . . . and
now "put myself in [the civilian's] shoes [to see] how he's thinking."[52]

When asked to suggest improvements in the complaints process, there was
a "strong consensus" in favor of an opportunity for face-to-face meetings with
complainants. Some saw this as an opportunity to confront complainants
("you're a liar"), while at least one other said, "I think people would have a
great respect for us if we just had a chance to talk to them." In this regard,
many officers had the same goal as many complainants. Others wanted the
CCRB to screen out the frivolous cases ("the garbage").[53]

Minneapolis Civilian Review Authority (CRA) developed a Quality Service Audit (QSA) process in 1998 (with the assistance of this author) which
provides both citizens and police officers an opportunity to evaluate their
experience with the CRA (see the excerpts in Figure 6-1). The Minneapolis
QSA is significant in two respects. First, it represents a pioneering institutionalized self-assessment process. Second, it surveys police officers as well as complainants. (It also surveys citizens who contact the CRA but who do not in the
end file a signed complaint.)

In stark contrast with the evaluations of the New York City CCRB, the
overwhelming majority of both complainants and police officers in Minneapolis expressed satisfaction with the CRA. About 80 percent of both
groups agreed with the statement that they had a chance to tell their side of
the story. Almost three-quarters (72.4 percent) of the citizens and 90 percent
of the officers felt that CRA staff members treated them with respect.[54]

Two Perspectives on Citizen and Officer Satisfaction

The work of scholars in the fields of the sociology of law and procedural justice provides two theoretical frameworks that help to place the different goals
of complainants in broader perspective.

One approach involves the different styles of law as defined by sociologist
Donald Black.[55] He characterizes the punishment-oriented criminal trial
model as a *penal* style of law. Mediation programs, or any other program
designed to facilitate face-to-face meetings, are characterized as a *conciliatory*
style of law. If a large number of complainants or potential complainants prefer the conciliatory style, then significant changes in complaint procedures are
warranted.

The field of procedural justice provides another useful framework for
understanding complainant goals. It makes a distinction between distributive
justice, which refers to outcomes (e.g., whether the complaint was sustained),
and procedural justice, which refers to how participants perceive the process
itself (e.g., were you treated fairly, or did you have a chance to express your
point of view). The fact that a significant number of complainants indicate

MINNEAPOLIS CIVILIAN POLICE REVIEW AUTHORITY
400 SOUTH FOURTH STREET, SUITE 1004
MINNEAPOLIS, MN 55415-1424
612-370-3800 Office
612-370-3846 Fax

Customer Feedback Survey

You were recently the subject of a complaint filed with the Minneapolis Civilian Police Review Authority, or were a witness officer in a complaint.

We are interested in your feedback regarding the quality of service provided by the CRA. We would greatly appreciate it if you could take just a few minutes to fill out the enclosed survey form.

Your response will be completely anonymous. Please do not indicate your name. The enclosed business reply envelope will mail your response to the City Coordinator's office.

1. Do you feel you had a chance to tell your side of the story?   Yes ___ No ___

2. Do you feel you were treated with respect?   Yes ___ No ___

3. If you accepted mediation of your complaint, was the mediation successful?
Yes ___ No ___

4. If your complaint resulted in a hearing, were you satisfied with the hearing process?   Yes ___ No ___

5. Do you feel the outcome of your contact with the CRA was fair?   Yes ___ No ___

6. Is there anything you would like to tell us about your experience with CRA?

_____

_____

_____

_____

For our records, we would like to know a few things about the nature of your complaint.

7. My complaint involved

___ Excessive Force ___ Inappropriate Conduct ___ Harassment
___ Inappropriate Use of Force ___ Failure to Provide Service ___ Theft
___ Inappropriate Language ___ Discrimination

8. I am: Male ____   Female ____

African American__ Asian American__ Hispanic/Latino__ Native American__
White__

Under age 18___   18–24 ___   25–34 ___   35 or older ___

Please return to the City Coordinator's Office, 350 South Fifth Street, Room 301M, Minneapolis, MN 55415, in the enclosed business reply envelope.
Thank you!

FIGURE 6-1 The Minneapolis Quality Service Audit (QSA)

that they want a face-to-face meeting, or simply an opportunity to express their views, suggests that procedural justice is more important than is distributive justice or the outcome of their cases.

Community Surveys

Surveying the impact of an oversight agency on the community at large poses a more difficult challenge. The obvious approach is to include a question or questions on this issue in standard public opinion surveys about the police. Do people know about the oversight agency? How much confidence do they have in it? Do these responses correlate with overall assessments of the police department? Unfortunately, this approach is not quite as simple as it might appear.

First, in any community the number of people having direct contact with the police complaints process will be very small. About 21 percent of the population has any contact with the police in any given year, and the vast majority of those contacts do not involve any conflict. A 1996 Justice Department survey, for example, found that police officers used force in only 1 percent of all contacts, and no respondent filed a complaint.[56] Thus, very few people in any community will have any specific knowledge about the complaints process upon which to base their opinion. Among those who do express an opinion, most will base it on secondhand information, either the testimony of someone who has had direct contact or hearsay about the complaints process, or the general reputation of the police department.

In this context, it is difficult to disentangle the exact source of attitudes about the oversight agency and/or the complaints process. If a department has received much favorable publicity (e.g., a community policing initiative, a skillful public relations effort by a new police chief) the result may well be a favorable rating for the complaint process, even though there is no substantive basis for that rating. By the same token, one particularly controversial incident, for example a disgruntled complainant who vigorously attacked the oversight agency (either with or without good reason) could contaminate public impressions of the agency. In Los Angeles, for example, the 1991 Rodney King incident had a short-term negative effect on public opinion about the LAPD, although attitudes eventually returned to their previous levels.[57]

An additional problem involves the cost and sophistication required to conduct regular surveys of public opinion. Some departments now contract for regular public opinion surveys, but the cost involved is a consideration for most departments.

Kerstetter and Rasinski's study of the Minneapolis Internal Affairs Unit Review Panel (1983 to 1986) offers a more hopeful perspective on the possibilities for using community surveys. The panel was established to audit the Minneapolis Police Department's internal affairs unit and make appropriate recommendations to the mayor and police chief (see Chapter 2). Kerstetter and Rasinski used a series of five annual public opinion surveys conducted between 1983 and 1987. The first three surveys included a 199-member panel that permitted assessment of changes in attitudes over time. Low-income and racial and ethnic minority households were oversampled. Respondents were asked (1) whether they thought the Minneapolis police department investigated complaints "thoroughly"; (2) whether they believed the department disciplined officers who were found guilty; (3) if the city had a Police Review Panel, and if yes, (4) whether they believed the Review Panel affected their confidence in the complaints process.[58]

The study found that public confidence in the police complaints process increased during the review panel's existence and then "fell precipitously" when it ceased operating. Awareness of the review panel began at 29.2 percent in 1983, rose to 47.2 percent in 1985, and then sank to 17.9 percent in 1987 a year after it ceased operating. Given the very low percentage of people who would have had any direct contact with the police complaints process, the almost 50 percent level of awareness of the review panel is particularly impressive. The review panel had a positive effect on public confidence in the complaints process. The percentage of those saying it gave them "a lot more" or "a little more" confidence rose from 26.5 percent in 1983 to 39.8 percent in 1985. Increases occurred among both white and minority respondents. In short, the mere existence of some form of citizen oversight had a positive effect on public attitudes.

Herzog's evaluation of the national civilian review board in Israel (the Machash, or the Department for the Investigation of Complaints against Police Officers) included a survey of about 500 randomly selected citizens. Over 60 percent (61.2%) could not identify the Machash, and 65.4 percent did not know how to file a complaint against a police officer. The lack of knowledge was far higher among Arab citizens compared with Jewish citizens.[59]

Oversight and Police-Community Relations

Since racial tensions have been the driving force behind the oversight movement, it is appropriate to ask whether an oversight agency has any impact on improving police-community relations. Although it did not conduct a community survey, the Vera evaluation of the CCRB concluded that "the CCRB in 1984 made no more than a modest contribution to improving police-community relations." It cited the poor public image of the CCRB, the small percentage of cases sustained, the lack of citizens on the board itself at that time, and the media attention to violent incidents involving the police that had not been resolved.[60]

Insofar as an oversight agency has any positive impact on public opinion, some of that effect should involve an improvement in race relations. The aspects of oversight that are most likely to have an impact on race relations are those related to community outreach. Police community relations are likely to be improved where an oversight agency actively reaches out to racial and ethnic minority communities, holds community meetings in their neighborhoods, actively publicizes the complaint process (with material in the appropriate languages). Positive effects are also likely where an oversight agency's policy review process listens to and addresses minority communities' special concerns about police policies and procedures.

Summary

The preceding discussion leads to several general conclusions. First, because providing a satisfactory experience to both complainants and police officers is one of the basic goals of oversight, all agencies—and internal police department procedures as well—should provide all of their clients an opportunity to provide feedback on their experience. A complaint procedure that fails to provide that opportunity cannot be deemed to be doing all that it can to enhance its effectiveness. Second, the client evaluation process is in many cases likely to identify problems with the complaint process (e.g., perceived unfairness or lack of feedback). Agencies need to act on that information, and any agency that fails to do so cannot be deemed to be effective. Finally, the available research indicates that conventional complaint investigation procedures do not necessarily meet the goals of complainants. More research is needed on this subject, and complaint agencies need to consider developing different procedures (e.g., mediation programs) to meet different needs.

AUDITING THE QUALITY
OF COMPLAINT INVESTIGATIONS

The quality of complaint investigations has been the central issue in the entire history of the oversight movement. Citizen oversight is based on the assumption that external oversight agencies will investigate complaints in a manner that is more thorough and fair than internal police complaint procedures.

The following section describes procedures that have been developed for auditing complaint review procedures to ensure that they meet the highest standards of quality. These procedures have been developed by several of the auditor models of citizen oversight. As explained in Chapter 3, auditor systems leave the responsibility for investigating complaints with police departments. This raises the question of how to ensure the quality of complaint investigations in Class I oversight systems that assume responsibility for investigating complaints. Unfortunately, many Class I oversight agencies have failed to take steps to ensure the quality of their own investigations. Consequently, *the procedures described in the pages that follow apply with equal force to internal police complaint procedures and external citizen oversight agencies.*

Two questions arise about the quality of complaint investigations: (1) What mechanisms should be used to audit investigations, and (2) what criteria should be used to evaluate the quality of investigations?[61] The auditor systems of oversight already institutionalize the audit mechanism as their principal role. For other complaint procedures, period audits should be established following the recommendation of the Kansas City auditor in 2000 (Figure 6-2). One of the most important parts of this process is a regular audit of tape recordings of

> 7. The director of the Office of Citizen Complaints should develop and institute a procedure to regularly test the complaint process, including monitoring intake procedures and reviewing tape-recorded interviews.

FIGURE 6-2 Recommendation of the Kansas City Auditor

SOURCE: Kansas City, Office of the City Auditor, *Performance Audit: Police-Citizen Complaint Process* (Kansas City: OCA, March 2000), p. 18.

interviews with complainants, officers subject to complaints, and witnesses. The auditor systems of oversight have over the years developed a set of proper criteria to be used in auditing complaint investigations. Issues include the completeness of investigative files, standards of thoroughness and fairness, and the timeliness of completing investigations, and they are discussed in detail in the pages that follow. Audit criteria are indicated in Figure 6-3.

Completeness of Files
- Are all proper documents in the file?
- Is there a log of investigative activities?
- Are all reports legible and easily readable?
- Are all files maintained in an orderly fashion?

Thoroughness
- Did the investigator take all the proper steps in investigating the complaint?
- Was a serious effort made to contact and interview the complainant?
- Were efforts made to identify, locate, and interview potential witnesses?
- Were efforts made to obtain any relevant physical evidence, including medical reports?

Fairness
- Were any persons interviewed asked hostile questions?
- Were any persons interviewed asked leading questions?
- Did investigators give unwarranted credibility to the testimony of any person interviewed?
- Does the file include derogatory information about any party to the complaint that is unrelated to the incident under investigation?

Timeliness
- Are complaint investigations completed in a timely manner?
- Does the agency have a set of goals and timetables for completing investigations?

FIGURE 6-3 Criteria for Auditing Complaint Investigation Files

Completeness of Investigative Files

Complaint files should be complete in the sense that all of the proper documents should be in the file, all investigative steps taken should be documented, all reports should be easily readable by an outside person, and the file should be maintained in an orderly fashion.

Many audits of complaint files have found that important documents are missing. The most important documents, of course, are the original complaint and reports of all interviews. In a number of cases, the audiotape recordings of interviews could be not be found, which raises in turn the question of whether interviews were recorded as required. All investigative steps should be documented. Proper documentation allows both supervisors and auditors to determine the thoroughness of investigations and whether or not important steps were taken in a timely fashion. All reports should be legible in case other parties (new investigators, supervisors, auditors, parties to litigation) need to review the file. Finally, all files should be maintained in an orderly fashion in order to permit efficient review of a file.

Auditing Investigative Interviews

In the judgment of this author, the single most important oversight activity technique that has developed in recent years consists of auditing the audiotape recordings of complaint investigations. In an increasing number of law enforcement agencies, interviews with complainants, police officers, and witnesses are routinely tape-recorded. Although some police departments may have initiated this practice to protect themselves in misconduct litigation cases, these tapes have become one of the primary tools for evaluating the quality of complaint investigations.

Evaluation Criteria

Through the mechanism of auditing complaint investigation interviews, criteria for evaluating the quality of investigations have emerged. These criteria and their applications are discussed in the following sections.

Thoroughness The basic criteria for determining the thoroughness of a complaint investigation involve the amount of effort expended and the specific investigative steps taken. The latter include (1) the effort to identify, locate, and interview potential witnesses, and (2) whether in the course of interviews the investigators asked the proper questions and follow-up questions. The San Jose Independent Police Auditor (IPA) has defined a set of reasonable criteria for assessing the quality of complaint investigations. An investigation is *very thorough* when "the investigator has taken every reasonable step to discover relevant witnesses or evidence"; *thorough* when "all the steps likely to discover important evidence" have been taken; *adequate* when investigators take "only the most obvious steps"; and *inadequate* when "not even the obvious steps" are taken. In 1997, it found that 8 percent of all complaint investigations by the

San Jose Police Department were "very thorough," 60 percent were "thorough," 21 percent were "adequate," and 7 percent were "inadequate."[62]

One dimension of the lack of thoroughness that has characterized citizen complaint investigations is that police investigators have not taken them as seriously as criminal incidents. Thus, for example, when an officer uses some type of force or is alleged to use force, sergeants and other supervisors have not attempted to collect relevant information immediately (as they would with an alleged criminal assault or robbery). Failing to act quickly can mean that potential witnesses are not identified and persons' memories are allowed to fade (this is a particular problem when investigations are initiated for months). The San Jose auditor raised this issue in 1998 and helped secure a new policy requiring supervisors to immediately collect evidence and interview all participants in cases where there is serious injury to either a citizen or a police officer. The auditor found 100 percent compliance with this new requirement by 1999.[63]

Locating and interviewing witnesses is absolutely crucial for a thorough investigation. As discussed earlier, most citizen complaints against police officers become "swearing" contests, with no independent witnesses or physical evidence. Investigators need to ask whether any witnesses were present, canvass the neighborhood to determine on their own if there were any witnesses, and then make a serious effort to locate any witnesses who are identified. It is also important to remember that in many cases witnesses are hard to locate. Many are likely to be poor, changing addresses frequently without leaving a forwarding address, possibly without a telephone, having poor English skills, or living in a neighborhood where there is a high level of suspicion of government investigators. For the lazy or overworked investigator, it is a simple matter to say there were no witnesses and close the case. Merrick Bobb found one use-of-force case in the Los Angeles Sheriff's Department in which the investigator failed to interview the physician who had treated the complainant for injuries suffered in the incident even though the physician was identified in the complaint file.[64]

Follow-up questions that probe for additional information and test the interviewees' version of events are particularly crucial. Such questions might include, "Then what did you do?" or, "When the officer told you to ___, what did you do?" or, "When the suspect asked ___, what did you tell him?" One obvious question is: "Were there any witnesses that you know of?" As in any dispute, the follow-up questions are crucial to establishing the context of the incident and determining the credibility of the various parties involved and the reasonableness of the actions by all parties. That, after all, is the function of cross-examination in a trial. Failing to probe a police officer's version of the incident, and accepting his or her initial statement at face value, is probably the most common shortcoming of internal police investigations.

Audits of complaint investigations can be used in several ways. First and most important, the exact nature of the shortcomings should lead to appropriate corrective action. This might involve retraining or eventual dismissal of particular investigators. Second, the general results of audits (with names of individuals not included, as these are personnel matters) should be published to inform the public about the quality of investigations and the fact that a quality control process exists. Such information appears in the quarterly reports of the Portland auditor.

One San Jose case illustrates how the tape recording of interviews not only can resolve subsequent disputes but also on occasion can work to the advantage of the police officer. A complaint had alleged that a police officer was rude to the complainant's friends and family at their home. After the case was closed by police investigators, the complainant called the auditor and alleged that there had been no formal investigation. The tape recording clearly indicated that the person had requested an informal process rather than a formal investigation. The auditor played the tape to the complainant, who then dropped his second allegation.[65] In the past, without the tapes, these are precisely the kinds of controversies that lingered on unresolved for months, if not longer.

The Portland auditor identified a number of problems with complaint investigations, the most important of which was a lack of consistency in precinct-level investigations. One of the most persistent grievances of police officers across the country, in fact, involves bias on the part of internal affairs. Many officers believe that IA protects favored officers but makes a serious effort to "get" those who are out of favor. Other problems identified by PIIAC auditors included absence of tape recordings in complaint files, poor quality of some tapes, and poor-quality written summaries of investigations. PIIAC returned cases to internal affairs for further investigation because the auditors "had no way of knowing whether the investigator had fully developed the nature of the complaint or what investigative steps had been taken."[66]

Merrick Bobb examined use-of-force incidents in the Los Angeles County Sheriff's Department in 1997 and found them to be "distinctly inferior, marked by incomplete evidence-collecting, scanty documentation, and a palpable bias favoring the accused officer." He also found light discipline for officers found guilty of using excessive force or otherwise violating department policy. A major part of the problem was that most investigations were done by the officer's immediate supervisor at the unit level rather than by the department's Internal Affairs Bureau.[67]

The level of investigative effort may have a major impact on the attrition of complaints. As already noted, many complainants fail to follow through on their initial complaint. The attrition rate in the New York City CCRB averaged 64 percent between 1992 and 1997 (that is, only 36% received a full investigation).[68] These cases are typically recorded as "complainant unavailable" or "refused to cooperate." The failure of a complainant to follow through, however, may be a result of how the oversight agency operates. Investigators may not make a serious effort to locate the complainant. As the NYCLU noted in 1996, a complainant's availability can be "a function of the extent to which the *investigator* is cooperative or available." The NYCLU also pointed out that police officers are paid to participate in CCRB process, while complainants may face loss of pay for taking the time to file their complaints or be available for interviews.[69]

A city auditor's report on the Kansas City Police Department illustrated the problems that arise from having no regular audit or monitoring of the complaint process. The auditor's report found that the police department "has no way of knowing whether all complaints received are actually investigated." There is no "method to account for all complaints, such as pre-numbered complaint forms." The OCC had noted a few years earlier that it received about two complaints a month from precinct stations that were "illegible" and thus could not be investigated.[70] Presumably, problems of this sort would be caught by the auditor systems in Portland, San Jose, Los Angeles County and brought to public attention with a recommendation for change.

Fairness Fairness is a particularly important criterion for complaint investigations. The challenge is to develop appropriate measures of fairness. A study of internal affairs units in two midwestern police departments identified several different examples of bias against complainants. First, cases were often interpreted as narrowly as possible, thereby excluding contextual elements that might favor the complainant. Second, allegations were often investigated selectively, focusing on the more serious use-of-force allegations, which are difficult to prove, and ignoring less serious ones that might be provable and reflect poorly on the officers. Third, the credibility of complainants was deliberately demeaned by including criminal history or mental health information that did not bear directly on the incident. Fourth, photographic evidence was used selectively, with photographs of uninjured citizens and in other cases medical evidence not collected even though mentioned by citizens. Fifth, investigators interviewed a smaller percentage of citizen witnesses (52.5% of all cases) than police witnesses (88.7%). Sixth, police officer testimony was generally given greater weight than citizen testimony. Seventh, investigators readily accepted exculpatory justifications on behalf of the officer (e.g., the officer was in fear of his or her life).[71] It is widely believed that such problems are endemic to complaint investigations. The auditor system of oversight provides a mechanism for identifying these problems and correcting them.

Audits of interview tapes can also spot bias in interviews. One symptom of bias is asking leading questions or supplying answers to police officers being interviewed. Questions posed to police officers, for example, may be worded in such a way as to suggest an exculpatory answer (e.g., "Wasn't the person drunk?"). Questions to citizens might be hostile or belligerent (e.g., "Weren't you actually drunk?"). It is quite possible for a third party to spot such biases and determine that an investigation is not fair. Portland auditors found that police internal affairs investigators were very uncomfortable when an officer did not immediately provide an answer, and filled the void by suggesting an answer themselves. They pointed out this problem and recommended corrective training for investigators. Subsequent audits found that the problem had largely disappeared. Other lapses in interviews were found: "a couple of interviewers appeared to assist officers frame their responses to questions," while "others did not demonstrate thorough questioning during interviews."[72]

Bias also involves including derogatory language or information about complainants. Portland auditors found police officers referring to people as "mental," and recommended that such terms be forbidden.[73] Referring to a complainant's past history (e.g., calling the person who always calls the police about frivolous matters a "crank") is also irrelevant to the incident in question. If information about a complainant's history is relevant, then a police officer's history is equally relevant. This history would include patterns of prior complaints. To include information about one party's history and not the other party's is evidence of a biased investigation.

An important aspect of fairness in investigations is the question of assessing the credibility of witnesses. Including derogatory information about complainants and witnesses is one traditional device for discrediting their testimony. In a five-year follow-up to the Christopher Commission report, Merrick Bobb found that investigators were willing to accept officers' accounts of incidents even when they were "highly unrealistic." Generally, there was a lack of "a principled basis for deeming a witness 'independent,'" and "officers were subject to less rigorous questioning than were witnesses."[74]

The Pittsburgh consent decree sought to eliminate bias by ruling that "there shall be no automatic preference of an officer's statement over a complainant's statement." Moreover, "in making credibility determinations, OMI investigators shall consider the officer's history of complaints . . . and disciplinary records and the complainant's criminal history for crimes involving untruthfulness."[75] Audits interview tapes can be used to identify patterns of bias toward certain witnesses.

Timeliness One of the most serious problems in complaint investigations is delay in completing investigations. In 2000, complaint investigations in Portland were taking an average of thirteen months to complete, a figure that virtually everyone regards as unacceptable.[76] The problem afflicts both police internal affairs units and external oversight agencies. Delay affects officers as well as complainants. The San Jose auditor reported in 1997 that both complainants and officers "have expressed their dissatisfaction with what are viewed as unreasonable delays."[77] In some departments, officers are barred from promotion while an unresolved complaint hangs over them.

One of the most significant contributions of several auditor systems has been to develop timelines for completing investigations. The San Jose auditor developed a series of timelines and by 1999 could report that 94 percent of all complaints were classified within the recommended thirty-day time period and that investigations were completed in 87 percent of all use-of-force Class I cases within the recommended 180-day time period. The continuous presence of the auditor was a major factor in raising the compliance rate.[78] The Boise ombudsman established a standard of completing complaint investigations within thirty days and in its first year succeeded in completing 62 percent within than time period. Only 16 percent took longer than sixty days.[79] The Portland auditor, meanwhile, found that delay in completing complaint investigations resulted in part from the lack of adequate staff in the internal affairs unit of the police department and recommended that an additional investigator be assigned to it. The Portland Police Bureau failed to act on this recommendation, however, and by 2000 complaints were still averaging an unacceptable thirteen months to complete.[80]

The different results in San Jose and Portland illustrate a general point. The function of an oversight monitoring process is to identify problems and recommend solutions. In San Jose, it appears that the police department responded to the recommendations and corrected the problem. In Portland, the police department failed to respond and the problem persisted for several years. In both cases, the oversight agency did its job. In this area, as with policy review, the responsibility ultimately lies with the police department. It should be added that we cannot automatically assume that oversight agencies with independent responsibility for investigating complaints will necessarily act in a timely fashion. The Minneapolis CRA disposes of complaints in a very timely manner, but the old Washington, D.C., CCRB allowed some complaints to languish for as long as three years. An important issue here is whether independent review boards effectively monitor their own activities to ensure timely dispositions.

Complaint Dispositions and Discipline

Another persistent criticism of internal police complaint investigations is that dispositions are not reasonably related to the evidence in the complaint file. Thus, a complaint is not sustained even though there is clear evidence of wrongdoing by the officer.

Systematic audits of complaint files can assess the appropriateness of dispositions. This procedure, of course, only raises anew the question of the thoroughness and fairness of complaint investigations. If an investigation fails to interview potential witnesses and/or conducts biased interviews, then the file that is subject to an audit is likely to indicate that the disposition was appropriate *given the facts presented in the file*. Thus, it is impossible to separate the issues of investigative thoroughness and fairness and the appropriateness of dispositions.

The next issue involves the appropriateness of the discipline imposed in sustained complaints given the misconduct involved. The Minneapolis Review Panel (1982–86), for example, found a number of such instances where the chief of police failed to impose discipline in cases where the complaint had been sustained.[81] The special counsel to the Los Angeles Sheriff's department, meanwhile, found that the department "often substantially reduces the level of discipline as part of a plea-bargain with the deputy, even when it has strong evidence."[82] Systematic audits, such as those conducted by the special counsel, can be used to identify patterns of inappropriate discipline.

A related issue is the allegation, voiced by rank-and-file officers, that internal affairs shows favoritism toward certain officers. The New York City Council reported that officers could obtain lenient treatment by befriending powerful NYPD officials or union leaders.[83] Some departments have addressed this problem through the development of a discipline matrix that specifies the discipline to be imposed for each offense, with some allowance for mitigating and or aggravating circumstances, and with some additional consideration of an officer's prior complaint history.[84] These discipline matrices are modeled after the sentencing guidelines currently in use in the federal courts and a number of states. The basic goal of both sets of guidelines is to control discretion and ensure uniformity in punishment.[85] On this issue as well, systematic audits of complaints and discipline can identify patterns of inconsistent discipline, bring the problem to public attention, and recommend appropriate solutions.

Summary

The quality of complaint investigations is essential to the integrity of a complaint procedure. The historic problem has been that police department complaint procedures have been biased—or at least have been perceived as biased. Citizen oversight is designed to provide more independent complaint review. Unfortunately, oversight agencies have not taken the steps necessary to ensure the quality of their own investigations. The auditing function described in the preceding pages, therefore, is equally relevant to both internal and external complaint procedures.

CHANGING THE POLICE SUBCULTURE

As indicated in Chapter 4, one of the key potential roles of citizen oversight is to change the police subculture, particularly with respect to reducing or eliminating obstacles to accountability. The two most important programs that have developed are early warning (EW) systems and programs to detect and punish officer lying.

Early Warning Systems

Early warning systems are administrative systems designed to identify officers with recurring performance problems, such as high rates of citizen complaints, and to provide some formal intervention, in the form of counseling or training, designed to correct the officers' behavior. EW systems consist of three elements: selection criteria, intervention, and postintervention monitoring. Some EW systems use only citizen complaints as selection criteria. Other systems, however, use a broader range of criteria, including internal use of force reports (both physical and deadly force), resisting arrest charges filed by officers, officer involvement in civil litigation, and other indicators of problematic behavior such as tardiness, sloppy reports, vehicle accidents, and so on. Because citizen complaints are such an underreported phenomenon and because the idea of EW systems is to spot problematic behavior early, a broad range of selection criteria is preferred.[86]

The intervention stage of EW systems raises a number of issues about which there is not yet conclusive evidence. In most programs, the intervention consists of counseling by an officer's immediate supervisor. There are serious and unresolved questions about ensuring that the proper counseling is delivered and that counseling is consistent across all supervisors. Some programs do not require even minimal documentation of the intervention. Some EW systems deliver the intervention through a group training class. The group approach has the advantage of efficiency and ensuring that all officers receive the same intervention, but it does not necessarily ensure that individual officers receive the counseling or training that is directly relevant to their problems. At present, there is no evidence that one approach is necessarily more effective than any other.

With respect to postintervention monitoring, most EW systems rely only on informal monitoring of officers' behavior. The New Orleans PPEP program, however, includes a formal six-month follow-up in which an officer's supervisor is required to observe him or her on duty and file signed bimonthly evaluations.

An EW system can help to change the police subculture by sending a clear message to officers that repeated misconduct will not be tolerated by the department. That message is communicated both through a process of special deterrence, directed toward officers subject to EW system intervention, and general deterrence, directed toward all other officers. At the same time, the counseling or training received by officers in the intervention stage will in fact correct the behavior that was giving rise to citizen complaints.

Citizen oversight agencies can play an important role related to the effectiveness of EW systems. The first issue, of course, is whether the police department operates an EW system. If not, the oversight agency can bring this issue to public attention and demand the creation of a system. In the absence of a system, the oversight agency can analyze the complaints it reviews and identify officers who are the subject of repeated complaints. It can use this information to lobby for the creation of an EW system. If an EW system does exist, the oversight agency can play an important monitoring role by collecting data on the subsequent performance of officers who have been subject to intervention. The San Jose auditor publishes this information in its annual reports.[87] The oversight agency can also help to enhance the effectiveness of the EW system by researching systems in other departments and ensuring that the local system incorporates the best practices found in other departments.

In short, the oversight agency can and should play a monitoring role with respect to an EW system. The effectiveness of the oversight agency depends on whether or not it plays this role.

Detecting Officer Lying

At present, programs to detect and punish officer lying are in a rudimentary stage of development at best. A promising program developed by Katherine Mader, inspector general for the Los Angeles Police Department, was interrupted by her resignation.[88] The other known program has been operated by the Commission to Investigate Corruption in the New York City Police Department. At present it is not possible to evaluate the impact of that program.

Because the integrity of the entire citizen complaint process depends on accurate information about incidents under investigation, and because officer testimony represents some of the most important evidence, reducing and eventually eliminating officer lying is an important role for citizen oversight. The effectiveness of an oversight agency can be judged in terms of whether or not it has taken steps to address this problem. Unfortunately, with the exception of the initial effort by Katherine Mader, the former LAPD inspector general, oversight agencies have not assumed this role.

CONCLUSION

The most important role that citizen oversight agencies can play includes the various activities related to monitoring law enforcement agencies. These activities are important because they are designed to change organizations, and in that respect they help to eliminate the problems that give rise to complaints. In assessing the effectiveness of citizen oversight agencies, it is important to distinguish between process evaluations and outcome evaluations.

Process evaluations are fairly easy to conduct. It is essentially a question of determining whether or not an oversight agency is engaging in the various monitoring activities described in Chapter 4 and this chapter. Oversight agencies that engage in few or none cannot be deemed to be effective. In such cases, the problem is a matter of formal authority and vision. Some agencies are not formally authorized to undertake such activities as policy review. To achieve effectiveness, they need to be given this authority. In some other cases, it is basically a matter of vision. The leaders of some oversight agencies simply lack a broad vision of their role and do not understand that they have an important role to play in monitoring and helping to change the law enforcement agency they are responsible for. There is no excuse for this failure of vision. Other oversight agencies have a broad vision of their role and it is simply a matter of following their lead.

Outcome evaluations of the monitoring role of oversight pose a more difficult problem. As this chapter explains, the long-term impact we are concerned about involves routine day-to-day police work. We do not currently have adequate data on this aspect of policing, and collecting such data on a regular basis is difficult and enormously expensive. This does not mean that we should abandon all attempts at evaluation. Some monitoring activities are relatively easy to evaluate, most notably the satisfaction of citizens and police officers subject to complaint systems. There is no excuse for not instituting the procedures for collecting the necessary data on this subject. In short, there are some evaluative tasks that are manageable and can be undertaken immediately. The more difficult tasks will require more thought and effort.

With respect to the criteria defined by Perez, the evaluation criteria related to the monitoring role discussed in this chapter are well-suited to determine whether a citizen oversight agency achieves independence of the police department for which it is responsible, achieves legitimacy by virtue of being perceived as being independent, and finally actively engages in a learning process likely to lead to improvements in the quality of policing.

NOTES

1. Douglas Perez, *Common Sense about Police Review* (Philadelphia: Temple University Press, 1994), 65–84.

2. Kansas City, Office of Citizen Complaints, *1998 Annual Report* (Kansas City: Office of Citizen Complaints, 1999).

3. San Francisco Office of Citizen Complaints, *1998 Annual Report* (San Francisco: OCC, 1999), 8.

4. Personal observation, author.

5. Samuel Walker and Eileen Luna, *A Report on the Oversight Mechanisms of the Albuquerque Police Department* (Albuquerque: City Council, 1997).

6. Portland Police Internal Investigations Auditing Committee [PIIAC], *First Quarter Monitoring Report* (Portland: PPIIAC, April 1998), 6.

7. Boise Community Ombudsman, *Year-End Report 1999* (Boise: Community Ombudsman, 15 February 2000), 12–13.

8. Wesley G. Skogan and Susan Hartnett, *Community Policing, Chicago Style* (New York: Oxford University Press, 1997).

9. New York City Council, Committee on Public Safety, *Beyond Community Relation: Addressing Police Brutality Directly* (New York: NYCC, 1998)

10. Skogan and Hartnett, *Community Policing, Chicago Style.*

11. ACLU–Southern California, *The Call for Change Goes Unanswered* (Los Angeles: ACLU-SC, 1992), 2.

12. ACLU–Northern California, *Failing the Test: Oakland's Police Complaint Process in Crisis* (San Francisco: ACLU-NC, 1996).

13. U.S. Civil Rights Commission, Maryland Advisory Commission, *The Baltimore Police Complaint Evaluation Procedure* (Washington, DC: Government Printing Office, 1980), 3.

14. Charles Winnick, "Public Opinion on Police Misuse of Force: A New York State Study," New York State Commission on Criminal Justice and the Use of Force, *Report to the Governor* (Albany, 1987), 21.

15. City of Portland, Office of the City Auditor, *Service Efforts and Accomplishments: 1995–96* (Portland: OCA, 1996).

16. Minneapolis Civilian Police Review Authority, *1998 Annual Report,* appendix, exhibits C and D.

17. Kansas City Office of Citizen Complaints, *Annual Report, 1993* (Kansas City: OCC, 1994).

18. San Jose, Independent Police Auditor, *Year-End Report, 1999* (San Jose: IPA, 2000), appendix J.

19. San Francisco Police Department, General Order #8.03, "Crowd Control" (3 August 1994).

20. San Francisco Office of Citizen Complaints, *1997 Annual Report* (San Francisco: OCC, 1998), 46–47.

21. New York Civil Liberties Union, *Five Years of Civilian Review,* (New York: NYCLU, 1998), 24–27.

22. San Francisco Office of Citizen Complaints, *Third Quarter Statistical Report, 1999* (San Francisco: OCC, 1999), 3–4.

23. Interviews, 1998.

24. Interviews, 1998.

25. Richard A. Leo and George C. Thomas, eds., *The Miranda Debate: Law, Justice, and Policing* (Boston: Northeastern University Press, 1998).

26. Thomas Y. Davies, "A Hard Look at What We Know (and Still Need to Learn) about the 'Costs' of the Exclusionary Rule: The NIJ Study and Other Studies of 'Lost' Arrests," *American Bar Foundation Research Journal* (Summer 1983): 611–90.

27. Stephen D. Mastrofski, Robert E. Worden, and Jeffrey B. Snipes, "Law Enforcement in a Time of Community Policing," *Criminology* 33 (November 1995): 539–63.

28. Lawrence W. Sherman, *Policing Domestic Violence* (New York: The Free Press, 1992).

29. The seminal works on this point are Wayne LaFave, *Arrest* (Boston, Little Brown, 196) and Albert Reiss, *The Police and the Public* (New Haven: Yale University Press, 1971). On the control of discretion, see Samuel Walker, *Taming the System: The Control of Discretion in Criminal Justice, 1950–1990* (New York: Oxford University Press, 1993).

30. Public Management Resources, *Auditor's Quarterly Report: Long-Term Compliance Audit for the Pittsburgh Bureau of Police, Sixth Quarterly Report* (San Antonio: Public Management Resources, March 1999), 3.

31. John Crew, interview.

32. Bureau of Justice Statistics, *Use of Force by Police: Overview of National and Local Data* (Washington, DC: Government Printing Office, 1999). The best discussion of the various data that might be used to measure police use of force, and the limitations of each set of data, is Kenneth Adams, "Measuring the Prevalence of Police Abuse of Force," in William A. Geller and Hans Toch, eds., *And Justice For All: Understanding and Controlling Police Abuse of Force* (Washington, DC: Police Executive Research Forum, 1995), 61–97.

33. Geoffrey P. Alpert and Mark H. Moore, *Performance Measures for the Criminal Justice System* (Washington, DC: Government Printing Office, 1993); Tom McEwen, *National Data Collection on Police Use of Force* (Washington, DC: Government Printing Office, 1996).

34. For a comprehensive discussion of the difficulties of systematically observing police performance, see Stephen D. Mastrofski, Roger B. Parks, Albert J. Reiss, Jr., Robert E. Worden, Christina DeJong, Jeffrey B. Snipes, and William Terrill, *Systematic Observation of Public Police: Applying Field Research Methods to Policy Issues* (Washington, DC: Government Printing Office, 1998).

35. Samuel Walker, Geoffrey P. Alpert, and Dennis J. Kenney, *Responding to the Problem Police Officer, A National Evaluation of Early Warning Systems,* Final Report, National Institute of Justice, 2000.

36. James G. Kolts, *The Los Angeles County Sheriff's Department* (Los Angeles, July 1992); Special Counsel, *11th Semiannual Report* (Los Angeles, June 1999), 85–86.

37. New York City Council, Committee on Public Safety, *Beyond Community Relations: Addressing Police Brutality Directly* (New York: NYCC, 1998).

38. Charldean Newell, Janay Pollok, and Jerry Tweedy, "Financial Aspects of Police Liability," *Baseline Data Report* 24 (Washington: ICMA, March/April 1992).

39. Samuel Walker and Eileen Luna, *A Report on the Oversight Mechanisms of the Albuquerque Police Department* (Albuquerque: City Council, 1997); Seattle, Internal Investigations Auditor Report (Seattle, January 1996), 4.

40. William L. F. Felstiner, Richard L. Able, and Austin Sarat, "The Emergence and Transformation of Disputes: Naming, Blaming, Claiming . . ." *Law and Society Review* 15:3–4, (1980–81): 631–54.

41. Samuel Walker, *Sense and Nonsense about Crime,* 4th ed (Belmont, CA: Wadsworth, 1998).

42. Hazel Glenn Beh, "Municipal Liability for Failure to Investigate Citizen Complaints against Police," *Fordham Urban Law Journal* 25:2 (1998).

43. Michele Sviridoff and Jerome E. McElroy, *Processing Complaints against Police in New York City: The Complainants Perspective* (New York: Vera Institute, 1989), 27–30.

44. Ibid., 51.

45. Mike Maguire, "Complaints against the Police: The British Experience," in Andrew J. Goldsmith, ed., *Complaints against the Police: The Trend to External Review* (Oxford: Clarendon Press, 1991), 191.

46. Samuel Walker, "Complaints against the Police: A Focus Group Study of Citizen Perceptions, Goals, and Expectations," *Criminal Justice Review* 22 (Autumn 1997): 207–26.

47. But some research has found significant levels of police abuse directed at homosexuals: Gregory M. Herek and Kevin T. Berrill, eds., *Hate Crimes: Confronting Violence against Lesbians and Gay Men* (Newbury Park: Sage, 1992).

48. Samuel Walker and Betsy Wright Kreisel, "Varieties of Citizen Review," *American Journal of Police* 15:3 (1996): 65–88.

49. Christopher Commission, *Report of the Independent Commission on the Los Angeles Police Department* (Los Angeles: Christopher Commission, 1991); Commission to Investigate Allegations of Police Corruption [Mollen Commission], *Commission Report* (New York: Mollen Commission, 1994).

50. The tables are found in Wayne A Kerstetter, "Who Disciplines the Police? Who Should?" in W. A. Geller, ed., *Police Leadership in America: Crisis and Opportunity* (New York: Praeger, 1985), 168–69.

51. Michele Sviridoff and Jerome E. McElroy, *Processing Complaints against the Police in New York City* (New York: Vera Institute, 1989), 47, 50.

52. Michele Sviridoff and Jerome E. McElroy, *The Processing of Complaints against Police in New York City: The Perceptions and Attitudes of Line Officers* (New York: Vera Institute, 1989), 19, 32.

53. Ibid., 36–38.

54. Samuel Walker, *Analysis of the Quality Service Audit Surveys: A Report to the Minneapolis Civilian Review Authority* (Omaha: University of Nebraska at Omaha, 1999).

55. Donald Black, *The Behavior of Law* (New York: Academic Press, 1976).

56. Bureau of Justice Statistics, *Police Use of Force: Collection of National Data* (Washington, DC: Government Printing Office, 1997).

57. Steven A. Tuch and Ronald Weitzer, "Racial Differences in Attitudes Toward the Police," *Public Opinion Quarterly* 61 (1997): 642–63.

58. Wayne A. Kerstetter and Kenneth A. Rasinski, "Opening a Window into Police Internal Affairs: Impact of Procedural Justice Reform on Third-Party Attitudes," *Social Justice Research* 7:2 (1994): 107–27.

59. Sergio Herzog, "Police Violence in Israel: The Police Complaints System on the Use of Force," unpublished Ph.D. dissertation, Hebrew University of Jerusalem, 1998. Table 3 is from Herzog, paper, American Society of Criminology Annual Meeting, 1998.

60. Michele Sviridoff and Jerome E McElroy, *Processing Complaints against Police: The Civilian Complaint Review Board* (New York: Vera Institute, 1988), 295–96.

61. A set of standards for investigations can be found in Lou Reiter, *Law Enforcement Administrative Investigations,* 2nd ed. (Tallahassee, FL: Lou Reiter and Associates, 1998).

62. San Jose, Independent Police Auditor, *1997 Annual Report* (1998).

63. San Jose, Independent Police Auditor, *1999 Year-End Report* (San Jose: IPA, 2000), ix–x, 68.

64. Merrick Bobb, *Five Years Later: A Report to the Los Angeles Police Commission on the Los Angeles Police Department's Implementation of Independent Commission Recommendations* (Los Angeles: The Police Commission, 1996), 40–41.

65. San Jose, Independent Police Auditor, *Year-End Report—1997* (1998), 43.

66. Portland, Police Internal Investigations Advisory Committee, *Fourth Quarterly Report, 1995* (Portland, 1995), 3, 10.

67. Use of force investigations in Special Counsel, *7th Semiannual Report* (Los Angeles, April 1997), 35.

68. New York Civil Liberties Union, *Five Years of Civilian Review,* 1.

69. New York Civil Liberties Union, *Third Anniversary Overview of the Civilian Complaint Review Board, July 5, 1993–July 5, 1996* (New York: NYCLU, 1996), 6.

70. Kansas City, Office of the City Auditor, *Preliminary Review: Kansas City Missouri Police Department,* 200–01.

71. Victor E. Kappeler, Peter B. Kraska, and Jeannine E. Marron, "Police Policing Themselves: The Processing of Excessive Force Complaints," paper, ACJS Annual Meeting, 1995.

72. Portland PIIAC: *Fourth Quarter Monitoring Report, 1995,* 3, 10.

73. Ibid., 5.

74. Bobb, *Five Years Later,* 39–42.

75. *United States v. City of Pittsburgh,* W.D. Pa. 1979.

76. PIIAC, *Quarterly Reports for 1999* (Portland, 2000); interview, Commander, Internal Affairs Unit, Portland Police Bureau, June 2000.

77. San Jose, Independent Police Auditor, *Year-End Report, 1997* (San Jose, 1998), 15.

78. San Jose, Independent Police Auditor, *Year-End Report, 1999* (San Jose, 2000), 36–37.

79. Boise, Community Ombudsman, *Year-End Report 1999* (Boise, 15 February, 2000), 8–9.

80. Portland PIIAC, *Fourth Quarter Monitoring Report, 1997* (Portland: PIIAC, 1998), 11; Portland PIIAC, quarterly reports for 2000.

81. Minneapolis, Internal Affairs Review Panel, *First Report* (Minneapolis, 1983); "Civilian Panel, Laux Differ on Discipline," *Minneapolis Star-Tribune,* 26 March 1994.

82. Special Counsel, *7th Semiannual Report,* 40.

83. New York City Council, Committee on Public Safety, *Beyond Community Relations* (New York: NYCC, 1998), 16.

84. Memphis Shelby Crime Commission, *The Role of Penalty Schedules in Managing Police Misconduct,* White Paper, 1:4 (September 1999).

85. Bureau of Justice Assistance, *National Assessment of Structured Sentencing* (Washington, DC: Government Printing Office, 1996); Samuel Walker, *Taming the System: The Control of Discretion in Criminal Justice, 1950–1990* (New York: Oxford University Press, 1993).

86. Samuel Walker, Geoffrey P. Alpert, and Dennis Kenney, *Responding to the Problem Police Officer: A National Evaluation of Early Warning Systems,* Final Report, submitted to the National Institute of Justice, 2000.

87. San Jose, Independent Police Auditor, *Year-End Report 1999,* 51–52.

88. Office of the Inspector General, *Sixth Month Report* (Los Angeles: OIG, January 1997).

7

Toward an
Accountable Police

SUMMARY:
THE ROLE OF CITIZEN OVERSIGHT

Citizen oversight of the police has been a major controversy in American society for half a century. Advocates of oversight believe that it is an essential and effective remedy for police misconduct. Opponents argue that it is both an illegitimate intrusion into the professional responsibilities of the police and ineffective in practice. The purpose of this book has been to determine the role, if any, of citizen oversight in police accountability. The evidence examined in this book leads to the following conclusions.

First, in a democratic society citizen oversight of the police is in principle a legitimate and necessary aspect of police accountability.

Second, properly designed and implemented, citizen oversight can make a positive contribution to enhancing police accountability.

Third, the effectiveness of an oversight agency depends heavily on the role it takes with respect to a police department; the monitoring role offers the greatest possibilities for achieving success. Many oversight agencies are not effective, either because of structural weaknesses or a lack of vision about what they might do.

Fourth, the monitoring role is particularly important because it focuses on changing the police organization, and not just punishing individual officers.

Fifth, there is relatively little empirical evidence regarding the impact of oversight agencies on the quality of day-to-day police work, and much research remains to be done on that subject.

Sixth, while it can make a positive contribution, citizen oversight is not a panacea and can be effective only as one element of a mixed system of accountability.

Each of these propositions is explained in greater detail in the pages that follow.

THE LEGITIMATE ROLE
OF CITIZEN OVERSIGHT

The traditional argument by the police that citizen oversight is an illegitimate intrusion into professional police matters fails on several counts. First, it is a basic principle of democratic society that citizens control and direct government agencies. The police, especially because of their awesome powers of arrest and capacity to use force, are not exempt from this rule. Moreover, elected officials—mayors, city councils, county commissions, governors, and presidents—already exercise control over law enforcement agencies: appointing chief executives, appropriating budgets, and making many important policy decisions. Citizen oversight simply creates a specialized administrative agency to focus on one particular aspect of policing. In this respect, it is no different than innumerable other administrative agencies.

Second, citizens have long exercised some input into certain aspects of police disciplinary matters. Civil service commissions and personnel boards routinely hear appeals of disciplinary actions brought by police officers. Police officers have never objected to these procedures because, to be blunt about it, they so often win and have disciplinary actions mitigated or overturned completely. Citizen oversight of the complaint process simply expands this long-established practice.

Third, the police themselves have welcomed citizen input through community policing and problem-oriented policing, the two most important new developments in policing in the last two decades. Both of these innovations emphasize the creation of "partnerships" between the police and community residents, with citizen input into the development of police policies and programs. Having embraced citizen input in this regard, the police cannot then turn around and argue that citizens have no legitimate role related to the very sensitive complaint process.

THE POSITIVE CONTRIBUTIONS
OF OVERSIGHT

Although many citizen oversight agencies have been plagued with problems, others have established creditable records of accomplishment. The effectiveness of citizen oversight should be judged on the basis of what the best and not the worst agencies have done.

First, many if not most oversight agencies have established more open and accessible complaint procedures than the procedures traditionally operated by police departments. In fact, police complaint procedures have traditionally been closed and often hostile toward potential complainants.

Second, there is persuasive evidence that many police departments have failed to investigate complaints in a thorough and fair fashion and to discipline officers guilty of misconduct toward citizens. In this respect, they have forfeited any claim to be able to police themselves without outside oversight;

Third, there is evidence that police departments have failed to use citizen complaints as a learning tool—that is, to treat them as indicators of problems that need to be corrected through new policies or training for officers.

On all three of these points, a number of citizen oversight agencies have very positive records. Several have active community outreach programs designed to explain the complaint process and reach segments of the community that have particular problems with the police. The San Jose Independent Police Auditor, for example, has an active program of meetings with community groups. The Minneapolis Civilian Review Authority receives very high ratings from both complainants and police officers regarding the fairness of its investigations. More important, it has opened itself to routine evaluation by its clients. The San Francisco Office of Citizen Complaints, meanwhile, has used individual complaints to examine police practices and to recommend changes in police department policy.

THE MULTIPLE ROLES
OF CITIZEN OVERSIGHT

For many people on both sides of the controversy, citizen oversight is little more than a slogan. In practice, however, oversight involves a number of different roles and activities. The original role involved the independent investigation of citizen complaints. As Chapter 3 explains, however, "independence" is an extremely complex matter. Achieving a genuinely independent process depends on both the formal structure of an agency and its resources and powers. Merely creating an oversight agency does not necessarily guarantee that it will be structurally independent, act in an independent fashion, or be perceived as independent.

As Chapter 4 explains, the role of oversight also includes, or at least potentially includes, a number of activities designed to monitor police departments and the complaint process. These activities include community outreach, providing customer assistance to citizens who contact the agency (e.g., explaining the law or police procedure), reviewing the policies and procedures of the police department and recommending policy changes, auditing the quality of complaint investigations, and finally, cultivating a culture of professionalism in the department through a variety of programs.

Two basic points need to be made about the role of oversight agencies. First, one crucial distinction between the more effective and the less effective agencies is the extent to which they adopt an expansive vision of their role and engage in a broad range of activities. Second, as is explained shortly, effective oversight is more likely to be achieved through the monitoring role activities.

The Shortcomings of Oversight Agencies

Although citizen oversight is good in principle, the plain truth is that many oversight agencies are not successful. Several different factors explain these shortcomings.

First, some of these failures are structural. As Chapter 3 explains, some agencies are by design not truly independent of the police department and have little meaningful power. The Kansas City Office of Citizen Complaints, for example, only reviews complaint investigation files that are compiled by police investigators. And unlike the auditor systems of oversight agencies of this sort, it does not have the authority to audit the quality of investigations. Consequently, there is no assurance that the investigations are fair or thorough or in any way better than they would be without the oversight agency.

Second, some agencies fail because of poorly designed procedures or poor leadership. The old Washington, D.C. Civilian Complaint Review Board, abolished in 1995, was so poorly managed that some complaint investigations were not completed for three years. The CCRB had no procedure for efficiently screening out meritless cases and concentrating its energies on cases that involved either serious allegations, or had solid evidence, or both. And as the case backlog developed over the course of several years, no one in the agency took effective steps to correct the problem.

Third, some oversight agencies are ineffective because they face unrelenting hostility from the police departments they are responsible for. The Philadelphia Police Advisory Board, for example, has been able to do little in the face of the determined hostility of the Fraternal Order of Police, representing the rank-and-file officers. Similarly, the New York City Civilian Complaint Review Board has had most of its sustained complaints rejected by the police department. In many of these cases, the police department did not conduct any additional investigation.

Finally, in many instances oversight agencies are ineffectual because of a lack of vision about the positive role that they could play. Many oversight agencies, for example, engage in no community outreach. They simply review the complaints that are filed and apparently have no sense that it is their responsibility to open up the complaint process and in particular reach out to segments of the population that are fearful of the police and reluctant to file complaints. Many oversight agencies do not engage in policy review. That is, they review the complaints that are filed but do not raise questions about the possible causes, such as the lack of police department policy on a particular issue or the need for training.

There are many activities that an oversight agency can engage in. Even though formal authorization by ordinance strengthens the hand of an agency, it is still possible for an agency to undertake certain activities on its own initiative. There is nothing, for example, preventing even a structurally weak oversight agency from undertaking either an active community outreach or a policy review program. The crucial element is a matter of vision and initiative on the part of the agency and its leaders. The broader the vision and the more active the role, the more effective an oversight agency is likely to be.

THE SPECIAL CONTRIBUTION
OF THE MONITORING ROLE

The monitoring role of oversight is particularly important because it focuses on changing the police organization. To an unfortunate extent, advocates of oversight have focused their attention on punishing individual officers. To be sure, an individual officer who is in fact guilty of misconduct should be punished. But to only punish the guilty leaves untouched the larger problems that are at the root of police misconduct. As the reports of Merrick Bobb, Special Counsel to the Los Angeles County Sheriff's Department, demonstrate very clearly, officer misconduct on the street is often the result of a series of management failures. These failures involve issues of recruitment, training, assignment, supervision, and discipline. All of these factors combine to create distinct organizational cultures within police departments. In too many departments, the organizational culture tolerates misconduct. In some instances, management practices actively contribute to unacceptable officer behavior. Merely punishing individual officers without addressing the underlying management problems does not result in lasting improvements.

Perhaps the most important monitoring activity is policy review. The San Francisco Office of Civilian Complaints, the San Diego Citizens' Law Enforcement Review Board, and the Portland Police Internal Investigations Auditing Committee send a steady flow of recommendations for policy change to the respective law enforcement agencies they are responsible for. No single one of these recommendations is likely to make a large difference in reducing misconduct. But the cumulative effect of such recommendations is likely to have two important long-term effects. First, attending to a number of small issues can have an important cumulative effect. We should think of this process in terms of "housekeeping" or "minding the store." Second, the process itself can change the organizational culture of a law enforcement agency, creating a climate of accountability in which the agency becomes accustomed to input from outsiders.

Also important is the process of auditing the quality of complaint investigations. In Portland, citizen members of PIIAC routinely audit the tape recordings of interviews with complainants and officers. In a number of instances, these audits identified biased or incomplete investigations. Not only were the cases sent back to internal affairs for additional work, but supervisors were notified of the problems and investigators were given additional training.

This auditing process is extremely important because it focuses on the nitty-gritty aspects of the quality of actual complaint investigations—and includes a process for improving their quality. The San Jose Independent Police Auditor, meanwhile, identified and helped to correct a number of problems with the classification and reporting of complaint data. These and other steps help to improve the professionalism of the complaint process.

THE LACK OF RESEARCH
ON THE IMPACT OF OVERSIGHT

Although a number of oversight agencies have creditable records of success, there is a serious lack of research on the activities and effectiveness of oversight agencies. Many issues have not been investigated at all, while others have been investigated inadequately. The shortcomings of research to date are many. First, only a few of the published studies have taken into account the many different roles, or potential roles, of oversight. To an unfortunate degree, discussions of the effectiveness of oversight have focused on the sustain rate, the percentage of complaints disposed of in favor of the citizen complainant. An important related problem is that, as Chapter 5 explains in detail, there are too many problems with official complaint data to allow us to use the sustain rate as a performance measure. It is relatively easy, however, to research the extent to which citizens and police officers are satisfied with a complaint procedure. The Minneapolis Civilian Review Authority's QSA system, in fact, collects data on this issue on a regular basis.

Second, there is a lack of *comparative* research that would allow us to make meaningful comparisons between different types of agencies. Generally, the debate on oversight has been framed in simplistic terms of citizen oversight versus police internal complaint procedures. The relevant question, however, is whether any one oversight agency or type of oversight agency is more or less effective than particular police internal affairs units. For that matter, there is no research on whether specific internal affairs units are more or less effective than others. And it should be added that there are good reasons for believing that some internal affairs units are in fact more effective than others.

Third, there are a number of important obstacles to measuring the impact of any oversight activity on day-to-day policing. What is required is some independent observation of police work to determine the nature and extent of misconduct. This is necessary if we seek to ascertain the impact of any change in policing (citizen oversight, community policing, a new chief) on the quality of police services. Two basic problems inhibit this approach, however. First, systematic observation of policing is prohibitively expensive. The cost of even short-term observations of single departments run into the hundreds of thousands. Second, even with such data it is extremely difficult to specify the impact of any one of the number of changes that affect a police department at any given time.

OVERSIGHT IN A MIXED SYSTEM
OF ACCOUNTABILITY

Even in the best of circumstances citizen oversight is only one part of a mixed, multifaceted system of accountability. To put it another way, citizen oversight is not a panacea and cannot achieve police accountability by itself. Or, to put it bluntly, no citizen oversight can save a truly bad police department where the department itself is not committed to accountability. This point, in the considered judgment of this author, explains the failures of the citizen review boards in New York City and Philadelphia. And conversely, the effectiveness of the Minneapolis Civilian Review Authority and the San Jose Independent Police Auditor in recent years result in large part from the fact that they serve police departments that have made serious commitments to accountability.

A mixed system of accountability includes a variety of internal and external mechanisms. First, and most important, the police chief executive has to make a serious commitment to accountability and to ending officer misconduct. A commitment to accountability means more than mere rhetoric. It means developing and maintaining the recognized best practices in police management and discipline. These include an early warning system to identify officers with recurring performance problems, a consistent and tough pattern of disciplinary actions, and the development of an organizational culture committed to "learning" from problems or indicators of potential problems.

Second, responsible elected officials must also insist on high standards of accountability. In practice, this means that mayors must make accountability the highest priority in selecting and retaining police chiefs. In the judgment of this author, one of the reasons that the oversight systems in Minneapolis, San Francisco, and Portland are more effective than others is that the mayors in those cities have taken strong stands on police accountability and are strong supporters of citizen oversight. Mayors in New York City and Los Angeles, on the other hand, have been relatively indifferent to the problem of police misconduct and have not supported citizen oversight.

Finally, the public needs to make police accountability a high priority. The public can act both through the political process, supporting mayors and other officials committed to accountability, and through private civic groups: the local bar association, the NAACP, the ACLU, and other groups that have direct knowledge about alleged police misconduct. One of the reasons that the New Orleans Police Department developed such a terrible reputation for corruption and brutality in the mid-1990s is that the public is cynical about official misconduct throughout the city and the state.

INTERNAL INFLUENCES		EXTERNAL INFLUENCES
Formal Policies And Practices	Informal Practices	
Recruitment		Responsible political direction
Pre-Service training Academy Field training		Improper political influence
	On-the-job socialization	
Official policies Deadly force Physical force Domestic violence Pursuits		Civic activism The media
Supervision Performance Evaluations	Officer subculture	The courts
Discipline Investigation Disciplinary Actions		Citizen oversight
Rewards Commendations Preferred assignments Promotions		

FIGURE 7-1 Influences on Police Accountability

The basic point is that with respect to police accountability citizen over-sight is only one of many influences. Figure 7-1 illustrates these different influences. Some are internal to police departments and some are external; some are formal and some are informal. Most experts on policing would agree that the informal internal influence of the police subculture has a particularly powerful impact on the police. To a great extent the police subculture has negated the intended impact of reforms that take the form of formal external influences. This book has argued that certain aspects of citizen oversight have a potentially positive effect on the police subculture. In the end, realistic expectations are necessary. Citizen oversight is no panacea and cannot single-handedly improve policing, but it does have the potential for making a significant, positive long-term impact.

FINAL THOUGHTS

This book opened with brief accounts of three instances of police misconduct in recent years. Similar incidents across the country have fueled the movement for citizen oversight of the police over the past half century. After years of controversy, including the rejection of numerous oversight proposals and a number of unsuccessful experiments, citizen oversight has established itself as a permanent feature of the American criminal justice system. Most of the large urban police departments in this country are subject to some form of oversight, and the concept is expanding to include many medium-sized and small agencies.

The purpose of this book has been to describe and evaluate citizen oversight of the police. The question that is continually asked is: "Is it effective?" Having reached the end of this book, the answer is a clear, "It depends." The effectiveness of an oversight agency depends on its formal structure and the powers it possesses, the activities it engages in, the quality of its leadership, the support it receives from the public and the responsible elected officials, and the attitude of the law enforcement agency it is responsible for overseeing. But embracing all of these elements, and ultimately more important than any one of them, is the vision that guides an oversight agency. That vision must include a commitment to holding the police accountable for their actions and the administrative wisdom to create the policies and procedures to ensure that accountability will be enhanced.

As a final thought, we should warn again that oversight is no panacea. Police misconduct will not disappear overnight. Nor should we realistically expect that it will ever be completely ended. But we can realistically expect that it can be substantially reduced, to the point where ordinary citizens can expect to be treated with dignity and respect by the police and not have to live in fear of physical abuse or rude and insulting treatment. And that, ultimately, is the goal of citizen oversight of the police: a civilized society served by a civil police.

Appendix

A Model Citizen Complaint Procedure

Standards for Citizen Oversight Agencies and Police Internal Affairs Units

OPERATING PRINCIPLES

The basic operating principles for citizen complaint procedures are openness, integrity, and accountability.

These principles, and the Standards that follow, apply equally to complaint procedures operated by police departments and citizen oversight agencies.

Openness

A complaint procedure must be open and accessible to the public. Complaints should be welcomed, and even encouraged, and regarded as indicators of problems that need corrective action. Openness means that at the point of intake all complaints should be received, reserving for later determination about the merits of particular complaints.

Integrity

A complaint procedure must maintain integrity in the sense that complaints are investigated thoroughly and fairly. Internal procedures are necessary to eliminate any and all forms of bias for or against complainants and police officers subject to complaints.

Accountability

Complaint procedures must be accountable to the public and to responsible public officials. Accountability means that complaint procedures must develop and maintain internal procedures designed to insure integrity, and be subject to regular audit by outside investigators.

I. OUTREACH

Standard 1.1. Informational Material

The agency shall publish and disseminate informational materials describing the citizen complaint process. The material shall include brochures, pamphlets, posters, copies of complaint forms, and other materials as deemed appropriate.

The material shall be written in plain language that is readily understandable to the average person. The material shall be disseminated as widely as possible throughout the community.

Copies shall be available in all police department offices, community centers, public libraries, and other appropriate locations.

Standard 1.1.2 Languages

Informational material shall be available in all languages appropriate to the population of the community served.

Standard 1.2 Community Meetings

The agency shall conduct regular public meetings with community groups for the purpose of explaining the complaint process and for hearing citizen concerns about policing. Such meetings shall be held in local settings in all neighborhoods of the community. Special efforts shall be made to hold meetings with groups known to have special concerns or criticisms of the law enforcement agency.

Standard 1.3 Regular Audit of Outreach Activities

The agency shall arrange for regular independent audits of outreach activities. Such audits shall include unannounced visits to determine that informational material is available in accordance with Standard 1.1. Audits shall also include attendance at community meetings (Standard 1.2) to assess attendance at meetings, the subjects covered, and the tone of such meetings.

II. COMPLAINT INTAKE

Standard 2.1.1 Complaints

The department shall receive and investigate all complaints that are brought to its attention. Complaints do not have to be filed by the alleged victim of police misconduct. The department shall receive and investigate allegations from witnesses or third parties to the incident. It shall also receive an investigate anonymous complaints.

Standard 2.1.2 Citizen Inquiries

The agency shall document all inquiries from citizens that do not result in a formal complaint to be investigated. The agency shall also document the service rendered to each inquiry (e.g., referral to another agency, information about police procedure, etc.).

Standard 2.2 Locations for Filing Complaints

Citizen shall be able to file complaints at various convenient locations throughout the community. Such locations shall include police department offices, other government offices, community centers, and so on.

Staff members at nonpolice offices shall be instructed on the proper procedure for receiving complaints and for forwarding completed complaints to the appropriate law enforcement or citizen oversight office. Officials at all offices shall be instructed that they are not to discourage citizens from filing complaints (see Standard 3.1, following).

Standard 2.3 Telephone Intake

Citizens shall be able to file complaints by telephone, fax, or e-mail.

Agencies in large metropolitan areas shall consider the feasibility of establishing toll-free telephone hotlines for receiving complaints.

Standard 2.4 Responsibilities of Sworn Officers

All sworn officers in the agency shall be instructed that it is their responsibility to be informed about the complaint process and that it is their responsibility to provide complete and accurate information about how to file a complaint to all persons who ask.

Standard 2.4.1 Responsibilities of Patrol Officers

Patrol officers shall carry in their patrol cars copies of informational material about the complaint process, including official complaint forms. It is the responsibility of patrol officers to inform citizens about the complaint process, if asked, and to provide copies of the informational material to all persons who request such material.

Standard 2.5 Notice to Complainants and Police Officers

All persons filing formal complaints shall receive prompt written notice that their complaint has been received.

Police officers subject to complaint shall receive prompt written notice that they are the subject of a citizen complaint.

Standard 2.6 Regular Audit of Complaint Intake

The agency shall arrange for regular independent audits of the complaint intake process. Such audits may include unannounced testing of the intake process, including random visits to complaint intake locations and telephone calls to offices requesting information about the complaint process. Such audits shall also include unannounced inspections of patrol cars to determine that informational materials are currently available.

III. RECORDING, CLASSIFYING, AND REPORTING COMPLAINTS

Standard 3.1 Recording of all Inquiries and Complaints

The agency shall make an official record of all inquiries about complaints against police officers. Intake personnel shall make no judgments about the merits of such inquiries. Citizen contacts that do not result in a formal complaint shall be classified as "Inquiries" (see Standard 2.1.2). An official record of such inquiries shall record the nature of the inquiry and the ultimate resolution (e.g., citizen appeared satisfied after being informed of provisions of municipal code).

Standard 3.1.1 Official Policy on Not Refusing Complaints

The agency shall have an formal policy stating that officials may not refuse to accept any complaint. Judgments about the merits of complaints shall be made by complaint investigators and not intake personnel. Each complaint must be finally resolved in some fashion within a prescribed time period, and every final resolution must be approved by the commander of the internal affairs or professional standards unit.

Standard 3.2 Complaint Classification System

The agency shall have a complaint classification system (e.g., Class I, Class II) that recognizes different levels of seriousness of alleged incidents. The criteria for classifying complaints shall be specified in a written policy.

Intake personnel shall be trained over the proper classification of complaints.

Periodic audits shall be conducted to ensure that complaints are properly classified and that serious allegations are not improperly placed in a less serious category.

Standard 3.3 Numbered Complaint Forms

Official complaint forms shall be numbered sequentially. Forms that are discarded because of mistakes shall be marked "Discarded" and filed with completed forms.

Standard 3.4 Reporting of Complaint Data

The agency shall publish regular reports on complaints received. Such reports shall include detailed information of the types of complaints received, the geographic areas where complaint incidents occurred, demographic data on complainants, the disposition of complaints, and the discipline imposed.

Standard 3.5 Regular Audit of Complaint Intake

The agency shall arrange for regular independent audits of the complaint recording, classifying, and reporting process.

IV. COMPLAINT INVESTIGATIONS

Standard 4.1 Investigation Manual

The agency shall develop and maintain an official Investigation Manual outlining the proper steps to be taken in investigating citizen complaints.

The Investigation Manual shall be revised and updated periodically.

Standard 4.2 Thorough and Fair Investigations

Complaints shall be investigated in a thorough and fair manner, free of bias for or against complainants or police officers.

The agency shall develop an official policy stating that the investigation of complaints shall be conducted in a manner free of bias against complainants.

In the case of conflicting testimony, there shall be no automatic presumption in favor of a police officer's testimony as opposed to a citizen's testimony.

Investigative reports shall not include any derogatory information about a complainant that is unrelated to the incident under investigation. Such derogatory information includes prior criminal history, prior history of mental illness, race, gender, national origins, immigration status, sexual preference, social and economic status, clothing, grooming, or personal hygiene.

Standard 4.3 Investigating Collateral Misconduct

In the course of some complaint investigations, investigators discover officer misconduct that is not part of the formal complaint. Such misconduct has been labeled "collateral misconduct," or colloquially, misconduct "outside the four corners."

Investigators shall investigate all instances of apparent collateral misconduct. In such instances, investigators shall create a separate complaint file, labeled "agency-initiated complaint." Officers subject to collateral misconduct complaints shall be promptly notified of the nature of the complaint.

Standard 4.4 Police Officer Cooperation with Investigations

All complaint investigation agencies shall have sufficient power to gather all relevant facts related to complaints. Sworn officers shall be required to answer questions posed by complaint investigators as a condition of employment. Citizen oversight agencies shall have the power to subpoena officers and compel their testimony. The Fifth Amendment protection against self-incrimination shall be respected, and any compelled testimony may not be used against an officer in a criminal proceeding.

Standard 4.5 Location of Interviews

Interviews of complainants, witnesses, and police officers shall be conducted in a manner and in a location designed to maximize convenience and confidentiality. No complainant or witness shall be required to visit a police facility to be interviewed.

No interviews shall be conducted at the homes of complainants, witnesses, or police officers unless the individual specifically requests such a location.

It shall be the responsibility of complaint investigators to secure a convenient and neutral location for all interviews.

Standard 4.6 Tape Recording of Interviews

All interviews with complainants, subject police officers, and witnesses shall be tape-recorded.

Tape recordings of investigative interviews shall be audited on a regular basis to ensure that investigations are thorough and free of bias against either complainants or officers.

Standard 4.7 Timelines for Completing Investigations

The agency shall develop a formal set of timelines for completing complaint investigations.

The timelines established by the San Jose Independent Police Auditor are indicated below. Other agencies may wish to set stricter limits.

30 days—All complaints properly classified
120 days—75% of all complaints investigated and closed
300 days—100% of all complaints investigated and closed

Standard 4.8 Notice of Status of Investigations

The agency shall inform both complainants and police officers about the status of investigations when investigations fail to meet the timelines defined in Standard 5.7.

Standard 4.9 Customer Feedback Procedure

All citizen complainants and officers subject to complaints shall be provided with an anonymous survey form that offers the opportunity to comment on how complainants were treated by the investigative process and whether they were satisfied with the outcome.

The survey forms shall be preaddressed and returned to an office other than the agency itself (e.g., mayor's office, community relations office). The office receiving the forms shall sequentially number returned forms, noting the date received, and forward them to the agency.

Standard 4.10 Mediation of Complaints

The agency shall develop and maintain a program for the informal mediation of citizen complaints. The program shall be voluntary on the part of both complainants and officers, and no person shall be coerced into accepting mediation.

Use-of-force complaints may not be subject to mediation. Officers with two or more complaints in the previous 12 months shall not be eligible for mediation.

Standard 4.11 Audit of Investigations

Complaint investigations shall be regularly audited. Supervisors shall conduct such audits on a regular (e.g., monthly) basis. The agency shall arrange for the periodic (e.g., quarterly, semiannually) audits by independent auditors.

Audits shall consist of a review of complaint investigation files to determine that (a) the files are complete and in good order; (b) that all investigative steps were taken; (c) that investigations are free of bias.

Audits shall also consist of a review of tape recordings of interviews. Such audits shall seek to determine that interviews were thorough and free of bias.

V.   COMPLAINT DISPOSITION

Standard 5.1 Disposition Separate from Investigation

The decision related to the disposition of complaints shall be separate from the investigation of complaints. Investigators shall be expected to gather all relevant information related to a complaint. A different individual shall review the investigative file and make a determination as to the proper disposition.

Standard 5.2 Preponderance of the Evidence Standard

In determining whether or not to sustain an allegation in a citizen complaint, the preponderance of the evidence standard shall be used.

Standard 5.3 Notice of Disposition

Complainants and subject officers shall be promptly notified of the disposition of complaint investigations.

VI. STAFFING AND RESOURCES

Standard 6.1 Adequate Staffing

The agency shall be staffed at a level adequate for completing its official duties. With respect to the number of investigators, the San Francisco Office of Citizen Complaints standard of one investigator for every 150 sworn officers shall serve as the ideal. The agency shall also have an adequate number of clerical and other necessary support personnel. Provisions shall be made for the use of additional investigative staff for particularly complex cases.

Standard 6.2 Selection and Screening of Investigators

The agency shall maintain procedures for the screening and selection of applicants for the position of investigator.

Candidates for the position as investigator must demonstrate that they are fair-minded and free of bias against any categories of persons. Candidates shall demonstrate the qualities of diligence, hard work, and attention to detail.

For citizen oversight agencies, no automatic preference shall be given for persons with prior law enforcement experience. At the same time, persons with prior law enforcement experience shall not be excluded from consideration.

Appropriate written and oral examinations shall be used to ensure that persons hired as investigators shall be free of any and all bias related to race, ethnicity, national origins, gender, sexual orientation, and social class. Persons employed as investigators shall not be biased for or against law enforcement officers.

For police department internal affairs units, candidates for investigator positions shall understand the importance of citizen complaints and shall not exhibit bias against complainants.

Standard 6.3 Training of Investigators

The agency shall arrange for preservice training of all new investigators. The training shall be specifically related to the investigation of citizen complaints.

For police department internal affairs units, prior experience in criminal investigation shall not be deemed completely sufficient for the investigation of citizen complaints. Additional training related to the investigation of citizen complaints shall be provided.

VII. EARLY WARNING SYSTEM

Standard 7.1 Early Warning System

The agency shall maintain an early warning system to identify officers who are the subject of multiple complaints. The agency shall use a variety of performance indicators, including but not necessarily limited to citizen complaints, use-of-force incidents, resisting arrest charges, being named in civil suits against the agency, neglect of duty, tardiness, and involvement in domestic violence incidents.

Standard 7.2. Intervention

Officers identified by the early warning system shall be required to attend an informal counseling session with his/her immediate supervisor, the commander of the internal affairs/professional standards unit, and the commander of the officer's current unit (e.g., patrol, field operations).

The purpose of the intervention counseling shall be to identify behavior problems and to recommend appropriate remedial action. Remedial action may include personal counseling, retraining, or reassignment.

Standard 7.3. Postintervention Monitoring

The performance of officers subject to early warning intervention shall be monitored for a period of 12 months following the intervention. The immediate supervisor shall be responsible for monitoring the subject officer's performance. In the event that the subject officer's performance continues to demonstrate problems, the commander of internal affairs/professional standards shall be notified.

VIII. POLICY REVIEW PROCESS

Standard 8.1 Policy Review Process

Citizen oversight agencies and police internal affairs or professional standards units shall review all citizen complaints for the purpose of identifying areas of police procedure that are in need of corrective action. Such corrective action may include the development of new official policy, the revision of existing policy, retraining of officers in certain areas, or the development of new training.

Standard 8.1.2 Law Enforcement Agency Response

The law enforcement chief executive shall be expected to respond to all policy recommendations in writing. In cases where a recommendation is rejected, the reasons shall be explained in detail.

Standard 8.2 Audit of Policy Review Process

The agency shall arrange for an independent audit of the policy review process on an annual basis. The audit shall determine the number of policy recommendations made, the areas of law enforcement in which recommendations have been made, the status of implementation of policy recommendations. A written report of the audit shall be prepared and published.

Index